Consolation

Consolation

The Spiritual Journey Beyond Grief

MAURICE LAMM

THE JEWISH PUBLICATION SOCIETY
Philadelphia 5764 • 2004

The Jewish Publication Society
2100 Arch Street
Philadelphia, PA 19103

The publisher would like to thank the following publishers for permission to quote from the sources listed:

Red Wheel/Weiser for permission to use excerpts from Molly Fumia's book, *Safe Passages*; Jonathan David Publishers for permission to quote from Maurice Lamm's *The Jewish Way in Death and Mourning*; Hampshire House Publishing Corp. for permission to reprint the song "I Believe"; and *The New Republic* for permission to reprint Leon Wieseltier's translation of the poem *My Place Is with You* by Hayyim Nachman Bialik.

The author and publisher have made every attempt to properly credit people and works referred to in this book. If we have inadvertently overlooked any, please notify us and we will make the correction in the next edition.

Design and composition by Pageworks, Old Saybrook, Connecticut
Manufactured in the United States of America

04 05 06 07 08 09 10   10 9 8 7 6 5 4 3 2 1

Library of Congress Cataloging-in-Publication Data
Lamm, Maurice.
       Consolation : the spiritual journey beyond grief / Maurice Lamm.— 1st ed.
             p. cm.
Includes bibliographical references and index.
ISBN 0-8276-0764-4
       1. Consolation (Judaism)   2. Grief—Religious aspects—Judaism.   3. Bereavement—Religious aspects—Judaism.   4. Death—Religious aspects—Judaism.   I. Title.
BM729.C6L36   2004
296.7—dc 22
                                    2003021156

The publication of this book is dedicated

In memory of
our beloved
Hanna Sarah Cohn
1952–2002

She lived by the teaching

צדק צדק תרדף

Compassion, commitment, and joy marked
all of her days.

Elsie and Martin Cohn
Sandy and Larry Cohn
Jerry Wein and Eli Cohn-Wein
Sandy and Rick Thau, David and Michael
Judy and David Gilberg, Anne and Danny
Amy Chosky and Joseph Cohn and Molly
Eve Collen and David Cohn, Sarah, Joseph, and Jonathan

To my brother,
Norman.
His rivalry was a goad,
his accomplishments a goal,
his excellence a guide,
and
his loyal brotherliness a lifelong gift.

Contents

Acknowledgments

The writing of a book is never a solo experience. What the contribution of ideas does for inspiration, the contribution of talent from editors, family members, and colleagues does for getting just the right words on paper. Sometimes the contributing is done sparingly, but not in this case, not for *Consolation*. Everyone has been most generous with their time, knowledge, and skills.

The editorial staff of The Jewish Publication Society has been unwaveringly enthusiastic about this book from the very start, especially the editor-in-chief, Dr. Ellen Frankel, whose editorial skills and leadership combine with her intensive pursuit of excellence. In this, she and I were well served by the talented and loyal publishing director, Carol Hupping. Both were simply a delight to work with.

I owe a great deal to my brother, Dr. Norman Lamm, for his many insightful recommendations. And to my wife, Shirley, who was, throughout the months of writing and rewriting, my primary sounding board, as she has been for every book I've written. Her suggestions touch every chapter and her patience approaches saintliness. Also, I thank my friends Sol and Ruth Teichman of Los Angeles, who provide me every year with an island of time amidst swaying palm trees so that I can crystallize my thinking in total tranquility. I've written the core of the book in their home.

I owe much to my long-time assistant, Caryn Starr-Gates, not only for the preparation of the manuscript in its numerous emendations, but for her stylistic insights as well.

Naturally, I am in debt to those publishing houses that have given me permission to reprint excerpts from their works, especially to Jonathan David Publishing Co. for allowing me to quote my own words from *The Jewish Way in Death and Mourning*.

Of the many sources I cite in this complex subject of grief and consolation and its slippery moorings in the human soul, one author stands out preeminently. She is Molly Fumia, whom I have met only by telephone. She wrote *Safe Passages*, a book of insights about the grief process. It is profound and filled with soul. Not only do her thoughts resonate in my mind, her emotions quiver in my soul. I recommend her book to all readers of this book.

Introduction

When I wrote *The Jewish Way in Death and Mourning* I did not fully appreciate the depth of Judaism's relationship with grief, and I assumed that the laws of mourning were self-explanatory. But now, older and I hope wiser, I understand much better the subtleties of our mourning laws and rituals and the comfort they can bring. I also now know the difference between comforting and consoling, and I have come to a disturbing realization: I have not satisfactorily consoled a single mourner during my entire rabbinic career.

How do I know this? Because I finally realize that there is no effective consolation without God's intervention, that real consoling is beyond the capability of mere people. To *comfort* is human; to *console* divine. That is why the traditional Jewish farewell is: "May God console you." In other words, "May God console you because I cannot do it by myself." This belated and jolting realization is the first reason I had to write this book: to enable me at long last to help mourners find their paths to true consolation.

Second, in my pastoral work I have seen time and time again that most mourners just want to "get through it," they want to "just suffer and then let it go," "make it go away," "get back to myself." For most of us, mourning is something to be endured, and we are thankful when it's over. We don't entertain even a fleeting thought that bereavement could be an enriching experience, even as it is a sorrowful and often tragic one. Instead, we become passive spectators of our own pain, and we see our grief period as a spindly mound that we must climb over. When our hearts are shattered, we aren't interested in deriving spiritual teachings from the experience. I hope that my book will help mourners not just *get* through their grief, but also *grow* through it.

Third, most of us believe that it is our moral duty to console mourners, but we perform this duty mindlessly: stammering a hello, rambling through a good-bye, and then just glad to get out of there. We prepare no plan or agenda for interacting with the griever, for choosing words that could be reassuring. We care deep but think shallow. We're clumsy at this business of consolation, not because we don't care but because we believe there is nothing intelligent or effective that we can really say anyway. I hope my book will also help consolers—help them to listen and speak with their hearts and learn how to console more effectively.

❧

My book speaks to mourners and to consolers on two different levels. This is because we all live on two levels, or, as I prefer to say, in two geographies: the geography of material things, which demands down-to-earth solutions to complex daily problems; and the geography of the spirit, where every human being has a transcendent dimension that searches for relationships, not reasons.

Parts One and Two are devoted to our emotional, psychological, and cultural sensibilities; Parts Three and Four to our spiritual, mystical, religious sides. Part One is a description and explanation of a mourner's pain. No one can "explain away" the loss; we are not God. But mourners may be able to view this frightful experience from a new vantage point that they never before considered. After a death they are sucked into a vortex of turbulent emotions and complicated arrangements, and simply describing these emotions may help them to see that such feelings are universal and they are not alone in their grief.

Part Two weighs the striking differences between pain and suffering and offers the possibility that personal growth can actually come even from unspeakable tragedy. There are healing strategies that Judaism provides us through its laws and customs (particularly shiva) and the rituals and death narratives in the Bible, in legends, and in literature.

Part Three focuses on spirituality, the earliest and most effective source of consolation. In spiritual discourse, we find answers not in deductive logic nor in the results of scientific, philosophical, or theological analysis. Here we encounter not theories to be analyzed and judged, only emotions and the ideas they stimulate.

People are usually more sensitive to spirituality during grieving periods than at other times of their lives. Spirituality seems to be inherent in all grieving. Here they confront God, or some higher power, with theological questions of "Why?" "Where is my daughter?" "How can I help her now that she is not here and doctors can do nothing for her?"—implying that a transcendent power actually exists and cares. In the secular arena there is no complaint desk, no address that receives messages, but in religion one can always cry out to the one in charge, always know where to look when questioning God. The task of this book is to sensitize mourners to this spirituality and awaken them to its positive energies and promises, so that this power can bear them on its wings in the journey beyond grief.

On the spiritual plane, we communicate through mental and visual images, metaphors, legends, and anecdotes, which reveal more than they say because they speak directly to the soul. And so it is in these chapters that I touch on matters of heaven and life after life, and of what tradition says about the continuing relationship between the mourner and the deceased. Here, words and meanings move far beyond mere definitions.

Part Four concludes the journey from grief to healing and is the climax of the book. It explores the possible outcomes of bereavement: passive endurance, simple transition to the next phase in living, reaching for transcendence, moving to greater growth and awareness through transformation, and finally to the achievement of the celebrated historic Jewish art: wringing blessing from curse.

An accompaniment to the book is a collection of readings close to my heart. This section, at the back of the book, is called "Words for a Loss, When at a Loss for Words." I hope that it will provide comfort for mourners and guidance for consolers, focusing on the deeper meaning of *nechama* (Jewish consolation), and on the Jewish protocol for visiting mourners.

Here mourners and consolers will find "Palliatives," suggestions for finding and giving comfort by transforming the spiritual ideas of an ancient faith into contemporary language. Then there is "Parables," a group of moral stories and fables that illuminate our complicated lives; "Pearls," meditations from the depths of human experience; and "Portraits," a gallery of unforgettable traditional images that speak to our souls during times of mourning. And finally I identify a variety of "Platitudes" and "Peccadilloes," inappropriate comments that well-meaning but flustered consolers commonly offer mourners. Such awkward, impulsive remarks often hurt or anger those they are meant to comfort. I suggest explanations that may help mourners better deal with such inadvertently hurtful speech and may also provide consolers with alternative expressions that are more appropriate and that they can use when they are looking for the right words to say.

What I have tried to do here, most of all, is to help all those who walk the path of grief to find their way to consolation—and then beyond, to an appreciation of the blessings and opportunities that present themselves to us when we confront loss. Although grief can be a demanding teacher, its hard-earned lessons do repay us throughout our lives and enrich our relationships with all those who remain behind with us in the land of the living. If we heed these lessons well, we can begin to be healed by consolations and be ready for the journey beyond grief.

September 2003
Maurice Lamm

PART I

THE GRIEVING HEART

Chapter 1

The Night Raiders

The darkness engulfs us in a deepening shade and frost penetrates our marrow. So with the lamps all put out, the moon sunk, and a thin rain drumming on the roof, a downpouring of immense darkness began. Nothing, it seemed, could survive the flood, the profusion of darkness which, creeping in at keyholes and crevices, stole round window blinds, came into bedrooms, swallowed up here a jug and basin, there a bowl of red and yellow dahlias, there the sharp edges and firm bulk of a chest of drawers.

—Virginia Woolf

Y ou have placed a loved one into the earth; friends have sprinkled their bits of wisdom upon you and have gone, the condolences have evaporated, and the tumult has suddenly deadened. Night falls. Suffocating, you confront the blanket of darkness and the thick silence with stunned disbelief. Is this happening to me? Is this what it always feels like? The unanswered questions hang. Awareness begins to emerge and loneliness sinks deeper into the subvaults of your soul. The golden chain of human lineage is severed and swings wildly before your eyes. Bone weary, you contemplate the meaning of life. You feel bereft. You are left incredulous, speechless, bewildered, adrift, inconsolable, and, above all, abandoned.

But truth hammers away at you: This is irreversible. Only a child would not understand how irreversible. "Grandpa went to heaven" does not seem to dismay children. They think, "He'll come back from heaven." For you, the prospect is more dismal. No matter the anger, the refusal to believe, the injustice, and the tears—your loved one is buried in that earth, never to return. The loss is not the world's loss or society's loss or even the family's loss; it is your own.

It is an assault on your reality. With no one else will you ever share the same routine, the fondness and friendship; no one in the entire universe will have that voice, that face, that touch, and your world will never again be quite complete. No longer is there any possibility of hoping against hope that "everything will somehow resolve itself." You realize that, truly, this is happening to you—you are bereft, alone, at an end—and this awareness begins to infiltrate your fragile soul and secret thoughts. "The catastrophe is not what is visible to the eye, so much as what is visible to the heart."

As you realize that life has permanently changed, you sense that you will revisit this scene, that time and again you will absorb the same first brutal shock and the same horror will play itself out. In Albert Camus's graphic words, "The weight of days is dreadful." Or, as the Psalmist asked thirty centuries ago—not waiting for, not expecting an answer: "My God, my God, why have You abandoned me?" (Ps. 22:2) Is not this the most persistent and penetrating conundrum of grief?

The busyness of the days immediately after burial crowds out the ghosts of grief, and not thinking about the magnitude of your loss enables you to while away the dreaded hours. Or so you believe. But trouble, grievance, and anger will not vanish by being ignored. In the dark, when the shades are drawn, the doors shut, the room still, and you are alone, the Night Visitors lurk on the cusp of your imaginings, prepared to create havoc. They come and go fitfully as they wish, inflicting wounds—self-pity, anger, loneliness, guilt, and fear—and they crowd your imagination, sometimes going so far as to trigger thoughts of ending your own life. It is night and the image won't fade, it will grow sharper: "Midnight. No waves, no wind, the empty boat is flooded with moonlight."

We all become depressed in such moments. We deserve to be. Such depression is not symptomatic of mental illness; it is a sober indication of our very normalcy. Sigmund Freud described this kind of depression with a more elegant term: "melancholy." Melancholy allows for reasonable sadness, a genuine deserving sadness, rather than a comprehensive, pathological state. Health professionals are often quick to identify this behavior as depressive and therefore undesirable, but in the mourning process, depression can be adaptive, allowing the mourner the time and space to adjust to new circumstances.

The roots of grief arise from wounds deeper than we may anticipate, deeper than our cultural, psychological, or even spiritual resources. They grow from the cavern of assumptions within us—beliefs on which we have unconsciously based our lives, what we have intuited that we can and cannot expect from life; beliefs about the boundaries of our abilities, about the purpose and value of our existence; and, in the very last analysis, about what our earthly experience means to us.

Everyone's mourning experience is unique, but there is a commonality. Some expressions rise naturally above others in articulating our grief. They are the night visitors who inflict their damage in the small hours of life.

I lie awake at night, tortured by a barrage of questions that pick at my flesh like tiny birds with sharp beaks—why me, what now, what did I do to deserve this, what could I have done to prevent this cruel parting? Unanswerable questions. I just let them flow through me, rather than pick raw my tender skin. Oh yes, here they are again, my night visitors.

—M. Fumia

Numb

Numbness is a very frequent reaction, whether a death is sudden or long anticipated. As mourners, we feel paralyzed and motionless, perched precariously above a bottomless gorge. We are unable to concentrate, feel irritable and restless, and are unwilling to talk. We stare, but do not see; we hear, but do not listen; we mutter shallow greetings, but we are hardly there; instead, we are adrift in a sea of nothingness. We have few desires, little appetite, no interest even in being helped. "I am dead inside. Nothing matters. Leave me alone."

It is not unusual for mourners to experience psychological numbness. Going into shock is like being injected with a general anesthetic; however, the opposite may occur first. With adrenalin pumping, an initial response may be "flight"—running to escape the pain or even fainting on the spot—or "fight"—berating doctors, nurses, rabbis, whoever brought the news. Very often, however, it is neither fight nor flight, but "freeze"—the inability to feel, react, think, or even believe that such a terrible thing could happen. Disbelief in such moments is common because the mind has great difficulty absorbing such overwhelming news. Shock at such a time is actually a protective mechanism, an emotional sedative that eases the pain.

Intellectually, we mourners know exactly what happened. But the fact is stuck in our brain and does not reach our emotions, which shut down. The shock blocks the processing of the gruesome reality. Our faces are wrapped as if in a blanket, and the world outside is muted. Cognitively, we appear to accept it, but this reaction is only a shield that protects our vulnerability. It is for this reason that religious custom, which prizes shared grieving, advises family and friends not to console mourners in the immediate aftermath of a loss. The mourner's soul must visit its own self and slowly break through the cocoon of grief and self-absorption.

The Book of Exodus describes the reaction of Moses' brother Aaron to the sudden death of his two sons—the bright stars and hope of his life—in one word, "va'yidom." "And Aaron was silent [numb]" (Lev. 10:3). Va'yidom is confected of two words—dom (silence) and dam (blood). It is as if to say that Aaron's blood had congealed, his vitality was sapped, his tongue was frozen. Aaron's mind could not process this sudden descent into the hell of grief. The twelfth-century commentator Rashbam looks into Aaron's soul and says that this is not a conscious silence, but that he is paralyzed in a reflexive disconnect between cognition and affect. "Light grief can speak; great ones are dumb," the Roman philosopher Seneca said.

Va'yidom—the only other place this word occurs in the Bible is when Joshua commands the sun to stand still in Gibeon (Josh. 10:13). Va'yidom—nothing moved, not even an acknowledgment. Aaron was like the sun standing still. The universe was numb.

Weeping

Crying is a blessing. Feel for those who cannot bring themselves to weep after a tragedy. Crying opens a vent in the heart to release the pressure building up inside us, so crying is a perfectly suitable response. Most tragedies are inexplicable. The common lament on learning of a death is, "Why him? Why now? Why this way?" Our loss is complicated by an apparent senselessness. Crying is a burst of raw emotion, inarticulate, beyond reason, offering no logic, no solution. We respond to the impenetrable with unintelligible lament.

Both numbness and weeping are inchoate, inarticulate, spontaneous, and rudimentary reactions to stark tragedy. Such an incoherent answer is often the only suitable response—a primal scream, a forced expulsion, a raging reaction to the uncivilized. The difference between numbness and weeping is that in numbness we inhale the grief; in weeping we exhale it.

Abraham responded to his wife's death, *"lispod le'Sarah ve'livkotah"* (delivering a eulogy for Sarah and weeping over her; Gen. 23:2). A eulogy is a rational assessment, weeping is emotional. He did both. The word for "weeping" is written in the Torah scroll with a diminished middle letter as though to say "not an outburst but a dirge." Abraham's strong emotional reaction may seem surprising since Sarah was, after all, an old woman, yet his display of grief sets a model for the appropriate attitude of the Jewish mourner. Although this is the first mention of weeping in Torah, Abraham surely did not invent tears. Adam, facing the first sundown and having never known a sunrise, must have cried. Noah, confronted by the mass destruction of the raging flood, was no doubt moved to tears. But in the Torah it was Abraham who first applied the human capacity for weeping to the death of someone close to him. Weeping is a eulogy, a mark of love and reverence.

Weeping, far from being thought of as weakness, is considered a manifestation of deep love. When King Solomon built the ancient Temple in Jerusalem, he built two gates—one entry for wedding parties and one for mourners. Outside the mourners' gate, people would gather to say, "May the One who dwells in this House console you." This custom is replicated today in many synagogues. On Friday evening, mourners formally enter the synagogue in the middle of the service—after the joyous Sabbath psalms are recited and before the night service begins—and congregants greet them with the prayer that God should console them. It is quite touching to hear an entire community consoling its mourners. "The holiest attribute of a temple," the Basque poetic metaphysician Miguel de Unamuno noted, "is that it is a place where men weep in common."

Crying is more than respect, it is a godsend. That is how I understand the phrase of Alfred de Musset that I have carried with me since college French: *"Le seul bien qui me reste au monde est d'avoir quelques fois pleuré"* (The only good left me in this world is having at times wept).

Weeping may hold meanings beyond normal comprehension. Such is an insight of South American writer John Welch: "With my tears I would water roses, to feel the pain of their thorns and the red kiss of their petals." Is it possible for a griever's tears to water the roses—to feel the pain and also the kiss?

Unraveling

The "torn-apart-ness" of sobbing is often followed by a "coming-apartness," when we address the sad realization that "it has happened to me." Nothing is falling into place. The fabric of the family, the order of life, is simply unraveling. The knots of relationships—arrangements, expectations, goals—are loosened; some are even untied.

Chaos is what we as mourners experience when our accustomed order is suspended or destroyed. How precarious and unstable are the illusions in which we live—the fantasy that people we love will never leave us. Chaos is the effect of the deceased's absence on everyone who instinctively pictures the family photo. Our personal feelings are built on assumptions and givens, until a child's future is taken away, a grandparent is no longer a perennial feature of our lives, or a spouse's support and comfort abruptly ceases. Life seems to unravel. "Everything nailed down is coming loose." What we carefully constructed based on a network of relationships, tacit agreements, half-spoken go-aheads—all of the tentative arrangements—is now turned upside down.

Of course, the unraveling is not expressed in logical terms, as weeping is not, but the heart is left hunting vainly for some order, system, meaning—for a life that is not insanely descending into chaos. Ralph Waldo Emerson likened this disarray to a broken string of beads: Once the string breaks and the beads scatter, the necklace cannot be made whole again.

Angry

In bereavement, swarms of unanswered questions drone around us like angry bees. The honey of acceptance does not attract us. True, it is an occasion for sadness, regret, and disbelief, but this is also a time of suppressed rage, of inflamed emotions, of blame and guilt.

As mourners, we are often racked with feelings of guilt toward the deceased. This guilt triggers blame, which in turn leads to unfounded anger—for every possible reason, toward every conceivable individual. Unconsciously, we feel that someone must pay for this horrific event. It would be a mistake for those who try to comfort us at this moment to take offense, as if the anger represented a rational and considered proposition. But at whom are we truly angry?

We are angry with ourselves. We may feel personally guilty for having had important words that should have been spoken and not saying them. The opportunity will never come again. We are disappointed and upset with ourselves for not battling harder. We are angry for being alone, for being a survivor.

When we are bereaved, we inevitably feel responsible and believe that we should have or could have done something to prevent the death. We punish ourselves because we didn't do all of the perfect things. Secretly, and sometimes quite loudly as though in expiation, we blame ourselves for not paying enough attention, for not apologizing about one thing or another, for not being "there" at some precise moment, or for not accompanying our loved one on this last journey—for not joining him or her to the "the last syllable of recorded time." We blame our "fate" that life is nothing but a sad, frustrating, raging insult, a series of inexplicable tragedies that we inherit simply by being born into this vale of tears.

We may be angry with God, who is omnipotent but seems incapable of intervening on our behalf. We blame God for allowing this terrible event to happen in the first place. Is this not the unjust consequence of an uncaring God? But instead, the very first traditional utterance after death is "God is a true judge" and the very first religious declaration after burial is "*tzidduk ha'din*," (The justice of God's edict.) These spiritual proclamations are necessary because they are likely to be primary in the mourner's mind, even if not automatically on the mourner's lips.

Although we duly recite these formulaic declarations of God's justice, our anger cannot simply be dismissed. Judaism understands the anger, anticipates it, and deals with it. That is why visitors to a house of mourning do not offer greetings of *shalom* (peace), to which the mourner would respond in kind. The tradition says that this is because "*Shalom*" is one of the classic names for God. Hurling the word in a griever's face might well trigger a reaction of cynicism, mockery, or defiance. In fact, because of this anticipated reaction, tradition calls for no greetings at all to be spoken in a house of mourning. The front door is left ajar or at least unlocked precisely to avoid the necessity for greetings.

At this moment, we may vent our anger on the loved one we lost—for neglecting health concerns, for leaving too little insurance, or for abandoning us. And we are angry with others who seem to be living on effortlessly in the midst of healthy families and intact lives. We rage at the indiscriminate distribution of death—that it was *our* loved one who was ripped from family and friends. And why does the whole world seem to go on undisturbed in the face of such horror? How is it that others haven't noticed that nothing will ever be the same again? Don't they realize what's happened?

From there, blame and anger spread to others for causing the illness or the death, hastening it, aggravating it, being unable to prevent or delay it, not making the dying more comfortable, or being indifferent: to the doctors who didn't pay enough attention, to the hospital that allowed careless mistakes to happen, to certain family members who didn't go out of their way or didn't seem to care, to clergy who didn't provide solace, and to friends who didn't visit often enough. Someone must bear the blame for such an inexplicable tragedy.

There is often evidence of this at the funeral itself. Family and friends are resentful; otherwise close relatives are not speaking to one another. Some who came to mourn are filled with anger and complain, *sotto voce*, when they might otherwise focus on the deceased and the welfare of other mourners. Grudges sometimes begin here and are not forgiven and not forgotten, even many months later.

Mourners may find that they cannot move on emotionally because they feel so guilty—about the death, about the life, about all the people who seem to have caused them grief. Often mourners cannot be persuaded by logical analysis or psychotherapeutic insight that the world is not to be blamed and that death does not require the naming of a scapegoat. Most mourners, however, know this in their hearts and, knowing it, will get past the anger and manage this aspect of grief in time.

Abandoned

A train is leaving the station and all are aboard. It roars down the track into open space. When the last thundering iron car rolls past, a child is left on the platform. Chiseled in our early memories is some feeling of being deserted, hopeless, lost, and vulnerable. It is very nearly universal. It is particularly poignant in a society riveted by memories of the Holocaust. Survivors—children left on the platform—tremble at the threat of being abandoned. It is providential to be alive; it is heartbreaking to be alone.

Abandonment normally implies a deliberate dereliction of responsibility. But, other than in cases of suicide, grievers intellectually know that their deceased did not die out of spite or on purpose to escape. Yet, children often view a parent's death as deliberate neglect of their need for protection. Spouses are often so tightly bound together to make a life together and raise the children that a partner's death may be taken as an abdication of responsibility, leaving the living to fend for themselves, abandoned and helpless. Even in suicide, when death is deliberate, the implied rejection of family and friends may be far from the truth.

It is quite difficult on an intellectual level, let alone on the level of sentiment and affection, for us to be convinced that the deceased did not deliberately desert us, or even out of some malicious intent. Indeed, we have seen that the dying quite often need "permission" from family and friends to let go and separate from this world because they sometimes see their own deaths as an abandonment of responsibilities and relationships and expectations.

Feeling abandoned is a cruel twist on an already dreadful event. It is so universal, so human, that it should never be underestimated.

Alone

"Alone" and "lonely" are two words that seem to mean the same thing, but they do not. Even mourners who do not feel abandoned may feel alone—horribly alone. We are alone when we feel isolated physically, believing we have no one who cares for us, no one on whom we can lean, no intimate friendship, no special love, and no lifelong partner. In bereavement, aloneness is especially heartrending and palpable. The words of one mourner echo through the generations: "My sweetheart left me for good. I have nobody else."

Aloneness can rear its head even in the middle of a crowd. We feel alone as though we were in fact forsaken physically. In grief, we can feel absolutely bereft, even though family and friends surround us, because we feel that our relationship with the deceased was unique and therefore incommunicable, separating our beloved from everyone else. We think: "It's no use telling this to anyone." This loss is uniquely our own, not because we were closer to the deceased (we may not have been), but because we related to the deceased in a unique way. The philosopher Arthur Schopenhauer said: "The deep pain that is felt at the death of every friendly soul arises from the feeling that there is in every individual something which is inexpressible, peculiar to him alone, and is, therefore, absolutely and irretrievably lost."

The fear of being lost and alone is among our earliest insecurities, triggered perhaps when our mother left us for a split second. Later, as parents, afraid of losing a child in a crowd or having a child spirited away from us, we experience a similar kind of terror. It is why our hearts crumble when we see a lost child crying.

Aloneness is this kind of corrosive emotion, eating away at us, perilously close to feeling abandoned. As adults, in order to decrease our chances of becoming lost or left alone, we create an impressive array of ego markers related to job, address, and credit card; in hospitals we wear an identity bracelet, and everywhere we are armed with cellular phones and beepers. We must be connected at all costs, or else we are alone. Yet, despite all these safeguards, we sometimes feel lost. We feel intensely alone when we feel uncared for.

We may also experience aloneness because we suddenly feel cut off from God, exposed to strange fears, and no longer sheltered by faith in times of trouble. Mourners may not be able to fathom—no matter what we say—why we lost our beloved, why God's face is hidden. "Would it have hurt God to let this one person live?" We may believe we have fallen out of favor with God and that our trusted relationship with God is at an end. No matter our complaint to God, we ultimately need God's protection, and that is a trigger of loneliness.

Loneliness is qualitatively different from being alone. Loneliness is an escape. Loneliness does not want company; when we mourners are lonely, we are busy with ourselves. "I can't get out of myself." This is not an enforced solitude of finding oneself alone but a choosing to be left alone. We want to solve our problems through our own devices; we want to work them out and arrive at a satisfying end.

Indeed, loneliness, unlike aloneness, is not necessarily destructive. In fact, loneliness can become a compelling spiritual challenge. Like its first cousin, aloneness, loneliness is sometimes painful. But it can prove to be stimulating and enriching, making us want to reach out to others and to better understand the scope of our tragedy. Loneliness may provoke us into probing deeper into God's purposes, imploring God's compassion, or even criticizing God for inflicting an "unjust" tragedy. In this case, loneliness is really solitude that, as we shall see later, is a strategy that can avail us in self-healing, help us dig deeper within ourselves to make the darkness comprehensible, aid us in understanding other people's alienation, and ultimately bring us the comfort we seek. And it is good to remember that solitude can, in fact, make us feel connected. (That is why later in this book we consider solitude part of the solution rather than part of the problem.)

Afraid

Grieving sparks the embers of fear, many fears, actually. In mourning, some of us are afraid that we will not be able to manage life physically: Bereaved husbands worry about caring for their families, bereaved wives worry about carrying on the business, older spouses may worry about being able to maintain daily chores, and so on. We may be afraid that we will pine for our beloved so intensely that we will not survive the ordeal of our grief. These fears and many, many others are quite understandable

There is another fear, seldom mentioned yet pervasive, thrusting itself upward from our inner depths. It is the fear that death will strike again. Folklore has it that death strikes families in threes. For those who take this superstition to heart, there is no changing their minds, even though it is patently baseless. Nevertheless, people often act as though death were contagious. This is apparent in a little-known custom that when shoveling the earth into the grave after burial, the shovel is not passed from hand to hand, but is used, then replaced into the earth, so that one person does not touch another in the cemetery. It is not the superstition that is important to the mourner; it is the fear.

Fear is the reason that the Talmud cautions that when a person dies, friends should be careful about their own lives. Fear is the reason that the Talmud describes the gruesome imagination of grievers as the vision of a sword dangling before them as they walk in the market, receding only as time goes by.

As we witness a relative descending into the grave, we instinctively ask ourselves whether we may have the same genetic predisposition, whether we may be prone to similar accidents, whether we may share a similar fate.

Grieving is as complex as human nature itself. The character of our grief is a reflection of all our interactions with the deceased, all our hopes for, and expectations of, our beloved; everything this person ever stood for; the talents and loyalties, the deep, multidimensional character that was a composite of our loved one's total experience. And now that person has disappeared. How can we *not* be afraid?

Such are the night visitors who inflict their damage in the small hours after a death.

Chapter 2

The Wounds They Inflict

She went to the fence and sat there, watching the gold clouds fall to pieces, and go in immense, rose-colored ruin toward the darkness. Gold flamed to scarlet, like pain in intense brightness. Then the scarlet ran to rose, and rose to crimson, and quickly the passion went out of the sky. All the world was dark gray.

—D. H. Lawrence

When someone dear to us dies, our inner being is shattered; we are torn apart, as though the dead person had been ripped out of our body. Our own life temporarily dies. Our suffering is unlike any other, not only because we feel bereft of a loss that will never ever be recouped but also because we are broken up, falling apart, because the loss has opened a black hole in our own life.

To fully grasp the depth of this grief, we need to understand a fundamental difference between suffering and pain. Both are endemic to the human condition, but the two are not the same. A person can endure pain without suffering—as a mother in childbirth is in excruciating agony, yet deliriously happy with the baby who is the very cause of her pain. And a person can suffer without having any measurable pain—as when a young woman, deeply in love, discovers that her fiancé has been unfaithful.

Suffering is the psychic equivalent of physical pain. Pain is neurological. Suffering is spiritual, psychological, and existential. Pain can be treated with medication; suffering can be softened by another person, a healing relationship. Pain seeks cure; suffering looks for healing. Ultimately, most pain can be fully controlled or even entirely eliminated. But humanity has never found a solution to suffering and it never will.

While the roots of suffering are many, one stands out as most important, especially to mourners: the threat to a person's intactness. A stroke victim may become hysterical because of the loss of speech; a diabetic may feel that life is over when a leg is amputated. This type of distress is triggered by a crack in our integrity; we are no longer a whole being. The gestalt of the whole person, of normalcy, wholeness, tranquility, sense of soul, is fractured. "I went to pieces," "I am not the same person." If this kind of suffering remains unresolved, it gets expressed— even some decades later—as sadness, anger, depression, grief, melancholy, rage, and withdrawal, sometimes as a yearning for reunion with the deceased.

In bereavement there is very clear evidence of such loss of our intactness. When a loved one is torn from our arms—especially in cases of sudden death, child death, or suicide—our wholeness is shattered. "Who am I without my wife?" "Am I a mother without my baby?" "When he took his life, he took mine." At the extreme, there is the possibility, entertained by many even in minor crises, of losing our minds, losing control of our lives, and of being helpless to prevent these things.

In addition, there is a distinct and dangerous effect that comes into play when our spiritual wholeness is threatened. We sense that our soul is becoming fragmented in the deepest vaults of our humanity. We are spiritually broken, wounded in a war with God or with fate or, indeed, with our own self. And that is why in mourning we often grieve for our own life, even though we are not always conscious of it. The great scholar Rabbi Joseph B. Soloveitchik sharply observed that our initial response upon hearing of a close death is malice toward our own self: "Maybe my time is up?" "Who needs this life anyway?"

We can find many signs from mourners themselves that this is indeed so. In the act of comforting, we need to pay close attention to a mourner's choice of words: "I should've died." "What use is this life, it's no longer worth living." "I might as well be dead." "I should go with the one I love." "I'm next." Upon reflection, the grief for a loved one turns to anticipatory grief for the mourner's self. Indeed, perhaps much of the grief we express for others is a grief that anticipates our own death. When in Leviticus (10:3) Aaron the High Priest goes numb after hearing of the sudden death of his sons, what resonates in him is the silence of the dead, and he identifies with the fate of the deceased. He dies—momentarily—together with his sons.

The mourner becomes the victim—in place of the deceased—like Gabriel in James Joyce's "The Dead": "We're all in the act of becoming the past." At the very least, we are burdened with two griefs that are intertwined: one for the deceased and one for our self. We not only brush up against the specter of death, we become infected by it. We lose our physical, psychological, and spiritual intactness, and our very existence is threatened.

Ancient sources in Talmud and Midrash refer often to this shattering of existential intactness. "If one in a group of friends dies, everyone in the group worries." "To what can this be likened?" asks the Jerusalem Talmud. "To a stone arch, where the stones are pressed closely and support one another, if one stone is shaken loose, all of them are loosened and threaten to fall to the ground."

There is a Jewish law, very touching in its effect, that says that the first meal that mourners eat upon their return from the cemetery must be provided by friends and relatives. It is called *"seudat havra'ah"* (a meal of health), or re-enlivening, or resuscitation, and it is provided only for the immediate family of the deceased. In other words, it is definitely not a banquet to thank guests for attending the funeral but an act of support for the mourners, rescuing them from their desire to starve and descend into the earth to follow on the heels of their departed. The insight of Rabbi Yeruchem is that "The mourner worries and groans in anticipation of his own death, and he will therefore not be careful to take food by himself—because he too desires to die!" The great medieval legislator Levush offers another reason: "This meal is also a form of consolation—we console the mourner, assuring him that we will not abandon him when he dies."

In the Jewish law codes, we learn that at the start of the seven days of shiva, the mourner imagines a sword is lodged between the shoulders. From the third to the seventh day, it is hanging in front. From the seventh to the thirtieth day it constantly moves, accompanying the mourner through the streets. For a full year, the mourner perceives it in his or her imagination and considers the family in danger. The image of the sword is evocative. Mourners see the threat of death to their own lives receding day by day, as they are able to reintegrate themselves gradually into normal life. The sword stalks them, but they overcome it—and eventually it vanishes. The medieval poet Sh'lomo ibn Gabirol said: "Everything that grows begins small and becomes big; but grief starts big and becomes small."

The ritual observances of mourning also address this subtle fear that is very often present and very rarely expressed. We cover mirrors in the house of mourning during shiva to make ourselves invisible, to delete our presence, as it were. During shiva, we do not indulge in sexual play because copulation is a dynamic symbol of the life force. In this first week following a death, we do not go to work—in a society that always associates "full productivity" with a "full life" and "maximum output" with saintliness, in which inactivity reflects lifelessness. Even the sitting during shiva, the dominant position of the mourners during this period, is a statement of confirmed passivity, approximating the ultimate homeostasis, death—the perfect balance of the body at rest, just as the deceased was laid to rest. What's more, mourners traditionally sit lower to the ground, to be physically closer to the jaws of the earth that have swallowed up the one being mourned. It is the ultimate conquest of Thanatos over Eros.

The idea of "self-mourning" is profound and is seen often in literature. A person often needs to symbolically experience a personal virtual death, and thereby work it out of the unconscious, where it may be blocking emotional maturity. We do not know when we will die, of course. In T. S. Eliot's words: "to apprehend the point of intersection of the timeless with time, is an occupation of the saint." But we must live until we die, and we need to recognize that, in crucial circumstances, in order to live free of the fear of impending death we need to undergo symbolic demise. The return to normalcy is the recognition that the first imperative of life is to live.

They Disorient Our Inner Compass

Our personal relationships are like threads that bind us together. Through numerous ties and knots we become entangled in one another's life. The Bible describes the father and son: *"nafsho keshurah ve'nafsho"* ([The father's] own life is bound up with his [son's]; Gen. 44:30). When these ties are severed, it disrupts virtually everything in life and moves everything off center. We are left bereft—most often in incomprehensible ways. By the end of a month, a year, or more, the bindings of the relationship begin to relax. No longer taut, they gradually disentangle and a new phase of the old relationship begins. Memory moves into the vacant space.

Before this happens, we experience an uncommon confusion—not necessarily delirium or chaos or even bewilderment but rather dislocation, a form of discontinuity. We sense that something is out of sync, but we cannot quite decode it: "I don't know where I am sometimes." "Often I stop suddenly not knowing where I'm headed." "All the old landmarks are gone." During our loved one's lifetime, we were safe within a circumference of images and memories—the departed and the family and our friends—and now this world is simply not the same. We are disoriented.

The word "disorientation" derives from "Orient"—the Eastern world. Peoples of the Western world use the verb "to orient" to mean "face eastward." Jews pray to Jerusalem in the Orient, Christian churches are directed toward Nazareth in the Orient, Muslims to Mecca in the Orient. "Orientation" signifies a direction—as, for example, maps and compasses are "oriented" to north. The word has become a metaphor for clear direction. It is logical that we should measure where we stand by our relationship to a fixed spot—and what more permanent direction than the East and its holy places?

Orientation implies finding a position outside ourselves, beyond our own ken, by which to measure place and time and to locate where we are and how we fit into the universe. Orientation is such a basic need that many people are not aware of it until it is compromised or absent. Child psychologists have found that even newborn babies have an instinctive orientation toward their mothers, probably based on the sounds of the mother's voice and other sensations that each child comes to discover, even when in the uterus. Normal growth and development are, in a very real sense, the maturing of orientation to persons, places, and times. Mental adjustments are often made so quickly that people fail to realize how often they go through the processes of reorientation. That is, they fail to realize this until they encounter an experience to which they cannot readily adapt, such as a death.

A person who is disoriented has lost direction, is wandering without a compass, and is unable to reach appropriate goals. Death very often kicks our minds off balance, pushing us off the straight road. Our fixed spot has vanished. The most critical aspects of reorientation then are relationships to other people, to the physical surroundings in which they live, and to the time context in which activities take place. Anyone can become disoriented momentarily when something unexpected is encountered, but normally orientation is quickly recovered as we refer to a familiar person, place, or time. We find our orientation by measuring what is new against what is known.

The disorientation that most people feel after the loss of someone they love can be deeply frustrating. We find it difficult to think clearly and often sense a general malaise. From this perspective, the world is in disarray and any subsequent hint of disorientation becomes ever more frightening as we struggle to regain or maintain normalcy. For some, the disorientation may be so profound that we "feel crazy" or are perceived by others to be just a touch off center. To be reoriented becomes our most important goal.

When everything is as shifting as an ocean, finding a constant is the only way to measure where we are, how far or close we are to our goals. When the buoy is in place, we are able to find ourselves in rough seas. But when it's not there, where are we? Where should we go? We are in danger of drowning. The Bible reduces it to four Hebrew words: "*Histarta fanekha, hayiti nivhal*"—When You hid Your face, I was terrified (Ps. 30:8).

The sensitive balance of our minds is nudged off its prepared course. As I noted, the Talmud says that our circle of family and friends is really an arch made of personal relationships that abut and hold up one another. When a family member is pulled out—whether we liked that person or not—we become unglued and insecure. So profound and universal is the disorientation felt by mourners that Judaism crafted a curious custom to respond to it: The immediate family, who usually sit in specific pews in the synagogue, change their seats when mourning so that their views of people around them become altered. They now see people in different contexts, in different sequences. And it is not confined to the synagogue; it also applies to the study hall and, by extension, to community events.

This place changing, *shinui makom*, an ancient metaphor for disorientation after loss, may seem at first like a trivial symbol. But this ritual should be placed against another long-honored and much-praised practice that teaches an opposite lesson. That is, the desirability of *makom kavu'a* (praying in a stable location), keeping your own seat in order to pray in a familiar background so that you are better able to concentrate on the prayers. Against this background, the policy of *shinui makom* has even greater significance and brings the idea of disorientation into bas-relief.

Since disorientation affects not only sons and daughters (who are in Jewish law the primary mourners), rabbinic decisors have applied *shinui makom* to spouses and other relatives, who feel that the loss has upset their coherent view of the universe. By the end of a year or so, however, relationships rearrange and the confusion that had dislocated lives becomes a memory. People return to *makom kavu'a*, their well-established place.

The Talmud tells about disorientation in an anecdote of a near-death experience: A young scholar fell into a coma. When suddenly he awakened, his grateful father, Rabbi Joshua, asked him what he experienced during that brief journey "to the next world and back." The son answered: "I saw an upside-down world" (*olam hafukh ra'iti*).

A world turned upside down affects all of life. From a physical perspective, when we cannot carry on as before we often neglect our health needs. We become distracted and preoccupied and find that making decisions is difficult. From a religious perspective, we lose our sense of who can be trusted, indeed, whether anyone at all can ever be trusted. As mourners, we become distrustful—even of God—often because we feel betrayed.

Therefore, it is generally unwise for mourners to change apartments, jobs, mates, and even friends during this period of disorientation. The absence of the departed and the re-formation of family relationships is change enough for any person. The mourner's task now is just the reverse: to stand still, find a footing, and slowly learn to walk again. There will be time in the future for making major change, but it is not now.

Disorientation leads to aimlessness, confusion, and muddled thinking. Reorientation will surely come, naturally and unnoticed. It will bring us back once again to thoughtfulness and purposefulness, and we can then resume our progress on life's fairly straight road. The Hebrew word *"kavanah"* means "intent" or "purpose" and is derived from *"kivvun,"* to orient yourself in a specific direction or to align yourself toward a constant, albeit distant, goal. The process of mourning should lead from disorientation to *kavanah*.

They Convulse Life's Meaning

"Life has no meaning anymore." "What is life all about, after all?" "If such a person could be taken in the middle of life, then life has no real significance, and we should not take it so seriously." When in mourning, we regularly use canned phrases, often unthinkingly, as verbal reflexes to the body slam of grief. But the fact that we use expressions that mirror vacant souls and meaningless lives indicates a latent, unarticulated fear that surfaces during severe crises.

In fact, Victor Frankl, the founder of logotherapy, considered this attitude to be the most salient characteristic of modern society: "The major existential neurosis of the modern era is meaninglessness; it creates an existential vacuum." True enough. While a sense of meaning alone may not bring peace to the victims or mourners, it may indeed ameliorate the sting of the episode and thereby pacify them.

As victims, our discomfort could be categorized as headache, heartache, or "God-ache." A headache is a transitory pain; heartache is profound suffering. But most serious is the spiritual suffering that comes with God-ache, an emptiness we feel in the deep recesses of our soul. We search our innards and find that life is just purposeless. The world makes no sense. Worse than merely being absurd, the world is unjust; chaos is everywhere and order nowhere. We seem victims of some random fate, without rhyme or reason. "What's the sense of it all?"

This emptiness is especially apparent after a death, when we lament that with the deceased gone, meaning is gone; that not only was the death senseless but life itself is senseless. This instinctive reaction to the trauma will surely diminish as our grief diminishes, but in the meanwhile, meaninglessness, at its extreme, can even lead to suicide. It is critical that we "make sense" of the world.

Of course, the feeling of meaninglessness during mourning is endemic to the human race. The horror of it is reflected in Scriptures. Ecclesiastes (1:2) scornfully looks at the world: "Utter futility! All is futile!" Some translate the Hebrew word "*hevel*" not as "futile" but as "wind." "All is wind"—just breeze and no content, meaningless life. The Psalmist, in a mood of despair, describes it so: "Man is like a breath, his days are as a passing shadow" (Ps. 144:4). Can there be anything less significant than a shadow? Yes, it is a passing shadow, one that brushes us with its fleeting temporality. Life is shown to be devoid of consequence, having no permanence, and making no difference. Gone. This theme is echoed by Shakespeare in *Macbeth:* "Life's but a walking shadow, a poor player that struts and frets his hour upon the stage and then is heard no more. It is a tale told by an idiot, full of sound and fury, signifying nothing." That is God-ache—a life that signifies nothing.

In mourning, as P. N. Furbank writes in his article "Unenlightenment," we often come to "lack what no human being can afford to lack—a narrative, a transcendent story that gives meaning to our world. We become, indeed, T. S. Eliot's hollow men:

> No loom to weave facts into a fabric,
> People with no gods to serve, hollow and
> Anxious, distrusting language, uncertain
> About even the most obvious features of
> Reality, lacking conviction, suspicious of truth.

When Meaning Is Sucked Out and a Vacuum Is Created

In the absence of a transcendent meaning, strange beliefs and customs can creep into the vacuum. For instance, during mourning, we sometimes exhibit a fear of contagion when dealing with death or even with any of the appurtenances of death. Some people are very strict about throwing away the deceased's worn clothes, as though they contained some communicable disease that might nefariously spread to the living. Jewish tradition does not approve of this wasteful practice. Clothing is better donated to the poor. The custom at the cemetery of not passing a shovel from person to person during the filling in of a grave but instead placing it into the mound of earth nearby could have grown from fear of infections and plague or from fear of a supernatural "contagion" of death, as mentioned in Chapter 1. And there is the custom that non-mourners should not drink of the "cup of consolation," the cup used by mourners for drinking wine on returning from the cemetery, certainly not before it is rinsed.

There are some peculiar customs concerning when not to visit the cemetery, too. One is discouraged from visiting when personal sadness conflicts with a communal Jewish festivity or a holiday or feast day and therefore is considered out of place. Several rabbinic scholars avoided visiting the cemetery after the dedication of the tombstone so as not to trigger the slightest possibility that they were imploring the deceased in necromancy; it is so easy to slip into the mode of "if only you were living, you would handle this terrible problem for me." But certainly the tradition nowhere suggests weekly visits or even condones it. Clearly, visiting the grave too often may obstruct the mourner's necessary acceptance that leads to eventual healing.

Other customs discourage women from attending funerals. This might reflect a fine degree of sensitivity for women's more demonstrative grief. But among some groups it demonstrates an aversion to emotional display, which they assume women will express and which they view as interfering with the serene atmosphere of the graveyard, disturbing its gravitas, as it were. Often, as in certain practices of the old Jerusalem community, youngsters and even adult children of the deceased are discouraged from walking at the front of the funeral procession, perhaps once again to avoid emotional display.

The fear of the unknown, the realization of our own powerlessness pitted against the awesome might of the Almighty in these matters, combined with an overwhelming sense of transcendence that is attendant upon every death, attaches formidable significance to rather insignificant matters. When such practices are handed down innocently from parent to child, they harden into custom and then evolve into religious tradition. While such practices never quite make it to the level of law, they become progressively more difficult to uproot. Indeed, preserving community tradition may be of paramount value in some settings and may even supersede certain individual needs. The more intensely religious the family, the more these feelings may find fertile ground. It is wise for mourners to consult an authoritative rabbi, one who understands the practices of mourning and makes recommendations in light of the individual needs, sensitivities, and overall setting.

Meaning Lost, Meaning Found

While it is true that the final question concerning our existence is whether it makes sense, it is a natural part of the process for meaning to be lost before meaning can be found. In grieving, we undergo a physical and psychological tearing down, a spiritual destruction and rebirth. This is not resolved either by rational analysis or by logical insight. We live our life in various realms of meaning, and our "meanings" are surrounded by a penumbra of mystery, impenetrable by reason. Nevertheless, as the intensity of bereavement recedes and the rim of the sun rises once again on our horizon, our minds are reoriented, the fabric of our inner thoughts is rewoven, the meaning of our life is restored, and our familiar places are regained.

The Open Wounds Will Close, but They Will Leave Scars

The wounds that the night raiders inflict are painful, sometimes appalling. Can we expect these wounds to be healed? If so, how long will our recuperation be? And if not, what measures can be taken to soothe them? If medications are not helpful, only postponing the resolution of grief, what spiritual or psychological means are there to treat these wounds?

For the first several days, the wounds of mourning are open and as sensitive as a severe burn. They cannot be touched or even approached without agony. The Sages wisely cautioned us not to comfort the bereaved when their dead still lie before their eyes. Fortunately, for most people the wounds heal sooner rather than later. In our heart of hearts, if not on our lips, we seek closure, and we therefore find it. Even as the vast majority of physical ailments heal themselves without medical intervention, so too the suffering of grieving. This is God's built-in mechanism for healthy people to recover naturally, miraculously, mysteriously, putting things back into place, despite death's deep disruptions.

In Jewish thought, God implements this healing through the medium of time. *"Mah she'lo ya'aseh ha'sekhel, ya'aseh ha'zeman"* (What the rational mind cannot accomplish, time will do). In fact, this adage does not stand as simply an assurance that in the end all will turn out well; it resonates in Jewish religious practice. The Rabbis said: *"Yishtakach min ha'lev"* (The deceased will recede from memory)—for parents in a year, for others in a month.

Even for the ancients, of course, this was an approximation. It surely is not an exact prediction, declaring that you will forget your beloved on a specific date in the calendar or that you are expected to do so. It only means that the sting of remembering will generally soften by that time. Indeed, the Rabbis venerated the remembered life, and this is why they instituted the yahrzeit, the anniversary of a death—for stoking the memory and pronouncing the *Kaddish*—and why the *Yizkor*, memorial service, is inserted into every major holiday service, a time when those who celebrate also suffer most the absence of their loved ones.

Yet, as we know, wounds heal differently, each taking its own time, presenting its own complications, and causing its own suffering. How long will it take for the death to be fully accepted and integrated into our being? Much depends on conditions. Were we conflicted about our relationship with the deceased? Were there other unresolved issues?

Each death carries with it some special kind of suffering. When a parent dies, we lose our past; when a child dies, we lose our future. If a child was killed or a parent dies neglected, we are bludgeoned by the guilt of not protecting our loved one—the most elemental obligation of being a parent or a child. We may feel guilty, as though the death were our fault, even if we know that it clearly was not.

Every death is different. Coping with the loss of an older child is different from coping with the loss of a younger one. Although as parents we love them both equally, our life experiences with them, our emotional investments in them, and our placements of them in the family album of our future are different. And the death of a spouse is different from the death of a child. The Rabbis said: *"Ein ishah metah elah le'ba'alah"* (A wife dies only to her husband); that is, the spouse suffers most—and this is an observable phenomenon despite the fact that a spouse is religiously mourned for only a month, not for the year that parents are mourned. And then there is the mourner who has lost a parent—whose grief people sometimes dismiss as natural, unexceptional, and therefore not so painful, even though it may be devastating to the mourner. They are orphaned adults.

But each loss is exceptional. Despite the fact that the wound will heal, the loss may leave a scar as the wound closes. That it does so is evident from the pictures that we retrieve from our memory and our dreams in times of crisis, when we reminisce and revisit the old days. All scars, in this sense, are different. Some leave signs of a deep gash that never fully fades. Some are lighter or less significant. Some are full on the face for all to see; others follow the natural lines of our creases and are well hidden.

Our scars are symbolized in Jewish ritual by sewing the garments that we tore in grief at the funeral. The wounds of grief are not cured, not gone, and not forgotten. They are healed, and life goes on. But the scar remains, and if we look closely we can see the stitches.

Chapter 3

Insights Essential to Healing

Were it possible for us to see further than our knowledge reaches, and yet a little way beyond the outworks of our divining, perhaps we would endure our sadnesses with greater confidence than our joys. For they are the moments when something new has entered into us, something unknown; our feelings grow mute in shy perplexity, everything in us withdraws, a stillness comes, stands in the midst of it and is silent.

—Rainer Maria Rilke

℞

A s mourners, we first must plunge into the thick perplexity of grief. And as we do, we should be aware of a number of truths.

Mourning Is a Cure, Not a Curse

Mourning is not grief but rather the way out of grief. Jewish tradition has molded many mourning procedures specifically to suit human sensitivities so that we can slowly and successfully adapt to a universe that is permanently changed.

The mourner's new world is now shrunken, bereft of a beloved person. When someone is torn from us it causes a rupture of relationships that our mourning customs sense exquisitely. Our customs wean the mourners away from the catastrophe by graduated psychological moves—first, through *"aninut"* (agreeing with the rage), and next, by relaxing its hold on the mourner between death and burial. Then by cutting mourners a wide swath, letting them spend a week in shiva, in the warm confines of their home, enabling them to heal their wounds privately, while strengthening them by bringing together family, friends, and community, armed with empathy, offers of physical and material help, and opportunities for socializing.

We Cannot *Not* Grieve

Human beings cannot outsmart grief. The experience of grieving cannot be ordered or categorized, hurried or controlled, pushed aside or ignored. Grief is as inevitable as breathing, as changing, as loving. As we enter the state of mourning we need to understand that the process of bereavement will happen—even if we try to ignore it, wish it away, or are confident that we are stronger than it is and that we can overcome it if only we are left to our own devices. Mourning may be postponed but it will not be denied.

The story of Arnold, a prominent social worker in Los Angeles, convinced me of this fact. Arnold told me that he simply could not understand how his mother had mourned his father. His father died twenty years earlier, leaving his wife, who absolutely adored him, and four young children. At shiva, Arnold's mother did not shed a single tear; later, she dove into the complexities of business and ran her household with enthusiasm. After her children married and moved out of the house, she remarried. But this second relationship was bitter. She grew to detest her second husband and was preparing to divorce him when he died suddenly. While sitting shiva for him, Arnold's mother broke down, wailed for her husband, and the flow of tears did not stop. Her children were stunned: Why did she grieve for a man she disliked so much but showed no sorrow for the husband she adored?

Arnold asked his mother why she didn't cry at the funeral of his father, whom she loved deeply. She said she was too focused on managing the family and the business, maintaining a face of courage and stability for the children, and simply could not afford the energy and time for grieving. He smiled sheepishly, nodding that he understood. His mother never overtly admitted to the anguish over the death of her first husband; she hid it from everyone and displayed a picture of strength. That was very brave, but there was this one problem: She could not grow beyond her grief, no matter how strong she was. When her second husband died she would not have shed a tear, but it was her first legitimate opportunity to genuinely mourn her first husband. Twenty years of grief burst from her heart and finally overwhelmed her. After two long decades, the dark chamber where she had stored her grief exploded.

Children Do Grieve

Mourning is especially traumatic for children as described in the book *Beyond the Innocence of Childhood*:

Death is not a mere possibility but a certainty for all of us. But for children, today's society unrealistically portrays childhood as a time of undiluted joy and freedom. Unfortunately, the reality of life may suddenly bring children face to face with tragic circumstances such as the death of their pet, the terminal illness of their parent, their own struggle with life-threatening disease, the accidental death of their sibling, or the suicide of a friend. The gravity of any of these situations takes children beyond the innocence of childhood and plunges them into a world that is frightening and full of uncertainty. Unfortunately, our perceptions and attitudes toward death do not equip children with the tools to help them cope adequately with such overwhelming experiences.

Adults spread their love among many meaningful relationships: spouse, friends, children, parents, and colleagues. Children, by contrast, invest almost all of their feelings in their parents. Only in childhood can death deprive an individual of so much opportunity to love and be loved.

Understandably, then, when adults look back at the time a parent died, they recall that it seemed like "my whole world disappeared." They suffered a loss that was irretrievable and irreplaceable. Sociologist Lynn Davidman writes: "When people under twenty-one years of age lose a parent, they never fully recover from that loss." The intensity and exclusivity of motherhood as it has been constructed in our society means that children who have lost their mothers feel they no longer have a stable foundation for their lives. The loss of a father entails other, but equally profound feelings.

Children certainly do grieve, but the process in children is opaque and more intricate than adult grief. This is made all the more complex because of their long silences, their hesitation to express a preference such as participating in the funeral and mourning, and their reluctance to express fear.

Many of the reactions children display in response to a loss are similar to those observed in adults, but the timeframe and overt process of grieving in the young are markedly different. Their cognitive abilities and personality structures are not mature. Children are more likely than adults to use more primitive defense mechanisms, such as denial and regression. These mechanisms put children at a substantially greater psychological risk. Denial, for example, may prevent a child from confronting and working through feelings of loss. Years may pass before the defense mechanism is released.

Underlying children's erratic, anxious, clinging, or obstinate behavior are common themes of sadness, rage, fear, shame, and guilt. Underneath these troublesome but reasonable feelings lurk disturbing unanswered, sometimes unarticulated, questions that haunt children who have lost a parent, such as:

Did I cause this to happen?
Will it happen to me?
Who will take care of me now?
Was this a deliberate abandonment?
Will a dead parent return and "get me" for my bad behavior?
Whom will death claim next?

We should seek professional help if our grieving children are sending any of these warning signals: Behavior that seems immature for their age; when the intensity and duration of grief do not abate at all or when what you perceive is sharply divergent from the normal (even though it isn't necessarily a pathologic response); persistent anxieties; fears of further loss of family members, friends, or pets; hopes of reunion with the dead parent or sibling; a desire to die, just as the deceased did; persistent blame and guilt of others or themselves; patterns of extreme hyperactivity; compulsive caregiving (a possible indication of self-blame for the death); proneness to accidents (may be a call for help); inability or unwillingness to speak of the deceased; an exaggerated clinging to survivors; a obvious absence of grief; strong resistance to forming new attachments; complete absorption in daydreaming; or prolonged dysfunction in school.

Many clinicians advise a time-limited intervention for all grieving children, and certainly for those who exhibit behaviors like those listed above. At the same time, we should not hold children under a psychological microscope and jump at the first sighting of a suspicious symptom.

When it comes to helping children through this difficult time, all professionals agree that promptness, honesty, and supportiveness are essential. Information should be geared to children's emotional and intellectual levels and ample opportunities should be provided for chil-

dren to ask questions about death. Children need rituals to memorialize loved ones (just as adults do) and they should be permitted to participate, in appropriate ways, in funeral or memorial services.

Often, children find solutions that seem logical to them but are simply the well-known "magic solutions" of young minds that are unable
to process traumatic information. Magical thinking, as it is called, is
motivated by the desire of children with incomplete cognitive equip-
ment to understand the world. Such thinking helps children develop
inaccurate conclusions about many aspects of death and grief—for example, that death is reversible, "like when daddy went out of town and
then came back." Such magical thinking can eventually deepen into
personality disorders. Psychological intervention may be required, often employing healing techniques such as developing safe spots, engaging in psychodrama, sculpturing, correcting distorted death stories, and
realizing the special cues of childhood to prevent the distorted magical
thoughts from taking hold. A very important goal of comforting children should be to reinforce the belief that the world is a safe, predictable place.

A major recent study supports the "keep-them-talking" strategy of
helping children after a loss. Children who felt that someone was listening to them and was open to their concerns were less likely to be
depressed or overly anxious following a death.

Children in mourning should not be compelled to behave in specific ways: to attend (or not attend) the funeral, to go to (or not go to)
the cemetery for the burial service, and they should not be compelled
to touch the corpse.

The profoundly sad moments of a family that must comfort a child
distressed by grief is expressed in this simple poem. It is from a classic
Japanese story in which a traveling poet-monk repays the hospitality of
a grieving family by writing them these lines:

Grandfather dies.
Father dies.
Son dies.

In the story, the family becomes outraged by the hurt they sense in this poem. In response, the monk explains to them that the poem reflects the proper state of nature: If you put the three lines of the poem in any other order, the result is tragedy. As we help children through the grieving, we and they can be comforted by the order of the poem, the order of nature. Any other order is only a deeper tragedy.

Some Grieve Even Those Still Living

More and more in our medically advanced age, we tend to witness slow, degenerative deaths that shut down lives in lingering ways. The suffering of the terminally ill, which can sometimes seem interminable, may prompt close relatives and friends to pray for their death. When the prognosis is not good, they begin to think of their beloved as never again leaving the sickbed. This is, as it were, equivalent to burying the deceased right there and grieving for the loss of the ailing person during the last days of life. Subliminally, it may even evoke the primitive human fear of being buried alive.

Judaism tries to avoid anticipated grieving by affirming that the first imperative of life is life itself. No overt mourning should be expressed while a person is still living. Jewish law advises that true mourning is not even possible while our dead lies before us. So even though we may mourn deep in our hearts for the terminally ill, formal religious mourning observances begin only after death.

There are conflicting theories as to the value of anticipatory mourning. Some distinguished psychologists decry it as overturning the grief process and intruding in the normal healing sequence. Others, equally distinguished, hold that it does nothing at all to impair the mourning process; quite the contrary, it affords us an opportunity to arrange a proper leave-taking of the dying person. Curiously, there is no similar debate relating to "postponed mourning," which refers to people who delay their grief because of pressing priorities, such as in the case of Arnold's mother. In such instances, when grieving is delayed it remains unresolved, often rearing its ugly head years or decades later—unexpected, merciless, and utterly unwelcome.

The "Beloved" May Not Be Loved

Not all our departed are truly beloved. For though we are told not to speak ill of the departed, no decree of etiquette can prevent us from feeling differently sometimes. To put it bluntly, those who give others grief during their lifetimes stir no grief in others after their death.

Clergymen commonly refer to the deceased, any deceased, as the "beloved." Yet ambivalence in relationships is universal. Surely, all who are involved in the process of mourning must seek to be respectful of the dead and to forgive their foibles. But casually referring to all deceased as "beloved" may sometimes spark anger, cynicism, and snickering in the mourner—or even cause more pain than solace.

Psychologists often observe that the quality of a relationship is the best predictor of the post-bereavement response. They maintain that a sound recovery after the bereavement of a spouse is more likely to occur in marriages that had been happy than in those that had been conflict ridden. On the other hand, Sigmund Freud held that the most important precondition leading to depression after a loss was an ambivalent relationship, not a negative one. But given the complexity of human relationships, few, even loving ones, are free of ambivalencies.

Should the deceased be mourned, even if she was unworthy of the honor, even if he did not do lovable or admirable things, even if she was downright repugnant? Not every person is a reliable friend, let alone an ideal family member. Friends choose one another out of mutual affection. But we don't choose relatives, and they may be disliked, envied, or resented for numerous legitimate or trumped-up reasons. By blood, all family members are kin; by preference, they may or may not be kindred souls. Can mourners for the "un-beloved" find meaning in our mourning rituals?

Here we need to accept the fact that an affectionate rapport with relatives is not the only paradigm for family life. Judaism is not a goody-goody faith, preaching lollipop moralism; it is a sensitive religion that is also moral and muscular. It understands human nature in the heights of its exaltation and also in the depths of its despair. As it provides psychological benefits through its mourning laws—without ever so much as hinting that these laws were designed for helping us—it also provides metaphysical comfort when we experience a profound feeling of alienation at the death of a close relative.

There is an existential crisis of the family relationship entirely apart from the psychological, the emotional, or spiritual. Even if we could not tolerate the deceased, we nonetheless have lost a family member with whom we may have shared our youth, our place in the family, mutual secrets, intimate insights, common concerns, or simply "space." After the death of any relative, there is a gap in the family, and the alienation that we may feel because the loss of an un-beloved is actually as terrorizing as the death of a truly beloved. This mourning often mystifies us. It is difficult to understand that there is something beyond "liking" and beyond "feeling bad."

It so often happens that when someone for whom we had little or no liking in life dies we still deeply mourn them. Baffled friends may ask: "Why do you grieve if you didn't love him?" The answer comes back: "But I miss him terribly." Friends may smile at hearing this, but it is not uncommon. Even a tarnished family relationship represents a shared life. The death of any family member can cause all other family members to shudder; the shrinking family diminishes everyone.

Another reason we bewail the death of even someone who is not very significant in our lives is the interconnectedness of all the grief events that an individual experiences. We come to every instance of death with all our other death experiences trailing behind us, informing our emotions, linking the melancholy, and sharing the grief. The mind lumps them together, and we can hardly separate them. When we cry for one, we do not cry for that one alone but for them all. In the end, it is not belovedness or un-belovedness that determines grief or the reason for grieving; every death inspires sadness.

PART II

REGENERATING THE HEART

Chapter 4

Shiva: The Habitat of Healing

Mourning is like re-entering the womb. We find a dark place where we can weep unheeded and become whole in our own time. Emptiness turns to hope in this safe refuge, this comforting cavern echoing endings and beginnings, slowly transformed again into a passageway to our other, older life.

—M. Fumia

Shiva is a sanctuary for grieving. It follows the course of suffering: It does not dismiss suffering with preachments of God's goodness nor cite easy assurances of desirable outcomes; it confronts rather than evades the pain of separation. In addition, it provides a profound though indirect healing regimen that leads us out of the entanglements of grief to a full acceptance of our loss and takes us even further, empowering us to growth and self-realization.

How does it accomplish such enormous tasks?

Carving Time Out of Eternity

Shiva responds to deep, rudimentary needs that are common to us all. It is Torah meeting us deep in our subconscious, in moments of profound despair.

We live in the infinite. We look up into a vast incomprehensible dome of billions of stars that are billions of years old—knowing that, even with our marvelous brains, we cannot comprehend the idea of a "billion." We stand at the edge of oceans, whose depths we cannot truly fathom, which stretch beyond the farthest horizon to the point where endless sea touches endless sky. We stand beneath wild mountain ranges that pierce the skies while they dwarf our souls, shrinking us to feeble Lilliputians. And we peer down into steep caverns.

Time and space both seem infinite. But we are mortal and finite, blips in the endless galactic stretches of the cosmos. To function in our world we need finite boundaries. To do that we must mark time and space. Boundaries enable us to orient ourselves; to navigate; to measure progress; to find meaning; to associate with ideas, with things, and with one another.

Because our lives, as we know them, are finite, we nail down special times—celebrations and commemorations—creating a grid that enables us to locate ourselves among the immensities and eternities. How far are we from this boundary, that end, this precipice? Though we are each created unique, we are not alone. How close are we to this relative, that neighbor, this friend? We base our relationships on intuition, voice quality, senses, logic, and a bewildering network of crisscrossing communications. Our personal distinctiveness is replicable in every person. But it is the fences and separations that enable us to identify and associate with others. This grid, with its limits, its exclusivities, and its foci, enables us to navigate. We have set boundaries in time and space that become our directional signposts.

Sigmund Freud noted that there is no innate grid of time and space in the unconscious; but as soon as we become conscious, we seek patterns in the continuum of time. William James explained that when we look at a wilderness we discern patterns that are not embedded in nature; our minds instinctively impose such a grid on the natural world. In fact, military map-reading courses teach this early on: If a geometric structure is detected in the wild, it is evidence that human beings have intruded on nature. The need for patterns, shapes, and boundaries is encoded in the human mind.

Not only do we need to measure time, we also need to invest it with meaning, purpose, and will. That is why holy days, memorials, fast days, and feasts, punctuate the calendars of all peoples—to commemorate historical events and to make sense of the morass of days. Professor Harvey Cox, author of *The Secular City,* called human beings *"Homo festivus"* for our built-in drive to mark significance through celebration. It is a spiritual counterpoint to our ever-present, ever-changing secular landscape.

When we apply these ideas to mourning, we discover that shiva is not simply carved from the calendar to sharpen our focus on what we have lost. It also enables us as mourners to locate ourselves and orient ourselves in an environment distorted by the disappearance of a signpost. Shiva anchors us firmly in a nucleus of stability, calm, and caring. Without the specific mourning periods—shiva, the thirty-day *sheloshim* period, the year of saying *Kaddish*—we would be lost in a morass of days; and in the end, we would free-fall into Shakespeare's "dark backward abysm of time."

Mindfulness

To appreciate the Jewish tradition of mourning, we need to understand the subtlety of mindfulness. To focus on a single event at a precise moment, we use our "acute awareness." We bring the event to the front of our minds, giving it our special attention. Other matters, peripheral to our immediate concern, reside in "latent awareness." For instance, when we feed our children breakfast and get them ready to go off to school, we hold them in acute awareness. When they are safely on the school bus, we may still retain them in acute awareness, but, generally, when we focus on work and other concerns, we move them into our latent awareness.

Grieving is so powerful and so mind altering that it demands acute awareness. When, too soon, we resume our workaday lives and marginalize mourning to our latent awareness, we also marginalize our feelings of loss.

Judaism is keenly sensitive even to our unarticulated needs. Ears do not hear the cries of the soul. Mourners may be convinced that they can just go on living; their upbringing may convince them that they can handle anything that comes and maintain their composure—but one day mourning will face them in their acute awareness. It is human. Grieving refuses to remain latent; it tugs at the human mind, demanding attention, even if it takes a lifetime. Diversion does not dissolve this difficulty. In this and other subliminal ways, the seven-day space of shiva synchronizes with mindfulness.

Reorienting

The Rabbis held that while shiva may be observed in a home that is most comfortable for the mourners and their visitors, ideally it should be observed in the house of the deceased, with the family sitting together. Where a person has lived, said the Sages, the spirit of that person continues to dwell for some time:

> It is, after all, in that home that one is surrounded by all the tangible remnants of a person's lifework, and it is only right that evidence of his life should be evident during shiva. It is therefore permitted to travel even long distances after the funeral in order to accomplish this. This is true even if no one has lived there but the deceased, and even if there are no mourners present; his spirit is there.

If this cannot be accomplished or is not suitable in present circumstances, the first alternative is to hold shiva in the home of the family member recognized as the head of the family (*g'dol ha'bayit*), who stands in place of a deceased parent. This replicates a traditional family structure into which we can reinsert ourselves as we did in our youth, learning—in that environment—to be empowered to leave that haven and proceed courageously to the next step of life.

In some cases, mourners come to sit elsewhere with other family members, helping those beyond the immediate family to rescript the future. On this level, the halakhah, Jewish law, provides boundaries, a space, to enable mourners to reorient themselves, even as we act out our disorientation.

During shiva mourners collide with clusters of the deceased's life: clothes, favorite pictures, furniture, hobbies, the accumulated stuff of life. In this collision, we are pressured to make an accurate measure of our distance from the departed, to locate our own life by reorganizing the very place we always met. In this way, we connect with reference points for reorientation, for learning where we are now and the direction we will be taking.

The deceased's soul is "present" in the deceased's home, hovering over the sadness and kindness. Jews of every kind, over a wide span of centuries, in a variety of Jewish communities, have found this idea comforting. In a contemporary sense, however, we can also see that the deceased's home—or the mourner's home—is the most natural place for us to reset our inner compass. Within the compressed experience of shiva, and within the invulnerable shield of our homes, we can recover our bearings and reformulate our lives. Call it "Habitat Shiva."

Adjusting the Focus

There is yet another way of appreciating the many-sided brilliance of Habitat Shiva. It is illuminated by our understanding of people, such as mourners, in transition. The anthropologist Victor Turner calls the transitional stage "liminality," meaning "threshold"—as "subliminal" means "below the threshold of consciousness."

Using Turner's concept, the mourner is a liminal person, literally on the threshold between one phase of life and the next. For example, in ancient tribal custom and often in modern practice, a person in transition from puberty to adolescence is in a state of liminality—living neither in the past nor yet in the future—and he or she exhibits strange characteristics common to all beings in a state of transition. In many cultures, liminal people may wear no distinctive dress that might reveal class or social standing, may not speak at all, may have no conjugal relations, may be mandated into total inaction, may allow their hair and nails to grow, and may exhibit no concern for social etiquette. The syndrome of liminality is characteristic of people deep in a transitional stage.

As mourners observing shiva, we are actually demonstrating a similar state of transition. We are no longer individuals belonging to a special class—we tear the fabric of our clothing to testify to that. We do not shave, we allow hair and nails to grow, we are bidden to be unconcerned with the niceties of etiquette—to not say hello or good-bye, but to grunt instead. We are foresworn from conjugal relations, and our posture guarantees passivity—we "sit" shiva. It is as though we were caught in a long, dark, serpentine hallway between two well-lit rooms. Before we emerge, we must brush aside the externals and everyday routines so that we can focus our acute awareness on surviving this transition and reaching the future. In a liminal sense, this hallway is a birth canal, a passage between one world and the next.

In this intermediate "no place," housed in the habitat for healing, mourners begin to acclimate to a future without the deceased and adjust their focus to the new environment they expect to find when finally they emerge from shiva.

Maneuvering for Stability

There are strange hidden remedies crouching shyly in the shadows of Habitat Shiva that promote the healing of grief in curious ways. These remedies are implicit in the observances of shiva, though we may be unaware of them.

I was once trekking up the base of a mountain in Vail, Colorado, when I came upon a long creek and could not get around it. The water was frantic but shallow. I found a path of stones balanced on other stones by which to cross the creek. As I stepped on the stones, I found they were shaky and would tip from side to side. With every stone, I had to switch from one foot to the other, back and forth, until I found my equilibrium. I could never have maintained my balance standing still; I had to move in rapid tilts to get from one side to the other.

For me, this was a graphic illustration of how we must keep our balance in life as we cross troubled waters. While we need to hold our heads high, experience teaches that to restore our equilibrium and get through tumultuous days, we may need to tilt and adjust, tilt and adjust, until we get to firm ground. Jewish law used this very paradigm for overcoming the tumult and disorientation of grief. Imperceptibly, it insinuated into the mourning process a surprising, even radical tilting of roles, of time, and of space.

Role Reversal

The medical breakthroughs of our age have altered the nature of dying, transforming it from catastrophic death to degenerative death. Lingering illness increasingly burdens relatives for longer periods of time—caring, worrying, calling, preparing, managing doctors and nurses, and transmitting daily bad news to other relatives. Even those mourners not directly involved in end-of-life matters carry the anticipation of this doomsday as a burden in their hearts for months. At death, the busyness turns to frenzy, and survivors must make major decisions, arrange the funeral, notify family and friends, and deal with myriad details: with hospitals, mortuaries, synagogues, and cemeteries.

Suddenly, the funeral and burial are over, the mourners recede from the fresh grave. And, just as suddenly, the tables are turned—they become death's victims and are at the center of concern, receiving all the compassion that until now was showered on the deceased. The transformation ritual is graphic and precise: Those at the grave site form parallel rows leading out of the cemetery, and the mourners wend their way through the line, receiving the muttered greetings of consolation. Halakhah made this specific moment a formal boundary in the burial ritual. Until the grave is covered and interment completed, every aspect, including the eulogy, must be directed to the deceased, the center of concern. But after the interment, everything undertaken must be supportive of the living.

The role of the survivors has dramatically reversed. The dying patient was the victim; now the mourners are the victims. The patient may have withdrawn gradually before death; now the mourners withdraw to the place of shiva. The patient may have been visited by the mourners; now the mourners are visited by others. The comforters become the comforted; the active turn passive; the ones who gave find themselves given to; those who fed the sick now find themselves being fed. In talmudic language, we go from *yekara d'shichva* to *yekara d'hayye*—shifting in a split second from "concern for the dead" to "concern for the living."

This silent turnaround tilts mourners dramatically, forcing them to seek the equilibrium that will enable them to navigate through the turbulence and eventually stand again on firm ground.

Time Warp

Between death and burial, mourners experience compressed time—there is a breathless rush to do everything to perform burial the very same day, or the next. This time is compacted by no less than three biblical demands to avoid leaving the deceased unburied. The consequences of failure, according to Torah, could turn into one of the most shameful moments of life, an infringement of the respect for the dead. Clearly, this is a time that is intended to be out of joint.

After burial, the velocity of mourning suddenly brakes. With purposeful suddenness, Judaism expands time and forces the clock to run slower. Shiva is slow paced, full of the listening, sitting, and chatting that requires much patience and much endurance. If the process of burial seemed too fast, mourning seems too slow. Physically, we dispose of the dead in double time; psychologically, we heal gradually. This time warp, built into Jewish mourning, allows grievers to heal at an emotionally healthy pace.

We are accustomed to the effect of jet lag on our internal clocks. It may both fatigue and energize us in a crazy-quilt pattern. We accept this as the cost of flying. Similarly, mourning is a lag on our minds. Death is the cost of life; suffering the death of close friends and relatives is the cost of having them. At the moment of loss, everything seems out of joint, feelings seem unexplainable, weeping seems inopportune, and our internal clocks seem thrown into frenzy. We cannot, and should not, combat the strange surges of our emotions, nor do we gain much by trying to explain ourselves to others or to ourselves. Let grief run its course, as it must. It will win, and—if we let it do so—we will win.

Space Switch

For mourners, space, like time, also changes. It may be altered on two levels.

The first is physical. In the case of prolonged illness, there is the dramatic switch from the broad landscape of hospital and cemetery to the narrow confines of a private home. As soon as the parallel lines are formed by family and friends leading mourners away from the grave to the house of shiva, diffused space becomes organized space. We are warmly tucked into home with those dear to us. On the surface this narrowing would seem to be a limiting factor, restricting our mourning. In truth, it is liberating because being home enables us to go back into our selves, to surround ourselves with people with whom we have affinity; and, what is more, much more, in this Habitat Shiva that encloses the start of our new life we begin to receive intimate guidance on every detail of mourning observance, an ancient tradition. Mourners are often at a loss over what is proper and appropriate, but Jewish law and tradition provide a strong hand that both limits and guides, bringing enormous comfort.

Essayist G. K. Chesterton illustrates this beautifully. Picture a plateau the size of a small house ten thousand feet above sea level. There are five children and a ball in this space. Where on this plateau are the children? They are huddled in the center, and the ball is not in play because the children are afraid that as they chase the ball they might fall off the mountaintop. Out of nowhere a helicopter lowers a fence that encircles the plateau. Where are the children now? Playing ball from one ledge to the other. The fence protects them from possible catastrophe.

Limitations keep us on a straight path, guide us, and require of us no effort. As Ralph Waldo Emerson observed, society's taboos are the guardrails on the bridge that spans the dangerous seas and prevent our drowning in our own excess. So the mourners, limited to the confines of walls, family, and friends, and constricted from the broad spaces of work and travel—the playing fields of society—are held firm, convalescing in familiar arms.

The second level is the "space switch" that we as mourners experience in the sudden change in the texture of religious observances from one day to the next. During the brief time between death and burial, all rituals are lifted from our shoulders. No prayers are required, no time-oriented, positive, religious practices need be observed, and even simple blessings are not permitted. We are encouraged to roam free over the day, possessed by our wild imaginings, suffused with gloom, and frenetic with the busyness of preparations.

Suddenly, from the moment we return home after the internment, we are channeled. To the grid of normal religious acts are added a cluster of customs specifically designed to express bereavement. The anonymous medieval author of *Sefer ha'Hinukh* says that the human purpose of these observances is that we as mourners act out our grief—not merely by expressing it through persuasion or right thinking but also by performing symbols and acting out the mood of grief, thereby weaning ourselves away from anguish. We go from the undisciplined savagery of death to the highly disciplined laws of mourning, and that is how we orient ourselves and return to family and society.

The Elastic Soul of Mourners

The elegant ritual of shiva is ingeniously designed to embrace not only the despair of mourners but the emotional and rational contradictions that are endemic to bereavement as well: denial and acceptance; solitude and shared grieving; silence and talkativeness; crying out against fate yet justifying God; and swinging wildly from spiritual negation on the first day to slowly realized spiritual affirmation in the days and weeks that follow. Shiva is superbly flexible, elastic enough to accommodate the wide variety of passionate responses to death, and halakhically tolerant of conflicting emotions and ideas.

This appreciation of the sometimes volatile nature of mourning is expressed by the halakhah's firm code, which, in circumstances such as death, is intentionally made malleable. The Rabbis, it could be said, were strict in enforcing the leniency of bereavement. The otherwise firm religious laws of living had to be tailored for the comfort of mourners. Life could not simply continue to be business as usual. When reality became taut, the Sages taught the wisdom of relaxing the strictures.

The Rabbis realized that a person's fiery emotions, passions, and hysteria could not be rigidly bound by specific times and or by religious fiat. Therefore, the final halakhic decision in a dispute over mourning practices follows the lenient position. Also, for example, in the laws of mourning, the principle inheres that "a partial day is equivalent to a full day." This means that a full "day" of shiva is downsized to a partial day—an hour or two. That is why the first day of shiva, which begins directly after the cemetery service, is nonetheless considered a full day of mourning, even though only a few minutes of daylight may be left. That is why shiva ends early in the morning on the seventh day, and this, too, is considered a full day.

This concept allows mourners to expand or compress the seven-day period to fit their inner need. Because the law is flexible in dealing with the grieving heart, it wondrously facilitates mourners in adapting to a rearranged universe, especially mourners at the two extremes—those believing themselves strong enough to dispense with grief and those that are too weak to manage the rigors of the grief period. It can accommodate mourners who have conflicting emotions and behaviors, seeking both solitude and sharing with others at one and the same time.

Grief Breaks into a Thousand Pieces

We tend to view mourning as a single unwieldy burden, a heavy load that we struggle under and are sure will finally wear us down. We just want to unload the heaviness from our hearts. But grief is likely to be triggered more by small details than by a solitary emotional upheaval.

During shiva, we stumble over seemingly insignificant things that stop us cold: an article of clothing, a familiar gesture, a sensitive touch, a giggle, a tone of speech, an article of faith, a preposterous mispronunciation. These trifles unexpectedly detonate explosions of memories, forcefully transporting us back to roads we thought we had already trekked. This fraction of our total loss may not be world shaking in itself, but it ultimately reaches into our core.

Healing Bit by Bit

The natural antidote to suffering piecemeal is healing piecemeal. The strategy of healing during shiva is not to reduce the severity of sadness but to confront the source of sadness: the death. By confronting the fact of death and our specific loss—frontally, shorn of the typical niceties of social life—we mourners ultimately find comfort through suffering. Only by exposing our wounds to the open air and the light of the day can we achieve timely closure. We get to the other side of the life cycle not by going under or by going over, but by going through.

The life now extinguished is examined in these days of fresh mourning, fragment by fragment. Bumping into the odds and ends of memory is not an annoyance, not an aggravation of an already painful situation, but a necessary step in reorientation. This is plainly observable and good theory, too. Freud, in his classic essay "Mourning and Melancholia," emphasized and reemphasized that the "work" of grief is in fact the slow resolution of the bits of grief the mourner suffers—the meticulous process that must be performed piecemeal.

Rummaging in the Closets of Yesterday

Facing our grief acknowledges the value of certain practices, not directly taught by Jewish law but implicit in its style. During shiva, especially in the home of the deceased, mourners may examine the drawers and closets that hold the treasures and the trivia of the departed's life. Some find that it is too soon after death to do this. Some can never do it by themselves but ask others to dispose of everything. There is no mandate either way; grievers should function on their own level of comfort in such matters.

We go through life leaving clues from room to room, whether what we do is noble or trivial, foolish or wise. The clues are always there if we look hard enough; they are either the inanimate evidence of physical left behinds—the letters and mementos, objects and odors—or the footprints of our activities, our life's journey.

Shiva is the habitat in which we mourners confront those pieces of the past. We bump into the remnants of life, such as the clothes and pictures; we listen to the stories of others; we have set aside seven days to contemplate the past; we touch things from the past that have unique aromas and textures. We begin to embrace the soul of the deceased, read cherished and dog-eared books, discover treasures in the picture albums, and listen to friends reminisce. In doing so, we take an unconscious inventory of the life of the deceased and tally the results—opening subjects and shutting them, finding closure by setting some aside and enshrining others in memory.

The healing of our angst is facilitated not by allusion to abstract principles and sage advice or by pills and needles, but by small, specific actions—the piecemeal disengaging from each association, the handling of each item that belonged to the departed. This is a powerful and beneficial aspect of mourning in Habitat Shiva.

Tracking the Tread Marks of Life's Journey

Just as we are surrounded by physical remnants of the past when we open closets, so we are soon surrounded by the deceased's outlook on life. If we go beyond chitchat with comforters and draw them out, they can help us reconstruct the biography of a person we thought we knew well. Why did the one we mourn take a particular direction? What were the achievements, the loves, and the angers our loved one prized? It is exceedingly rare to find no skid marks in a person's journey, to find that our loved one's life was smooth and that he or she just cruised through the years.

To track our beloved's travels on life's rough road, we can ask relatives and friends (who find comfort in helping): Where were the incidental stops and reverses, the sudden detours off the main road, and the times our loved one swerved? Where did he or she get lost? Were there times when she or he veered out of control? Shiva is a time for sharing information—to relate how our loved one managed to make a living and care for family or to hear stories of his early school years. What were her favorite movies, art style, or music? What effect did he have on the lives of others? This is the stuff of earthy immortality; these are the fragments we mourn.

Instinctively, as we reconstruct the biography, we make judgments; and as we smile or cry over foibles and stories never before heard, we begin to form a picture of a real person. Comforters often exaggerate when they speak of the dead, as though hyperbole and false estimates were solace to mourners. Yet it is possible that we can re-evaluate some of our original impressions, separating truth from glorifications, fables, and exaltations. The opposite is also possible. We may realize areas in which we perhaps underestimated or misjudged the deceased—and we may now feel free to recant some of the offhand criticisms made during a lifetime of judgments.

Ma'ase avot siman le'banim (The actions of parents are signs for their children). On its face, this means that children replicate the behavior and destiny of their parents. But profound phrases yield layers of interpretation, and this aphorism takes on an additional meaning in mourning: that the actions of the parents can be signposts for children to use—or perhaps disagree with—so that some of the pain that befell their elders need not befall them.

Habitat Shiva Is a "Heart of Many Rooms"

No two people mourn in the same way. There is a masculine way, a feminine way, a children's way, a parent's way, a grandparent's way, a sibling's way, and a host of ways for friends. Also, especially at death events, we express ourselves in a way that resonates from our unique psychological makeup. There is no one way that is the approved style of bereavement. Healing proceeds ineluctably and imperceptibly when we face terrifying small griefs in personal ways, especially when we finally accept our griefs and integrate them into our futures.

As complex as we are in our physical makeup, we are equally complex in our psychological beings: We have unique fingerprints, eye reactions, voice qualities, and DNA. Even more complex is the bridge between two unique individuals. That is why there can be no single answer to the problems of grief that so frequently stump us, and no single medication to stimulate our soul's immune system to immediately squash the disease called grief. Grief is an accumulation of energy in a person, and a major purpose of mourning is to successfully release that energy—idiosyncratically.

There are gender differences in how such grief is expressed. Men are less comfortable than women with a dramatic release, preferring slowly and deliberately to chip away at grief. Male mourners often intentionally suppress their sadness during certain times and then consciously bring it up later. Some psychologists call this practice "sampling"; other psychologists have referred to it as "dosing." Men are likely to heal through silence and solitude, with little of the therapy or group support that women favor.

Traditionally, the female style of grieving focuses on crying, hugging, talking it out, and using therapy and support groups. In our times and culture, this is often viewed as "the right way" to mourn. And yet, scholars on the cutting edge of grief research are finding that the masculine style has its own benefits, too, and is no less effective. It emphasizes thinking it through, acting soberly, and exercising emotional control. The two modes appear to be contradictory, but on a profound level they likely complement one another. In fact, the expression of mourning—male or female—may be more affected by other matters, such as a complex mélange of each mourner's background, fears, closeness to the deceased, and experience with previous death events.

Mindful of the elasticity built into shiva, the halakhah empowered people to respond to the life-shattering experience of loss in keeping with their own personality. One simply could not mandate talkativeness to a normally quiet person or silence to a verbose one. The style of each person's coping with grief must emerge from inside out—within the general framework established by the tradition. This ingenious arrangement, in synergy with the elasticity of the shiva laws and customs, and the strivings of each person's soul, provides the best possibility for restoring the mourner's health. It is sound, therefore, to take the advice of the Talmud—"make yourself a heart of many rooms"—and apply it to the management of our grief. Habitat Shiva includes the contrasting moods of many "rooms," each room calling forth its own spirit and style.

But the Habitat Is a Sukkah, It Is Only Temporary

Most people who have gone through the mourning experience can testify that Habitat Shiva, despite its magnificence, is notoriously unstable. The sukkah was a temporary dwelling or hut built by the Israelites and used by them during their wanderings in the desert before they reached Canaan. The ritual sukkah that we Jews build today is a hut, specifically built to be fragile by using see-through reeds or slats that enable rain to fall through, reminding us that our fate is in the hands of God.

Similarly, Habitat Shiva is a temporary shelter that stands for seven days, affording us limited protection until our strength begins to return.

It is exactly what the Psalmist sought: "[God] will Hide me in [His] Sukkah in the day of trouble" (Ps. 27:25).

In the day of our bitterness, we take refuge in this spiritual sukkah of healing, shielding us for the short trek until, by ourselves, we can reach our promised land.

Chapter 5

The Conflicting Agenda of Healing

Each substance of a grief hath twenty shadows.

—William Shakespeare

Mourning practices in Judaism enable us to respond in our own way and to heal as we instinctively prefer. That is why Judaism provides the time and the space for contradictory approaches to healing from mourning. For example, it nurtures our profound need both for silence and for storytelling, both for solitude and for shared grieving. All approaches to healing reside comfortably in the habitat for healing and, indeed, not only during shiva but sometimes also extending into the thirty-day *sheloshim* period.

Virtually all of the religious mourning observances and prohibitions flow from the recognition of the complex need for silence and solitude. They describe where the mourner stands at this raw, unprocessed moment after death: wanting to be left alone to commune with his or her own self, undisturbed. But silence and solitude are not only descriptive, not only self-indulgent; they are also prescriptive. They lead to gradual healing. Unaided and undisturbed, they can marvelously unravel the knots of internal agonies and conflicted feelings of grief.

61

Silence emulates the profound stillness experienced by the prophet Ezekiel, who was commanded *"he'anek dom"* (sigh in silence). From this, Jewish law derives its most notable mourning bans. Sighing in silence implies there should be no greetings, no study of Torah, because of the joy Torah offers. There should not even be any playing with infants, which bespeaks the most rudimentary enjoyment, and no participation in any form of rejoicing, no attendance at parties, festivals, and personal celebrations.

Solitude follows the same religious configuration. The mourner's urge to be separate from society accounts for the temporary abandonment of social niceties such as haircutting, grooming, laundering, and such, and it lasts until friends are annoyed by the mourner's wild appearance and self-imposed isolation. They say: "We are going on an important trip, *come* with us," implying that it is time the mourner returns to the community, breaks out from the shell, and no longer acts "like a leper" or an ex-communicant, living outside society.

In both cases, the halakhah institutes a curious religious process, exquisitely attuned to the grieving heart. It acknowledges the correctness of the mourners' behavior and at the same time it institutes practices that draw mourners out of these shells and move them from here to there, as though it were resuscitating them after their identification with the deceased, then leading them to a new plateau from which they can launch their return to normalcy.

The halakhah recognizes the need for silence by urging visitors to wait three days before consoling mourners—because while the memory of death is fresh, in the first raw moments, their solitude must be protected from outside diversions. Later, as the tightness eases, Jewish law strives to relieve the stark solitude by mandating that others to go into the mourners' home and share their grief.

To jump-start the process of self-healing, the halakhah indulges in yet another apparent contradiction. It recognizes the need for silence by instructing the consolers that the first thing they must do in the house of shiva is—nothing. They should be silent and let the mourner be the first to break the silence. And it prompts comforters to draw out of mourners the story they have just lived through, allowing them to unburden themselves of their suffering.

There are thus four approaches to healing, and they need to be understood separately.

Silence: The Numbness Dissolves

Words are the shell; meditation the kernel.

—Rabbi Bachya ibn Pakuda

The silence of mourners is natural and profound. The silence that Judaism ascribed to them is formally recognized, though it is never specifically mandated. Judaism emulated Ezekiel. It learned from the prophet's behavior, considered it to be a paradigm of grief, but did not translate it into a positive mitzvah of mourning. Nevertheless, it was so respected by visiting consolers through the ages that I refer to it as "Ritual Silence" since it is not only the lack of chatter that it embraces, but a silence ritually adopted, even in the midst of company.

Ritual Silence is a protected state. Mourners often sit quietly in the center of garrulous company, their hearts in another world. Here solitude is not silence. Although "solitude" actually means "privacy"—no questions, no answers, no company, no dialogue, no explanation, no good wishes—in mourning there is an additional need: actual silence, even among others.

As I mentioned before, silence is characterized by a biblical figure, one more prominent and much earlier than Ezekiel: the High Priest Aaron, Moses' brother. When learning of the sudden violent death of his two sons, Aaron responded starkly. His reaction is recorded in two Hebrew words: "*va'yidom Aharon*" (And Aaron was silent [numb]; Lev. 10:3). For Ezekiel, silence was a fasting of the mind. But the silence of Aaron was instinctive, not reasoned or planned. It was beyond silence; it was numbness.

Ritual Silence promotes several important values to mourners. Fore-

most, it is a barricade against the invading reality. It protects the grieving from the shock of recognition that they are bereft of someone very
close: a parent, who is a person's front line of defense against dying because they usually die before children; a mate, who has most often
"abandoned" his or her spouse and frustrated their mutual plans; a sibling, who has been a companion longer than any other relation; a child,
whose death is an unspeakable horror that defies intelligent articula-
tion.

Second, Ritual Silence enables mourners to live within their own
persona, where they can hear the "voices" and the familiar sounds of the
departed—the cry of pain or the rollicking laughter—and also replay in
their mind sequences of the departed's actions: a unique intonation, a
joke, an insight, or a blessing. In this silence, mourners can talk to the
deceased aloud, almost as though the loved one were present.

> *I sometimes hold it half a sin*
> *To put in words the grief I feel;*
> *For words, like nature, half reveal*
> *And half conceal the Soul within.*

> —Alfred, Lord Tennyson

Many of us are disturbed by the silence of others, reacting as if it
were a criticism. Living in a world of support groups and chat groups and
frat groups, and groups of groups, we sometimes think that silence is a
primitive or pathological reaction. In the past, however, society often
encouraged extreme manifestations of a withdrawal into silence. One
of these withdrawals was called the "rest cure" and its successor was
"continuous narcosis." The goal of these therapies was to keep people
quiet by literally putting them to sleep for twenty hours a day to allow
nature to mysteriously overcome a trauma or bereavement. Somehow,
it was thought, a vacation from awareness regenerated one's mind.

Well-meaning friends and relatives sometimes misunderstand the
mourner's simple need for a period of total silence and denigrate this
behavior as being "escapist" or as living by "wish fulfillment." But there

are actually several noteworthy ambiguities or indiscretions that silence hides.

In Silence No Struggle

A silent thought or a nonverbal nod to a knowing friend is worth a thousand words. In the context of such silence, we as mourners heal by mental shorthand—one nod for a thousand words—enabling us imperceptibly to reorganize the many pieces of the puzzle created when the life of our loved one exploded. Silence has this distinct benefit: healing when not being watched or checked can proceed at its own pace. There is no persuasion, no prodding, and no push in the midst of stillness. It is like the fourth of Deepak Chopra's seven Spiritual Laws of Success—the Law of Least Effort. You do not struggle against the moment, you flow with the circumstances. "Grass doesn't try to grow, it grows. Fish don't try to swim, they just swim." In silence, we don't try to convince anyone of anything; we just allow the healing to move through us at its own velocity.

Grief Exaggerates When Nobody Is Present

The dead do not become saints overnight. But love tends to exaggerate the deceased's stature, looks, brain power, kindness, generosity, and other attributes. Inflating these aspects buttresses our sense of loss and provides us with comfort, which may enable us to leapfrog the first moments of grief. But this is best done in silence. We should tell these things to ourselves, where there need be no outside test of truth and no strict absolute justice, and where no statement ever needs a defense. Exaggeration does not do well in public; it is for the mourner's ears only.

Intimacies Are Not Public

Silence is a retreat, a refuge, and a veritable asylum for refreshing worn hearts. Silence is also a haven for intimacies that are inexpressible, for mysteries that may not be verbalized—for hidden events, unspoken attitudes, remembered embarrassments, and closeted histories, which are not for public consumption. Indeed, ethics demands that we not divulge such matters, just as we do not speak ill of the dead, regardless of the truth. Silence is thus a *sanctum sanctorum* for intimacies, financial status, inheritances, marital relations, embarrassments, feelings of guilt, secrets, unknown faults, and other hidden circumstances that we would expect those who mourn us to shield from others. Many remembrances are not taboo, but they should be recalled in silence, not shouts. Yes, it is true that at its extreme silence is also an asylum for scoundrels who cannot make peace even with people already resting in peace. But that does not detract from the great benefits of solitude and silence in the matrix of calamities.

Silent Partners

The classic biblical mourner, Job, was visited by his three friends, who sat "with him" on the ground for seven days without uttering a single sound. Essentially, that is how God Himself consoled Job: "He set His presence alongside him" (as implied in Job 42:5–6). Ancient custom required that visitors sit silently on the ground with, and like, the mourner—an expression of "suffering *with*" that forms the word, "sym+pathy," together + feeling, and also "con+dolence," together + grieve. Although we practice this differently today, how elegantly simple is this "sitting alongside," and how it can relieve the sharp sting of solitude.

Ecclesiastes observed that there is a time to keep silent and a time to speak. Midrash to that verse records that the wife of Rabbi Mana died. His colleague, Rabbi Abin, came to pay a condolence call. Asked Rabbi Mana: "Are there any words of Torah you would like to offer us in time of grief?" Rabbi Abin replied: "At times like this Torah takes refuge in silence." In this spirit, Maimonides cautions visitors that they not speak too much because all words have a tendency to generate a spirit of frivolity that is contrary to the spirit of shiva. The Talmud assumes this when it says, "True reward comes to one who is silent in a house of mourning and talkative in a wedding hall."

And This, Too

Tristan, in Thomas Moore's memorable image, had no rudder and no oar and sailed the silver seas by the sound of his harp. Silence prompts us to inhale the cool air of the open spaces and permits us to flow with the music of our souls.

Telling the Story: Making Sense of Sorrow

Suffering in silence requires a suspension of feeling, which in turn leads to soul death. The hero of the American frontier was the strong, silent type; he could never become a psychotherapist's role model. To be "good" and silent is unnatural—to be a "good" patient or a silent sufferer is bizarre. This is not a Jewish path, and this appellation, "good," in no way describes a Jewish hero. If we are not to suffer, we must reach out to God, to the physician, to visitors who come to console, and anyone else who will listen, and tell the story of our fears and worries, thereby re-establishing our connectedness with life. It is a Jewish understanding that giving voice to our grief may dissipate the grief, and not only because it is cathartic.

When comforters talk, they air out a raw wound that will otherwise fester. This may sometimes seem sadistic and it may often leave the mourner crying, but the suffering will be less intense with each discussion, and talking will impart strength and increasing degrees of acceptance. Talk can begin the process of internalizing the departed.

The Power of Narrative

Storytelling is a basic tool of history and tradition. Society, like the individual, needs stories to define itself. All religions have rituals that involve storytelling, particularly about historical events, the changing of the seasons, holidays, and life-cycle occasions (such as births, marriages, and deaths). From ancient times, we Jews have enshrined the supreme value of storytelling by designing rituals that formally tell our classic formative narratives.

A good illustration is the biblical mandate that Jews tell and re-tell the story of the Exodus from Egypt, the central event of Jewish history. The Sages said of it: "The more one speaks of the Exodus, the more praiseworthy." The "telling" is in our prayers every day, but a special telling occurs on Passover eve, at the seder meal. Every Passover, seder participants are called on to recite the traditional words that describe the Exodus. But curiously, they do not simply repeat the biblical account, they relate a narrative that elaborates the story and emphasizes parts of the story to attract adults and children, and places different weights on different values. Those who sit at the seder build a new haggadah on the old haggadah until everyone integrates into his own memory a personally coherent story. The narrative itself asserts: "And all who expand [the Exodus story], are praiseworthy" because as they elaborate on the original story, they shed new light on God's work and relate the Exodus to contemporary events. Participants ask novel questions and provide novel answers. The story must seem new on every Passover, just as on every Passover it is basically the same.

Telling our story is not only useful, it is indispensable for human development. We are a narrative species. We survive by storytelling; that is the way our culture is transmitted. And this is profoundly true for individual survival: We must tell the story. It defines us; it gives us the immortality we crave.

In November 2000, the Russian submarine *Kursk* sank, drowning 118 crewmen. One man, Lieutenant Captain Dimitri Kolesnikov, felt compelled in those terrifying moments to tell the story. He wrote a dying message to his wife, which was miraculously recovered from the wreckage. In it he described his position and how he was trapped. Roger Rosenblatt, writing in *Time* magazine, noted that this impulse to tell our story is so enduring that it occurs in most such events. As a JAL airliner was nose-diving to destruction, the passengers wrote letters to loved ones. In the Warsaw ghetto, even after individuals saw their entire families engulfed in flame, they still left scraps of paper on which they wrote poems, thoughts, apologies, and hopes, and slipped them into crevices in the walls.

Narrative shapes nearly every human endeavor. It connects the dying with those who live on in the hope that the story or the note will someday be found. "We use this," Rosenblatt wrote, "to break the silence, even of death, even when—in the depths of our darkest loneliness—we have no clear idea of why we reach out to one another with these frail, perishable chains of words." Kolesnikov himself aptly described it: "I am writing blindly."

Shiva provides the framework for telling the story, as we wind and coil until we slip into our tailored world once again in perfect fit, reshaping our worldviews. We mourn appropriately if we tell our story effectively. Comfort cannot be fostered by diversionary chitchat; it is achieved by purposive, directional, and therapeutic presentation.

An Episode Becomes an Epic

Telling the story has the reverse effect of being silent. In silence, intimacies and secrets are amorphous, floating in memory. Silence enables meandering, whereas describing the numerous details of the death narrative crystallizes memory. It imposes a grid over myriad minutiae, molding the facts, *ex post facto*, into a sensible, digestible, methodical pattern. And as with all storytellings, it endows the details with a beginning and an end. The very act of telling the story, no matter its content, requires that it must be purposive and distinctive, and it must make sense. Soon enough, the words are cast into soothing prose, high-sounding phrases, and homey jokes.

We tend to think of memory as a camera or tape recorder in which the past is filed intact, objectively, and from which it may be restored whole. But memory is not that at all. Memory is a storyteller, and like all storytellers it creates new shape and new meaning by emphasizing some things and leaving out others. Subconsciously it connects events that were not meant to be linked, suggesting new relationships and meanings. Most significant, it almost always places the person doing the remembering as the central figure in the epic journey toward the darkness, often cutting out other important people from the picture. This makes the story the rememberer's story, but hardly history.

Also, the narrative will change from time to time, not only because of who is listening—a doctor, close friend, or an old aunt—but because remembering is an unfolding process bent on reorganizing the teller's universe, giving it coherence, and reorienting a life that will now be lived without a loved one. By telling the story, the mourner often discovers that initial impressions of what occurred and in which sequence were incomplete or even inaccurate. In fact, the more unexpected the death, the more likely this will be true.

The end of the mourning period and its narrative shaping often yield surprising conclusions. The story may have developed an unspoken, perhaps unrealized, purpose: to demonstrate one salient point—my dad was smart, my daughter was charming, my husband was caring. It also makes apparently random events seem purposeful. Rehearsing and retelling the story convinces the mourner of its integrity and understandability, and the mourner's own life takes on a meaning never intended.

Question: What happens if a grief-stricken person cannot tell the story? The story may be too horrible, or the mourner may be too fragile, or perhaps the mourner thinks it is too unimportant to tell to others. The consequence may be that the mourner will indeed remain disoriented for a longer duration. The process of narrative is so important that, without telling the story repeatedly, the mourner may find it exceedingly difficult to recover a sense of order.

I find myself going over and over the details of his death with everyone I know. To speak and speak again of this event proclaims its awful truth to me ... and so I allow the repetition, knowing that words are possibilities—of explanation, of comprehension, of absolution. My testimony, once familiar, will reassure my trembling, still questioning heart.

—M. Fumia

As mourners, we need to understand several important points in order to derive the greatest value from telling the story:

- We should retell the same story. This should be done as often as possible—even a hundred times—because it makes the death more real. Every retelling is a bullet that is fired at the ghost of denial.
- We should rehash the details of the final days; it brings the talk back to the loved one, enabling us to begin the process of internalizing our deep loss.
- It is appropriate for us to talk not only about facts but also about feelings—not in minute detail, but in general outline.

Telling the story reveals a concealed truth. We are not only telling, we are also listening. And those here to console us are hearing it from someone who is to be trusted, who knows the truth. Mourners find themselves hearing explosive words, which don't fall comfortably from their mouths because they are bitter, words like "He left me" or "That damnable disease ripped my child from my arms." They say the words and say them again until the stabbing shock wears off and the event becomes less and less an unspoken, incomprehensible, intimidating ghost.

The possibilities implicit in storytelling open the door to many things:

- **Clarification.** By changing our story slightly with every new audience, we realize more details, and we are simultaneously teaching it, learning from it, and deriving fresh lessons from it— all from listening to our own story.
- **Comprehension.** Unconsciously we are analyzing the event as we are describing it. It will begin to make sense, and we may discover why certain things happened as they did. There may be a sudden stop in the middle of a sentence—"Oh, now I understand"—and the realization will dawn. Even adults want to

hear what a ten-year-old wants to hear before he goes to bed: "Tell me that story again."

- **Forgiving.** When we are slammed against something incomprehensible like death, we make it more acceptable if we blame someone for causing or precipitating it or for exacerbating its horror. After hearing ourselves tell the whole story, we begin to understand it better and slowly tend to forgive those we may have been blaming. We see that there probably was no death-causing negligence, no malice aforethought, and no evil purpose. Slowly, we begin to forgive others, even God. And then, *mirabile dictu*, we may even begin to forgive ourselves. With the evaporation of blame comes a melting of shame.

- **Being forgiven.** Accepting forgiveness is equally important. Curiously, people often come to conflict resolution prepared to forgive one another but not themselves to be forgiven. To forgive says: You have hurt me, but I will lay it aside and we can be friends again, as though it never happened. To be forgiven means: I committed the hurt and I accept your kind offer not to remind me again of my wrongdoing. People are not often ready to be forgiven, and this makes the reconciliation of a relationship after death more difficult. Even after death, mourners are not prone to accept forgiveness.

- **Confidence.** Telling the story reassures us that we are capable of confronting the event, face-to-face, without fear, because we have become so familiar with it by repeating it so often. Yes, the memory will revisit us time and again, as it must, but it will be less disorienting as the days and the stories move slowly into the future.

Solitude: The Protective Membrane

"I want to be alone." "I can't sort it all out in front of everybody." "I don't need your advice, I need my own." "Give me some space." As mourners, we don't just casually drop these phrases; we plead them.

Coming to terms with loss is difficult and painful, and it is often a solitary journey. Although friends honestly want to share the burden, the process is essentially private because there are, after all, so many intimacies that were never expressed or could not be shared when our loved one was alive. Human beings are the only creatures that can see their own death coming. Instinctively, we prepare for that death by shucking our everyday interests and cultivating instead our interior garden, as Anthony Storr describes it in his book *Solitude*. This applies, in precisely the same manner, as we anticipate the approaching death of a loved one and even more so afterward, when we experience a loved one's loss.

"Solitude" is an elegant term, and it applies to a person who has a capacity to be alone and to be comfortable and thoughtful in being alone. As mourners, shiva places us in the confines of our home and in a boundaried timeframe and then grants us the freedom of solitude—removing us from society, its hurly-burly of interpersonal reactions, its frenzied demands, its etiquette, and its niceties. The Hebrew word for mourner (*avel*) means precisely the condition of solitude—withdrawing from society to the warm, intimate setting of privacy. Even if the wish for solitude is not for the positive purpose of concentrating on our loss but for the negative need to escape its intense pressure, solitude can be a blessing and empower us to regenerate our tired and battered soul.

We Find Ourselves

This solitary time can become enshrined as one of the most significant moments of our lives. Instead of losing ourselves we may find ourselves and come to realize who we are, what is most important in our life, and how we can live in the changed world with different resources. But before we can reorganize our new lives, we have to incorporate into our life that mysterious black hole into which the deceased has vanished. We need to experience the sudden bewilderment of living without the deceased (sometimes we even absentmindedly reach for the telephone to call him or her) and to verify for ourselves that this tragedy has actually happened.

Solitude has the potential of producing fresh thinking, creativity, tranquility, and even a sea change in our outlook. This is because the freedom that solitude affords us enables us to turn over our mind at our own pace, rather than listening with a tin ear to unsolicited advice. Only solitude promises the possibility of new insights and realizations, as well as attitudinal and, ultimately, behavioral change. Perhaps the mind has to be left alone so that it can churn matters and realign the different emotions in a sort of "incubation." However, if solitude is enforced, it could become a kind of imprisonment, a solitary confinement. It may leave us with the impression that there is simply no one to accompany us on this awful journey, no one to share our burden.

And if solitude is not just an absence of others but a long sought-after need to become truly our own self, it transforms into a different dimension. It may well become an exercise in true healing, a replenishment of the spirit, a desire to get on with the future. In practical earthbound matters, solitude can lead to a refreshing of our mental energies, a restocking of our imagination. It is an asylum from the blandishments of a world that is too worldly.

A leading exponent of humanistic psychology, Abraham Maslow, wrote poignantly of "peak experiences" such as solitude that enable people "to become selfless, timeless, outside of space, of society, of history." We become free from other people, which in turn, enables us to become more of ourselves. The mourner's withdrawal to the shiva house is roughly similar to a spiritual retreat, seeking asylum from the thousand and one slingshots that puncture our grieving souls.

In solitude a realization may dawn on the mourner, from "nowhere," that meaning in life is not always tied up with interpersonal relationships; that intimate relations with the deceased are at an irreversible end; and that even without this personal intimacy, life can still continue to hold our interest and our hope.

It is curious, Anthony Storr says, that the natural state of the human is not as an individual. The word "individual" originally denoted "indivisible," which today is its opposite; if two people are indivisible they are not individuals. "Individual" was not solitariness but a union of one human with another. During the Renaissance, an inversion of the word took place. It shifted from meaning "indivisible and collective" to mean "divisible and distinctive"—moving from a sense of unconscious fusion with the world to a state of conscious individuation, separateness, solitariness—the very opposite from its original sense of the human collective.

Why We Choose Solitude

Many factors will determine whether an individual will turn toward others in grief or toward solitude and self. But it is not true, as many of us assume today, that interpersonal relationships are the only, or even the best, method of finding the answer to every possible distress. Our society has placed overwhelming emphasis on group participation, "milieu therapy." God forbid that a mourner should be allowed solitude—because, we fear, all solitude will be taken as abandonment. Yet by religious definition, mourners are closer relatives to the deceased than those who visit them; mourners have a history with the deceased that none of the visitors has had. Is it not possible that they may be able to learn from self-examination more than from a friend's well-meaning suggestions?

Solitude can be just as therapeutic as support groups for many mourners. In fact, it may be the most valuable resource individuals have. Solitude allows men and women to get in touch with their deepest feelings in the stillness of the night or in the quiet of the home, enabling them to come to terms with their loss. It may well result in modifying initial reactions, controlling anger, and repairing the damage to the soul. As it has been said, the owl is considered wise because while all of us can see when it is light—only the wise can see when it is dark.

Some people only see it as being happy with people or being lonely alone. With maturity another possibility arises: being happy in solitude.

Of course, we are essentially social beings who need to connect with others. But a human being can have interests as well as relationships and a rapport with the world of ideas as well as with people. In fact, it is generally recognized that people, as they age, are more inclined to focus on the larger questions of life rather than the incidental conversations with friends and relatives. Thoughtful people sometimes take long walks, without company, because there seems to be so much new in the world they haven't yet grasped, so much to wonder at and plan and worry over and try to disentangle. Solitude seems to have its own fullness, enabling us to be satisfied to be by ourselves, burrowing into time.

For those individuals who prefer solitude in the aftermath of a trauma, it behooves the community to appreciate this and to allow them to restore their composure according to their own lights.

> —When from our better selves we have too long
> Been parted by the hurrying world, and droop,
> Sick of its business, of its pleasures tired,
> How gracious, how benign, is Solitude!
>
> —William Wordsworth

Sharing Grief: Submerging Loneliness

There is a religious paradox that the Jewish tradition has known forever, and it is fascinating how our profoundly sensitive and streetwise tradition has solved it. On the one hand, the Torah calls the mourner "*avel*," which means "withdrawing." The Torah clearly understood a mourner's desperate need for solitude. Then, immediately, the Torah turns around and instructs friends and neighbors of the mourner to go to the mourner's house to relieve his solitude. The tradition is clearly saying that the one thing mourners desperately need is to have other people with which to share the burden, to draw them out, to listen, and to not leave them in solitary confinement. As much as mourners need to be alone, they need to be with others. Curiously, marvelously, the tradition sanctioned—indeed, encouraged—both solitude and shared grieving.

Of course, the inherent contradiction between these two needs is obvious. If you want solitude, you can't have company. If you are pining to be alone, it is self-defeating to invite friends to share your thoughts. And if you like company, by definition you will have no solitude. How can both happen at the same time?

Let me explain.

People require a human presence, a warm voice, and a sympathetic glance to reassure them that they are alive, that their thoughts are valid, that they are not alone in this wild, wild world. This may be an even more crucial need than solitude, especially following the worst tragedy of life. It is an ineluctable fact of the human condition.

The famous rabbinic authority Rashba tells of many friends gathering at a house of shiva—and no one was *menachem* (consoling). What should they say? he asked. Nonetheless, it is considered consolation, "even if there are no words of consolation, because the presence of friends, gathered in [the deceased relative's] honor, is itself a consolation."

Here, once again, the halakhah blends one quality into another, advancing the healing process without mentioning it; doing it in subliminal and elegant fashion. Solitude gradually and naturally leads into shared grieving—known as *nichum avelim*, "the comforting of the mourners."

Visiting mourners is not an act of courtesy or even a deliberate means of consolation so much as the performance of a supreme kindness, a biblical mandate: sitting silently with the grief-stricken until they break their treasured silence, listening to their story, relieving their solitude by sharing their grief, praying and hoping for their comfort, and offering them assistance should they need it.

If telling the story is the core agenda of Jewish mourning, shared grieving is its forum. All of the comforting and consoling takes place inside the framework of sharing grief. The mourner's desperate need of silence and solitude is matched only by the universally desperate need of company—the presence of other people—warm, compassionate, sensitive, listening, empathetic human beings.

Can it be that people at certain times in life want to be alone and to be together at one and the same time? Yes. The Oxford theologian and apologist C. S. Lewis desperately wanted to be alone after the death of his wife, but he couldn't bear to be alone. He asked his friends to come to his house—and to speak only to each other! He wanted solitude in the midst of visitors.

A graduate student of mine at Yeshiva University's Rabbinical School told the class that after his father died, he needed to be alone. And so, after returning from the burial, he sat down before a television set and turned the volume up high. One of the students snickered: "You call that solitude?" The grieving student answered without hesitation, "I had to have the television chattering in the background, to leave me alone." Human presence, a voice, a listening ear, conveys warmth and security; but it should not interfere with a journey that must be made alone and in silence.

The Best Way to Lighten a Burden Is to Share It

Jewish tradition assumes the idea that, in the shorthand of the street, misery loves company. As shallow and callow as this phrase is, it is generally true that mourners often suffer misery and almost always love company. So Jewish tradition brackets consoling the present mourner with all other mourners—she'ar avelei Tziyon vi'Yerushalayim (the other mourners of Zion and Jerusalem)—otherwise, if he turns a deaf ear to other mourners, his consolation visit does not fulfill strict halahkic requirements. In this way did Judaism bond the griever to the community of grievers—implying that we are never alone, even in the circumstance of a death. Connectedness is a visceral need of the unfortunate, and they seek at least a distant linkage. There is no exit from the throes of grief without the touch of others, whose mere presence can illumine the way. The possibilities of shared grieving present the mourner with the supreme blessing of the shiva mourning period—working through personal grief in tandem with the likeminded—and it is one of the most powerful advantages of the religious mourning procedure.

An insight discovered in the twentieth century's scientific frontier, genetic engineering, yields a similar conclusion. Not only is "no man an island," as the poet John Donne wrote long ago; no human or animal gene is either. Genes share their work in groups, and the performance and specific architecture of each one intimately affects the performance of others. Single genes have no singularity.

Friends and community must visit, even uninvited, those who find themselves isolated, imprisoned in a cell in the company only of pain, even though they may be only peripherally acquainted with the grievers. That is the center of the mandate to console mourners. Continued isolation is to some mourners the worst-case scenario of grieving, although they often instinctively pull away from a crowd, separating themselves from the very source of their succor.

Grief is a universal power that, since our beginnings, has linked all human beings together. It opens up to each one of us the connectedness of all human suffering and keeps us ever conscious of the healing possibilities of shared grieving.

Chapter 6

The Healing Rituals

While grief enters the house as a stranger, it often leaves as a friend. A messenger who brings unwanted news, grief stays to endure our disbelief, and to instruct us in the healing art of profound acceptance.

—M. Fumia

Ritual is the most maligned of religious values, for we rarely appreciate or even realize the benefits we get from it. Ritual is a superb emotional stabilizer for individuals. It is a remarkable unifier of people and of communities that may be separated by great distances. And ritual, more than any other behavior, transmits the values of one generation to another, because its shared language and meaning transcend time and place.

The word "ritual" is Middle English and derives from the Latin "*ritus*," meaning "to flow" or "to stream." A rite is the river itself. If our stories arise from deep inside our senses, rituals are the eternal rivers that flow through them, irrigating them with fresh vitality. If you think about it, the most pervasive feature of ritual in all faiths and in many social organizations is water—its purifying, refreshing, transforming, cleansing, and sustaining traits and its power to promote growth in everything. And so ritual's origins in streaming, *ritus,* is understandable.

Transitions, especially, are characterized by specific ritual behaviors that have their significance just below the surface of our consciousness. Ritual is subrational, not rooted in logical behavior but in a cultural system. Most Jewish ritual is ancient—either mandated in Torah or designed by Sages and scholars of our early history to deal with the crises of living and to implement major concepts of our religion. It is of the dark stuff that mysteriously flows to nurture our character, our style, and our faith.

Rituals perform a great service in Judaism, especially in our times of grief. They legitimize personal feelings, stimulate spiritual sensitivity, promote a spiritual relationship with the deceased, and build a protective fence that nurtures freedom; they coax a gradual healing, provide an authorized map to Jewish bereavement behavior, and release psychic energies that may have been repressed since childhood.

They Secretly Germinate Values

Sigmund Freud affirmed that small acts of ritual can mold a mourner's thinking and maintain mental health. He assigns to the "work" of mourning the rituals that are "evenly calibrated, methodical, and at almost an industrial pace." This characterizes Judaism's awesome contribution to the healing process of bereavement, as vivid today as it was three thousand years ago.

For example, the ancient requirement of sitting on the floor alongside the mourner recalls the instinctive action of Job's friends. Today, this is accomplished by sitting on a low stool. It works now as then to stimulate mourners to contemplation, rethinking, and retelling their story, until that which appears to mourners as passive and time wasting actually opens up a fresh personal space—a site of inchoate, deeply sunken grief into which they insert their ambiguous feelings.

Joshua Loth Liebman, author of the classic *Peace of Mind*, affirms that the halakhic observances of the mourning laws are in sync with the most recent psychological findings, encasing remarkable insights such as the shiva ritual. Dr. Liebman was a Reform rabbi who understood the value of ancient rituals and insights into the halakhic view of grief management.

Conversely, rituals also function as limits to expressing grief. They keep mourners within reasonable bounds—not permitting them to reside inside a cemetery (as in the City of the Dead in Cairo) or in the hollow base of pyramids or to spend a great deal of money on an elaborate casket and shrouds. Rituals also teach us how to commemorate; how much to celebrate other events, such as weddings, that coincide with mourning and contradict the grief work; how to keep holiday observances in the face of joylessness; and how much or how little to memorialize the dead to avoid both pathology and denial.

Jewish ritual weaves relationships. In day-to-day living at the table, it requires a minimum of three people to offer community gratitude. At prayer services, it requires a minimum of ten people to acknowledge the greater glory of God. Indeed, it is a mark of our aloneness today that, outside of our religion, there are very few community rituals for grieving.

Because Jewish ritual thrives on relationships, the observance of holidays for a mourner is particularly poignant. Holiday observances in the absence of a child, parent, grandparent, sibling, or spouse confer upon us a renewed sense of loss. We feel utterly bereft of our deceased at an event that customarily celebrates togetherness. And if we frequently shared rituals with the deceased in the past—especially spouses with whom we may have shared holidays for a lifetime—those holiday rituals will trigger many memories. We sense our lost relatives when we hear the *Kaddish* recited, when we see favorite holiday foods being prepared, and when we sit at the Sabbath table.

Rituals also have the power to transform an event like a funeral into something larger and more timeless, as participants join mourners who have performed the same ritual for generations. The recitation of the *Kaddish* at graveside, the tearing of the garment, and the lighting of memorial candles—especially with the whole family gathered—are community rituals that magnify the honor of the deceased and are expressions of love intensified by the collective power of all the souls present.

Rituals also enable mourners to walk more securely as they make their way, benumbed, through the funeral, the burial, and the grieving. When we mourn, we find ourselves in strange territory, no matter how many times we have suffered loss. We cannot express ourselves appropriately, unsure of what is proper, of how to express mourning, of how to greet guests, of even how to pray. The mourning rituals give us the reassurance that we are expressing our grief authentically, in a time-honored and legitimate fashion.

I had the clearest proof of this when I wrote *The Jewish Way in Death and Mourning*. The response to the book was uniform: gratitude for the consolation the book offered. There was only one problem, and that was that I actually offered no consolation at all. What really emerged was a new understanding: People could draw comfort from knowing what Judaism expected them to do. In a time of disorientation, the Jewish tradition takes mourners by the hand and walks them through their bewilderment. Knowing that "this is the way it has always been done" frees mourners from having to make numerous decisions and gives them the opportunity to indulge their sadness.

Thus Jewish mourning rituals carry an especially rich significance. They apply only to select moments, are targeted for specific personal events, and are therefore observed with a clear sense of purpose and care. The meanings these rituals convey are not of an intellectual nature but rather of enriched personal human experience, a fact that considerably heightens their value.

But here's the rub: There are masses of Jews who invest rituals with no transcendent meaning—perhaps out of lack of knowledge, perhaps because of their lifestyle or background—and consequently do not follow any of them. When that is their choice, no logical persuasion will help convince them to do otherwise. Staunch secularists should know, however, that when they confront a death in their own families or circle of friends, secularism offers no help—no new meanings, no words of comfort. Rituals are not magic, not abracadabra soul tranquilizers. They must be observed for authentic religious or cultural reasons; they are not effective merely as quaint customs. To be truly effective, rituals need to be played by the rules and not modified by personal predilection. Having said this, it might be wise for those who generally cannot abide rituals to cut themselves some slack; allow themselves a nonintellectual exercise; and perform the rituals for the sake of tradition, in honor of older generations and in respect to our millions of forbears who lived and died in spiritually meaningfully ways. Those who authentically do not believe that observing these rituals are necessary are equally decent and moral people, even though they do not feel bound by specific ritual behaviors.

Tearing It Up and Sewing It Up: *Keriah*

A tear in the fabric of the family has historically provoked the grief-stricken to tear something, or to rage and rip, to strike out, even to wield a hammer. Throughout successive ages and cultures we have witnessed people cutting gashes in their skin to express the horror of a loss or spilling their own blood in sympathy for a relative's spilled blood. Judaism never tolerated such behavior. But it did enact a symbolic gashing—on the clothing that mourners wear over their heart. In our day and age, this rending is often performed on a small black ribbon, but here I speak only of the halakhically mandated tearing of clothes, the ritual as prescribed by our Jewish legal tradition.

The Ritual of Tearing: Permissibility of Rage

Biblical law decrees that we as mourners make a tear in our clothing when learning of the death of a relative, teacher, or prominent scholar; for a cataclysmic tragedy, such as the burning of a synagogue; and for a family or community disaster. The tear is called *keriah* and it is one of the most striking Jewish expressions of grief. Jacob stabbed his clothing when he saw Joseph's bloody coat and thought that his son had been killed; King David tore his clothes when hearing of King Saul's death; and Job, who knew death too well, stood up and formally rent his coat.

"*Keriah*" means "ripping" as in the ripping of the fabric of a shirt, suit, or sweater—on the left side over the heart at the death of parents and on the right side at a distance from the heart for the death of other relatives. Mourners tear fabric, not skin, in an act of controlled agony that expresses deep frustration rather than angry vindictiveness. It is the one ritual that most obviously expresses the mourners' inner feeling. Indeed, the halakhah stipulates that the *keriah* be performed only during *chimum*, the "passion" of grief, rather than as a standard ritual observance. The law requires that the rending of the garments be performed while standing. The posture of first accepting grief in Jewish life is always erect, symbolizing both strength in the face of crisis and respect for the deceased.

Tearing the clothing as an expression of emotions deeply felt releases psychic energies of grief that might otherwise have been repressed and actually acts them out in a public display. This might indeed help prevent any real self-destruction that may grow wildly from the bottomless blackness of depression. *Keriah* expresses the grief but also prevents an untoward expression such as scarring one's face or tearing one's family apart.

In this we can see that rituals not only express feelings but also mold them and tame them, protecting survivors from the excesses of their pain. We can also see that the less society believes in a soul or spirituality, the more it needs to seek reassurance from rituals like *keriah*.

It is interesting that, because the law was concerned with the sadness over a death, it prescribed *keriah* not only for grief within families but also for grief over the death of teachers, scholars, and rabbis; they are our Torah "parents" and they too are mourned. Judaism placed this under the rubric of "*et tzarah*" (a time of terrible personal trouble), which is also a warrant for a lifetime of grieving for parents, children, and other beloved and respected relatives.

The Ritual of Mending: The Limits of Grieving

The laws of *keriah* address not only the tearing of the garment, representing separation and loss, but also the repair of that tear, which represents the closure of grief. *Keriah* is an expression of grief and also an expression of healing; the tearing and the mending are the sunset and sunrise of mourning. As it is expressed in Ecclesiastes (3:7), there is "A time for ripping and a time for sewing."

Traditionally, a daughter, for reasons of dignity and modesty, may baste the clothing that was torn as soon after the funeral as she wishes. A son may baste his clothing only after thirty days. After shiva, the rent clothes need not be worn. However, neither son nor daughter may ever permanently sew these clothes. The wound left by the passing of parents may be healed, but the scar never disappears completely.

For other relatives, mourners are required to perform the rending of the clothes but need not make the rend visible. Thus, if they change their clothing during shiva, they need not rend the new clothing. The clothes may be basted after shiva and, unlike when mourning for parents, sewn completely after thirty days. If a major holiday occurs during shiva, mourners may sew the clothes before sundown.

Clearly, no intimate relationship can ever be duplicated, but a parent is a special case. A parent literally cannot be "substituted for" as a spouse might be, not "replaced" as a young child may be, not "added to" as a sibling may be. The halakhah could not possibly respond to every nuanced and idiosyncratic trauma; it had to provide specific guidelines for masses of people in each generation, and the Sages surely realized the impossibility of replicating or cloning any individual loss. For example, Midrash recognizes that "a woman dies only to her husband"—the husband is the most affected—but still he sews up the tear rather than bastes it. Ritually, the tentative, hesitant, incomplete act of basting is strictly reserved for the loss of parents.

The mere fact that the halakhah took special note of mending and made specific requirements and subtle distinctions about how it is to be done and for how long speaks eloquently about the need for closure. Special times and rituals to express an emotion are difficult to accept, but they are important to establish if a ritual is to work for us at all. No one can be commanded to do anything at any time; people need exactitude and specific timing.

What determines the time of closure? The rabbis call closure "*yishtakach min ha'lev*" (forgotten from the heart). Certain mourning practices are done to ensure that the deceased not be forgotten; other rituals are limited because the deceased is indeed considered "forgotten." For example, mourning for parents lasts one year because that is how long they are "remembered"; for other relatives, mourning is for thirty days because they are "forgotten" more quickly. These are the ritual times for closure.

Now, obviously, the idea of "forgetting" cannot refer to forgetting a child in a month or forgetting a sister after thirty days. If anything, the Rabbis were more acutely aware of such sensitivities than we are and it is unthinkable to assume that the halakhah would venture such generalities. This is clear from the law that one who tears clothes in a moment of agony does not sew them up for a lifetime, except that the clothes may be basted, as a mourner does after a parent's death. What it means, rather, is that the sting or bite of the pain, the initial anguish and its wretchedness, begins to subside after thirty days for some relatives, whereas for parents it takes a whole year. The pain is not forgotten, but defanged. The duration of anguish, *et tzarah*, is what the Rabbis refer to as *yishtakach min ha'lev*—and such time estimates can be legitimately assessed in a general way, as emotional grieving cannot.

Sewing turns the fabric into one piece again; basting holds the two pieces together but the clothes are not fit to be worn. Sewing is tight, closed, and natural looking; basting is loose, open, and flimsy looking with long stitches, and not obviously closed up. Basting creates a porous fabric—it keeps everything in place, the Gestalt is whole; but between the stitches memory seeps through, oozing the deep regrets of the human heart the torn garment covers. On the right side, a little farther away, the tear is sewn, the interstitial spaces are shut. The world moves on.

Both tearing and mending have not fared well in our contemporary society. Tearing is not commonly done for reasons of fashion, dignity, and rebellion against any religious hegemony; mending is unusual because in our abundant economy we can replace our clothing instead of fixing it.

But the symbolic lessons—of both the tear and the mend—remain relevant and significant. Tearing is biblically mandated and, according to Jewish law, must always be done. Mending is not mandated; it is done only if the mourner wishes to continue using the garment. In practice, I counsel tearing, as required by the Torah, and mending, seven days later, rather than discarding the garment, for I view the mending as a graphic statement of closure. It seems proper to wear the sewn-up garment at least briefly before putting it aside.

Symbolically, all mending, whether sewn or basted, leaves behind a scar. The stitches of the mending remind us of the removal of a person from our lives. The scar proclaims that no death can be cured, only healed; that no family is made of whole cloth, never having suffered tragedy.

The Funeral: Confirming the Absence of the Absent

It seems natural that of all the rituals surrounding death, the funeral and burial service are the two that most hammer home the fact that the end has come for the deceased. Funeral rituals, more than any other, should erase any possibility of denying the death. Unfortunately, this is not always the case.

In the United States, the reverse is often true. Specifically, because the funeral is intrinsically a somber death notice, professionals—from psychologists to undertakers (with the complicity of unsuspecting consumers)—have ceremoniously masked every aspect of the end of life and taken the death out of dying. That is why we experience a profusion of solemn-sounding denials at funerals that can actually forestall a mourner's healing.

The dead person is all too often viewed in wedding attire, masked by cosmetics, stippled and stapled. The casket may be adorned like a luxurious bed. At the service, the family may sit behind a veil, separated from the casket and from their friends. At the cemetery, the grave and the mound of earth to fill it may be covered by a grass mat. A machine may lower the casket, and the grave diggers fill the hole after the mourners leave. A clean operation. In sum, unsuspectingly, mourners often don't lift a hand, don't shed a tear, and don't bury their dead.

Judaism says no. The traditional Jewish funeral service is noticeably simple and emotionally meaningful. The service does not attempt to comfort the mourners; that is done in the house of shiva. Our Sages cautioned against the foolishness of trying to comfort the bereaved when their beloved lies before them. Moreover, it is psychologically futile to effect reconciliation between mourners and their fate at the funeral itself. For Judaism, the funeral is a time for *yekara d'shichva* (honor of the deceased), focusing on the honor, fate, and value of the deceased—not to protect the mourners but to say good-bye to the mourned. Even the eulogy is strictly for the deceased's honor, not for the consolation of the gathered grievers. In fact, until recently, the family used to hire professional women "criers" to stimulate the mourners' sadness, rather than pacify it.

When honoring the deceased at a funeral, we implicitly acknowledge the reality of death and the natural expectation is that we accept the finality and irretrievability of the tragedy. That is why Jewish law allows no viewing of the body during the service, no cosmetics or adorned caskets, and not even floral arrangements to beautify the occasion. The funeral proposes practices that solemnify it, not mollify it.

The first function of a funeral, then, is to honor the dead and to affirm the absence of the deceased. This is why Judaism requires that friends and extended family fill in the grave themselves, if at all possible. The experience of hearing that worst of sounds, the thud of earth falling on the wooden casket, is horrific—a mind-clearing, no-holds-barred statement of bald reality—"dead end." In the characteristically Jewish manner of grieving, we confront the blackness, not color it.

Two Rabbinic Experiences

My first experience with the denial of death that is foisted on unsuspecting mourners came very early in my rabbinate in Long Island, New

York. The widow was elderly and had no children or relatives. As this was my first funeral as a rabbi, I remember the details clearly. We had completed the service in the funeral home and proceeded to the cemetery. As we drove up the hill, the procession stopped, the director came to the first car in which we rode, and asked if I wouldn't mind if the hearse went ahead so we could follow in several minutes. I was an unsuspecting novice and told him that it was no problem.

When we arrived, there were no signs that we were in a cemetery. I saw no monuments, no grave, no earth mounds, and no casket. There was a green tarpaulin canopy that shielded us from the sun and comfortable chairs for sitting in the park. I quickly saw that there indeed was a problem. I whispered to the director that he should remove the grass mat covering from the casket and from the mound of earth that we would shovel into the grave. He was terribly upset with me, the upstart young rabbi. No one joined me in filling the grave; and after moving three or four shovelfuls of earth, I left with the others. Remembering that day, I cannot believe that I allowed myself to participate in this playacting, which this congregation had been doing unthinkingly for years.

After shiva, the widow called to me as I was walking away: "Rabbi, where is my husband Shalom?" I went over to her side, trying to mollify her with the usual pastoral saccharine phrases of the day. She persisted: "Rabbi, I didn't see my husband. Maybe it's all a dream. I was thinking, maybe he is really alive somewhere? I must be going crazy."

I had another experience later in my rabbinate, in Beverly Hills, California. Bruce Geller, the television producer of *Mission: Impossible*, was killed in a plane crash in the Santa Barbara Mountains. His wife, Jinny, asked if I would conduct the funeral. The guests were mostly celebrities from the film industry, and I reminded her that as an Orthodox rabbi, I would insist on shoveling the earth into the grave. That is exactly what she wanted.

At the grave, after the service, I invited everyone to place a shovelful of earth onto the casket as an act of farewell. I do not recall ever having been so deluged with gratitude for giving people an opportunity to really bury their friend with their own hands. Jinny stood by, elegantly and in tears. She had buried her Bruce.

Early twentieth-century Austrian writer Franz Borkenau once classified the major cultures this way: the Hellenistic is death accepting, the Western is death denying, and the Jewish is death defying. Death denying is not Jewish and not sound.

A funeral should be what it was intended to be: a culmination. Sometimes it is in operatic style with dramatic flourish, sometimes in the prosaic style of Cyrano de Bergerac felled on a lonely street—but always it brings down the curtain on a life and the lights go dark. *La commedia e finita*.

A Funeral Should Express a Person's Worth

World literature is filled with the consequences of wrong-headed funerals. Today, we no longer experience the awesomeness of the ancient funerals of heroes. But still, one badly chosen word, one look that is less than sympathetic, or an inappropriate religious service, or the clergyman's using a wrong name can be devastating to the sensitive mourners whose raw skin at these moments turns on every word and whisper. The memorial service is designed to demonstrate the worth of the deceased, and that makes everything about it sacred.

The effects of inappropriate grieving rituals are described by Francine Du Plessix Gray in her article, which originally appeared in *The American Scholar*. She emphasizes that we do not fully appreciate the cultural inheritance that has always deeply valued the special arrangements for burial: for example, the Greek pantheon; the elaborate, operatic funerals of royalty; and the open tomb of Lenin. In fact, most of us do not realize that the Torah stresses, in three separate commandments, that if the bodies of the dead remain unburied, they suffer grievous shame. In Antigone's words, they are "unburied, a lovely treasure / for birds that scan the field and feast to their heart's content."

When reading Homer you are able to sense the ancient Greeks' idea of the disgrace of a person being insufficiently mourned or inadequately buried. If the deceased was improperly mourned, the Greeks held, it could cause malevolent mischief, such as devastating crops and destroying populations. Astonishingly, in the midst of the carnage of war, opposing armies arranged truces—not for saving children or gathering food, but for the proper burial of dead warriors and the washing and anointing of the corpses.

This is not just another figment of the fertile mythological mind or another ritual for an exalted hero that could be laughably dismissed. Sigmund Freud in the 1930s described the wretchedness that mourners may suffer if they cannot properly express their feelings over the deceased's death. The mourners, he says, may come to melancholy, to clinical depression, to self-hatred, and even to suicide.

The funeral, being designed for *yekara d'shichva*, should indeed honor the deceased—by paying tribute, by praying for his or her presence to come before God, and by hoping that this death might bring merit to his or her family. That is, it is a time to properly express the honor of the deceased and to serve the family by confirming the absence of the absent.

Covering Mirrors: The Fear of Becoming Invisible

The laws of Jewish mourning call for the covering of all mirrors in the house of mourning during shiva. The reasons for this custom are many, including avoiding the cosmetic dimensions of life during grief, remembering the felled "image" of God—the deceased—by avoiding anything that has to do with images, and discouraging grievers from transferring focus from the spiritual to the physical.

But, as in other areas of religious observance, an ancient tradition elicits ever-new levels of significance and interpretations. Today, we see an even deeper meaning in the act of mirror covering. It addresses a primitive fear, one not usually associated with grief. This fear is a silent predator: the fear of becoming invisible. Grief teaches a stark lesson:

Life goes on, and it goes on unperturbed, without the deceased, no matter how worthy a person we have lost. Unspoken, however, is that more intimidating lesson: Life will also go on without us when our time comes. This realization dawns on mourners suddenly and with a ferocity not commonly acknowledged.

This unspoken fear is one that lodges deep in the mourner's soul: Am I invisible? Am I the deceased a few years later? Each death matters to so few people. The essence of death is a drama of vanishing—for the deceased and also for the mourner.

My friend Jack Salzburg suffered the death of his younger brother. On the first day of mourning, he looked around at his family—an adoring and loyal family—and their friends who had gathered at his home after the funeral. They were chatting amiably. The mood was tranquil; Jack was terrified. What shook him was that suddenly he realized that this identical scene would probably be repeated after his family buried him. He shook his head in disbelief—he will have vanished without a trace! He asked me plaintively, "So Rabbi, what did I work for all my life?" I did not say a word.

The mirror responds to this fear. A mirror reflects the presence of a person, and the reflection, though it is of no material substance, takes on an existence of its own in his or her imagination. The mirror seems magical. Somehow it assures us that we are alive. This is why when someone speaks to you when you are standing in front of a mirror, he or she is often not looking at you but at it. The mirror's drawing power is magnetic; we simply *must* look into it. It confirms our presence, our life.

Looking in the mirror, mourners see their own image, proving that they are visible and hence alive. In this sense, the mirror evokes the image of Narcissus, staring into the lake and seeing his own image for the first time. It fixes his gaze, beckoning him to admire his beauty and to fuse with it. The mirror reflects our aliveness and transfixes our thoughts.

When we cover the mirror, we mourners no longer find a reflection. There is no proof that despite our loved one's death we remain alive.

During shiva, we tell ourselves that we, or some part of us, is dying too; "I'm dead inside." We become afraid, to the core of our soul, that we, too, will be invisible. When the mirror is covered and we perceive no image reflected, it is an affirmation of our vanishing.

But why does shiva not allay the fears of mourners by allowing us to keep our mirrors uncovered? The answer is that shiva, in all its customs, focuses on confronting, not accommodating, our inner thoughts. It prescribes: Remember, don't forget; face the dangers, don't cover them up; express your anger, don't swallow it. This is why Jewish law, despite well-meaning visitors and their protestations, instructs us not to rejoice, even by playing with little children. Shiva is not a time for alleviating sorrow but for meeting it head on. In this sense, covering the mirrors emphasizes rather than moderates our fear of invisibility.

True, we all tend to become invisible some time after death. *Yishtakach min ha'lev* (forgotten from the heart), we evaporate from the heart of those who knew us, said the Sages. But we should not apply this notion of invisibility to all of life. The American humorist Mark Twain was insightful in saying that a person could learn too much from an experience. It is said that he told the story of a cat who once leaped onto a hot tin stove—the cat never touched tin again. We interact with many people, and those for whom we have made a difference will not easily forget us. We loved, we learned, we taught, we fought for ideals; we reared children, contributed to the general weal, worked to better the lives of our neighbors, and strove to be decent human beings. We should not assume that no matter what we do, our lives will become invisible.

Still, life relentlessly pushes on—one generation goes, another generation comes, Ecclesiastes assures us. That is what God has ordained. It is part of the structure of humanity—the way the world works and has always worked. It is much like visiting the old neighborhood years after moving away. We're surprised to find that life is humming along, as it always has. In fact, probably nobody even noticed our absence; it is as though we were never there. "The world could get along without me and no one would miss me." "Did I make a difference to anyone?" Unlike the cat, we should not take too much from this lesson. Yes, we do make a difference, we do affect people in myriad unseen ways. And those people, in turn, affect others, and in that way we do change the society we live in. But the earth inevitably spins on, largely unaffected.

Covering the mirror helps us confront our fear in both directions: that it is real in the sense that life will go on without us, and that it is unreal in the sense that each of us always makes a difference.

Sitting Shiva: The Central Metaphor of Jewish Mourning

Despite the fears, angers, isolation, and confusion that accompany the death of a parent, spouse, dear friend, or child, the cultural message is the same: Move on. It is almost un-American to stay put or to stop and think. You have to drive yourself to succeed. It is, therefore, astonishing that the metaphor for mourning is not "move on," as one would expect, but "sit down."

Sitting during shiva is the most characteristic Jewish posture of the mourner; sitting is probably the most widely observed Jewish ritual of the seven days; and "sitting" is the figure of speech most closely associated with Jewish mourning.

What is the significance of a specific posture, sitting, that distinctly separates itself from every other physical movement? Why reject standing, the preferred position for prayer? Why reject walking, the preferred metaphor for halakhah, Jewish law? Why reject running, the preferred way to approach a mitzvah? Why reject bowing and prostrating, the preferred position before God? Why reject moving on, the preferred path toward modern progress? Sitting during shiva is precisely, specifically, purposefully sitting—not walking, standing, running, bowing, or lying prone. Why?

"Walking" implies forward movement, dynamism, goal seeking, and progress. It is a motor function, directional and energetic. *Halikhah* (walking) is the root of "halakhah," the term for Jewish law, because it symbolizes all of the above.

But "sitting" is, by design, the metaphor of Jewish mourning because it implies thinking, meditating, and contemplating. It is not at all interested in movement—backward or forward—or progress, dynamism, and achievement; it is only interested in reaching into the bottom of the soul. It is a still-life portrait—the picture of passivity, of pensiveness, of a preoccupied and melancholic mind. Sitting anchors the heart, keeping the griever from losing the sanctity of mourning in a whirlwind of activity.

Sitting also is learning and not doing. That is why "school" in the Jewish religious vocabulary is *yeshivah* (sitting) and not the action-oriented law, halakhah (walking). Sitting initiates self-examination, and it stimulates a struggle with your self, not with an adversary. It is not a training ground for "making it," but a sanctuary for tunneling into the soul, not mental exercise so much as spiritual exploration.

In addition, the active postures—standing, walking, and running—signify that a person has control of the situation. What we moderns fear most is losing control, which we equate with the end of life. A Jewish clergyperson testifying before the U.S. Congress in 1998 actually said that a loss of control is tantamount to a loss of life and, by itself, is sufficient reason to allow people to refuse medical intervention and commit suicide. For shame. In fact, this insight is one reason why people visiting hospitals should not stand next to a sick person who is lying in bed—the posture of standing erect, of looking down on someone lying down, does not comfort. Instead, it suggests control, superiority, self-will, and power.

The appropriate posture for grieving is sitting, precisely because it denotes *not* being in control. Mourners are at a loss because of their loss. We know deep in our soul that the deceased was not in control, else there would have been no death, and that we are also not in control, else we would not be in this situation—that the ultimate control is not with human beings but with God. Our very posture for seven consecutive days says so. Repeatedly, consistently, forcefully, it is an insight that strikes all people confronting the dark—"What could I do?"

Quintessentially, while sitting in silence and in solitude, we mourners will seize the opportunity of the moment—in the midst of the hurly-

burly of greetings and goings and consolations and in the midst of our
own tormenting questions and nuts-and-bolts worries—to allow our
bewildered mind to reset itself and to contemplate our new world. This
can only be accomplished while sitting, not rushing.

Kaddish: Chamber Music for Two Hearts

The *Kaddish*, the Jewish prayer recited after death, is a vigorous declaration of faith. It is one of the most beautiful, deeply significant, and
spiritually moving prayers in the Jewish liturgy. It is an ancient Aramaic
prose poem, a litany whose word-music, strong rhythms, stirring sounds,
and alternating responses of leader and congregation cast sheer hyp-
notic power over the listeners. Its rich texture is a communal recitation—a chorus of strange sounds that mesmerize mourners and form the
outer shell of our grieving persona.

Inside that shell, in the chamber of the heart filled with grief, is
music of another sort: the harmony of two hearts—the deceased and the
survivor—present together in a musical enclosure. The immortal words
of the *Kaddish* tie together heaven and earth; they form a sound box in
which our mourning minds float free, enabling us to connect with the
departed. When mourners end the *Kaddish*, we recite the last sentence
while taking three steps back, symbolizing our exit from the spiritual
world and our return to the earthly plane.

Jewish mystical teachings speak often of reuniting with loved ones
after death. The prophet Samuel said: "Those who are beloved and
friendly in their lifetimes, in death will not be separated" (2 Sam. 1:23).
Love is eternal, transcending even death. Love, of course, does not seem
to last forever. But not even a drop of the water that covers 70 percent
of the earth is ever lost. What evaporates from the earth comes back in
the form of rain, and so on. In an analogous sense, love too is never lost.
A person dies; love does not.

Ashley Davis Prend wrote:

In this universe nothing is ever wholly lost
That which is excellent remains forever a part of this universe
Human hearts are dust, but the love which moves the human heart
Abides to bless the last generation.

Saying *Kaddish* means nothing less than that the relationship, once vibrant and earthly, can continue after death—albeit on a new plane. Physically, the relationship is ended, so that ultimately spouses can re-marry, parents live on, and survivors of tragedies can resolve their grief and restart their journey into their future.

A spiritual relationship continues, however, with survivors remembering and cherishing the memories of the deceased as they resume a full life on earth. While death ends the physical relationship between people, it does not root out memories or affectionate feelings, and it does not break the bonds that unite hearts—whether as spouses, parents and children, or close friends. Especially, it does not end an ongoing spiritual relationship for as long as we cherish it. Neither should it stand in the way of new relationships on this earth—new marriages, new births, or new friends.

The intense spiritual relationship, so outstanding after death, naturally recedes with the passage of time, and by the good grace of God. But in the flush of death it can be constructive, comforting, and profound. This is an exceptional divine gift to human beings, and generally it presents with none of the raging conflicts one might predict.

After spending weeks clarifying for myself how *Kaddish* can become a platform for spiritual communication, I discovered psychotherapist Anne Brener's wise advice: After death there is still the possibility of continuing the conversation, of saying what needed to be said. *Kaddish* can be the vehicle for this mysterious connection, as we recite it in the spiritual presence of the departed.

I had this experience after losing both my parents in the space of three months. I had finished reciting *Kaddish* one evening, and the rabbi, a close colleague, called me aside to ask whether I was aware that I had been smiling while saying *Kaddish*, a dissonance he thought problematic. He was surprised when I assured him that this was natural for me, because during the *Kaddish* I could picture my parents in conversation with me, and in life whenever I spoke to them I could not put down the phone without smiling. They were a joy. *Kaddish* was my special time for communicating with them. When I started *"Yitgadal,"* in my mind I said, "Hi Pop" or "Hi Mom" and felt no intellectual discomfort whatsoever. What was important to me was not some otherworldly advice that I never asked for and never received or some request for their intercession. All that mattered was that I was in their presence.

Inside the rhythmic words of *Kaddish*, which we soon recite by heart, there is room for an encounter with the deceased that we would otherwise not have. In this safe refuge, mourners, if they so wish, can legitimately resume unfinished declarations of love broken off by sudden death or explain some unfortunate behavior. We can image a parent or child and, while reciting the sanctified sounds in an atmosphere of pure spirituality, complain or plead or reassure or confess some wrongdoing and ask forgiveness or offer forgiveness for a hurt that won't go away. *Kaddish* enables people spiritually to rewind the clock that is ticking relentlessly forward.

This view of *Kaddish* is something of a mystical flight; fortunately, most of us are blessed with a touch of mysticism. *Kaddish* can thereby become a source of comfort on a plane higher than its mere communal recitation. Rabbi Akiva, who conceived *Kaddish* as a spiritual vehicle for a child to redeem his or her parent, may well have imagined *Kaddish* as a renewal of a relationship between a father and a son. Might not this proposition be a precursor of mourners "meeting" with their parents— inside the *Kaddish*?

Many people believe that after a major loss you should grieve, accept it, and be done with it. Sigmund Freud promoted this idea in his influential paper "Mourning and Melancholia," explaining that for grief to be resolved, emotional energy must be withdrawn from the deceased and reinvested in something new. I subscribe to this. Freud, however, added that one must sever the tie, and end the relationship for good. For some, perhaps this is so; for most of us, however, in the time after death this spells too much of a rejection of a rich past and all its meaning.

Mourners need not completely sever ties with the deceased. A loved one remains in our heart, in our soul, intertwined in who and what we are. The deceased need not be evicted by force. In time, gradually, through the resolution of grief, we will release ourselves from the strong emotional energy that connected us to the person who is gone. But we will always and forever have a spiritual relationship with him or her.

When reciting *Kaddish* we hear truly sacred music, the harmony of the spheres. As we end the recitation, we take three steps back, re-entering everyday reality with a long release of pent-up breath or a fresh smile. The *Kaddish* serves as a mysterious gift, a balm for the soul.

Chapter 7

Man Comforts; God Consoles

A midrash: God will appoint Abraham as His emissary to console Jerusalem; but Jerusalem will not be comforted. God will then call Isaac, but with the same result. Jacob and Moses will fare no better. Seeing that Jerusalem refuses to be comforted by its patriarchs, God Himself will then approach to console the city.

Pesikta Rabbati 30:30

The strategy of healing in Judaism operates simultaneously on three levels. First, it establishes an atmosphere of healing for mourners, such as Habitat Shiva, in which the healing process is encouraged to grow. Second, it provides rituals, such as the recitation of *Kaddish*, which course silently through the mind and heart and infuse healthy spiritual attitudes. Third, it promotes direct comfort by a verbal tonic of consolation, which focuses on the needs of the mourner, such as when visitors come to the shiva house, inquire about the deceased, and bring the mourner their wishes that God may console him or her. All three strategies are effective because they are based on the finely tuned spiritual sensitivity of grievers.

Perhaps the most revealing insight that I have learned in my study of consolation is that, with all the religious and moral necessity for people to console, they in fact cannot do it. Surprisingly, giving and receiving consolation simply is not in the human makeup. My thoughts are echoed by one of the twentieth century's greatest Jewish ethicists, Rabbi Eliyahu Dessler, Principal of Jews' College in London, who says that even if there were a super-abundance of comfort given the mourner, it could not remove all his grief. It is simply beyond human range.

A mourner who must resolve a deeply felt trauma cannot be consoled unaided. Judaism holds that only God can effectuate this. God performs a separate miracle for each mourner. True consolation is a special gift of God, who tends to mourners whenever people bring the mourner their own best efforts to comfort him.

Consolation is a two-tiered healing process, both being referred to by the same word, "nechamah"; one is by man and one by God. On the first level, the visitor fulfills God's command to provide comfort, and this act of first-tier consolation becomes not only a source of comfort to the mourner, but an urgent plea to God to confer on the mourner a complete and lasting closure.

Isaiah hints at this two-tiered consolation when he declares "console, console" (nachamu, nachamu) in the opening consolation chapters of the Book of Isaiah. Midrash calls this kiflayim (doubling) and appears to convey, as one commentary hints, that Isaiah speaks of two levels of consolation: "console" by man, "console" by God.

At some point in each of our lives we will attempt to console mourners, and our words of consolation will appear to flow spontaneously and sincerely. Yet despite the universality of this experience and its seeming naturalness, I do not believe that any one person actually consoles another. A consoler may be able to relieve a mourner's anxiety, perhaps suggest a solution to a given problem, or distract a mourner's agony for a short time, but he cannot provide closure, or metaphysical answers, or theological judgments, or the inner strength to achieve a full spiritual resolution of grief.

For the simple truth is this: Man comforts; God consoles.

God Consoles Grievers Himself

As stunning as is the idea that God grieves for man and consoles him is the idea that God Himself consoles. It seems unimaginable, but that is the teaching of the Torah. It is understandable for God to instruct His earth-bound messenger, a prophet, to comfort His people. "Console ye, console ye, my people" are the words in the Book of Isaiah. But for God to "personally" console a human being is an idea that gives us a deeper understanding of Jewish consolation. The Torah refers to God as healer of the sick: "For I the Lord am your healer"(Exod. 15:26); as accompanying people when they are hurting: "I will be with him in distress" (Ps. 91:15); as consoling Isaac: "After the death of Abraham, God blessed his son Isaac. And Isaac settled near Be'er-lahai-roi" (Gen. 25:11); and "personally" consoling all mourners: "I, even I, will console you all." (Isa. 51:12) This action of God consoling the bereaved is interpreted to mean that God Himself—*b'chvodo v'atzmo* (with His own honorable presence) bestows consolation upon His suffering children.

What is the difference between God Himself consoling mourners and God bestowing His consolation through the medium of a prophet or anyone else? The self-evident answer is that a human being, even though he is a prophet, can comfort and assure and hope at best—but only God can provide consolation that is fully remedial. God's consolation stamps finality on the grief and brings an end to a griever's intense anguish. The best-intentioned clergy, bereavement counselors, and health-care professionals bring surcease and comfort during agony, but they cannot secure a firm end to the weeping.

The complex reintegration of our minds and souls into the normal texture of life by not allowing the grief to mummify us is the closure to grief that many attribute simply to the passage of time: *Mah shelo ya'ase ha'sechel, ya'ase ha'zeman* (What reason cannot do, the passage of time can do). But Rabbi Dessler wisely declares that it is not time but an act of God that operates unnoticed and insinuates itself into man's soul. It takes God to create the miracle that enables people to survive such horrific loss. God reveals it in time.

This is certainly not to diminish the vital importance of our comforting the bereaved; the Torah has framed it as a sacred moral principle! It is, after all, the best any person can do. But spiritually, what is most significant in our comforting is that it calls for God's attention and prays that He live up to His holy covenant of mutual affection.

"I Will Be the One Who Consoles the People"

The destruction of the Temple in Jerusalem was a cataclysmic event in Jewish history. Not only was this holy site in ruins, but the Jewish people were forced into exile, and the inevitable termination of the Jewish religion was a distinct probability. There was no future conceivable in those dark moments, and the Jews were therefore quite hopeless.

In these circumstances two major prophets, Isaiah and Jeremiah, tried to console the people, but alas, even their profound spirituality, their awesome leadership, and their legendary eloquence could not assuage the people's fears. Even though the prophets served at the command of God, the people still rejected their consolation: "Unhappy, storm-tossed one, unconsoled!" (Isa. 54:11).

When the future of a people is at stake, the situation calls for God's *own* intervention. The tragedy that befalls a whole people needs consolation from the Master of all people. Such a national grief requires closure guaranteed by God, a reversal of fortune, and a triumph. All three are provided by the sequence of seven *haftarot* readings from the last chapters of the Book of Isaiah, which follow the national fast day of Tisha be-Av, the Ninth of Av, commemorating the destruction of the ancient temples and the exiling of the Jewish people. In the face of such tragic loss, Jewish tradition directed the Jew to try to heal. It declared that seven chapters of consolation from Isaiah be read on each of the following seven Sabbaths. This corresponds to shiva, the seven days following a death, when we live in a "habitat of healing."

Strangely, the seven chapters are read publicly—but intentionally out of order! An ancient midrash explains that this reordering accurately depicts the spiritual drama of consolation and may not be altered. The chapters are recited in the following order: 40, 49, 54, 51, 54, 60, and 61. At the heart of this altered sequence is chapter 51, bracketed on either side by excerpts from chapter 54. In this interrupted order can be found a profound lesson in the drama of healing, hidden in the folds of the Law.

First, in chapter 40, God forcefully instructs the prophets to console the people: "*Nachamu, nachamu, ami*" (Console ye, console ye, my people!) (Isa. 40:1). The next chapter continues this motif. But the third reading, chapter 54, announces that the prophet's message of consolation has failed to comfort the grieving nation: "*aniya so'ara lo nuchama*" (unhappy, storm-tossed one, unconsoled!). In the fourth reading, chapter 51, God responds emphatically, reassuring the people: "*anochi, anochi, hu menachemchem*" (I, even I, will be the One who consoles the people). In other words, I, by Myself, will console you all. At the insistence of the people, the divine command to Isaiah—"Console, console"—is converted to "I, even I." The last three chapters extend this theme, concluding victoriously in a crescendo of hope: "I greatly rejoice in the Lord."

The rabbis wisely positioned this drama of consolation in the last weeks of the religious year, thereby linking the Jewish people's grief over their national losses with the following week's repentance on Rosh Hashanah. Thus, the last Sabbath of the old year enacts the people's transcendence over their grief; the first of the new year, the spiritual identification with God Himself.

Rachel Wins God's Consolation

The biblical figure of Rachel leaps out of the Torah parchment and becomes a heroine for all those who cry out for consolation. But she does it through the window of Jeremiah. Jeremiah, scouring the Torah for a fitting persona to persuade God to console His people, decides on Rachel. She is not only one of the matriarchs, the wife of Jacob, she is also the most beloved, the eternally young, and the most admired mother of the Jews. She suffers heartbreaking losses and is the victim of a conniving father and manipulating sister, yet she emerges as the hero of her own story. At the end of her life, dying in childbirth, with everything to live for, she calls her child ben Oni, "a son of my suffering." Her son's name becomes her epitaph. Remarkably, Rachel is not only a memory or symbol, but a vital figure in the history of the Jews, a private person become matriarch become historical personage. People who need an extra measure of compassion or hope visit her grave to this day; she is the quintessential fulfillment of motherhood, womanhood, and saintliness.

Centuries after her untimely demise, the Book of Jeremiah portrays Rachel pleading with Almighty God, her face soaked in tears, adamant that she will not stop crying until God Himself consoles her by bringing back her children from exile. She is portrayed in this classic pose: the grieving mother who insists on consolation from God Himself no less, not from His messengers, not from His patriarchs, not from His leaders, not from His prophets, but from Him (Jer. 31:15, 16, 17):

> *Thus said the Lord: A cry is heard in Ramah—*
> *Wailing, bitter weeping,*
> *Rachel weeping for her children.*
> *She refuses to be comforted for her children,*
> *who are gone.*
> *Thus said the Lord:*
> *Restrain your voice from weeping,*
> *Your eyes from shedding tears;*
> *For there is reward for your labor*
>   *—declares the Lord:*
> *They shall come back from the enemy's land.*
> *And there is hope for your future,*
>   *—declares the Lord:*
> *Your children shall return to their own country.*

Rachel's weeping over her children as they pass by her grave into exile is heard not only in Ramah, at the top of the mountain, but as the Zohar says, *"me'olam v'ad olam"* (from world to world). Her quarrel with God is not one of muttered grief, but a fierce entreaty to the heavens. Her rejection of just a human being's comforting is a gut-wrenching call from inside a thousand-year-old tomb that echoes her life scream, as when she pleaded with her husband, Jacob, for a child of her own: "If not, I am dead!"

Rachel's thrust is now aimed at Almighty God: *"Me'ana le'hinachem, ki ainenu"* (I will have none of this, God). She refuses to be consoled, because *ainenu* (they) are not here. This standard reading, however, is a sorry mistake. The Zohar declares that *ainenu* does not mean "*they* are not here." It means "*He* is not here," that is, God is absent from the scene. This is the plain meaning of Jeremiah's words, borne out by subsequent events, by the text's inner sense, and by the coherence of the dialogue. We can just make out her inaudible cry: "Your people are being driven out, but where are You? They're helpless and futureless, but *ainenu*, You are not here."

The medieval commentator Ramban describes the scene graphically: "As they pass the grave she rises to the top of her tomb and pleads for God to have mercy on her children." And "Rachel cries incessantly—the likes of which no one on earth has ever heard—and not only as her children leave now, but in every dispersion and for all her children who are in exile."

She reasons with God: *"Ribono Shel Olam,* Master of the Universe: Do You remember that I did not demand from You a solution for my own trouble? Though Jacob worked seven years for me, on my wedding night they substituted Leah for me; and I did not expose the ruse by speaking because Jacob would have distinguished between my voice and my sister's. I am only flesh and blood, yet I did not dwell on my grievances; certainly You, God, should not dwell on Your grievance that Jews worship idols and commit sins!"

She is resolute, demanding that God bring the exiles home. Though

Heaven and Earth mourn, they cannot bring the exiles home. Though angels of heaven, sun, and moon mourn, it is to no avail. But Rachel, who is inconsolable, prevails, forcing God's hand.

Then God swears that the Jews will return and tells Rachel: "You can stop your crying now. Wipe away the tears from your eyes because your efforts have achieved their just reward. Your children will return from their captivity. The children are coming home! Therefore, do not read, "Rach-el (Rachel) cried over her children," read: "Ru'ach el (God's spirit) cried over her children!"

And so, Rachel wins.

The heart of true spiritual consolation is the consolation that is delivered by God Himself, *b'chvodo v'atzmo*, in all His Glory and His Persona.

Jews affirm this very idea through the formula they recite when they leave a house of shiva: "May God comfort you among the other mourners." For though we are bidden to console mourners, we paradoxically admit our inability to do so in these scripted words of comfort.

Man gives comfort; only God consoles.

A Protocol for Comforting Mourners

Jewish law is clear: *mitzvah le'nachem*—visiting mourners at home is not a courtesy call, it is a command, a mitzvah. During this brief encounter, visitors need to choose between consoling in a hands-on manner or being sympathetic spectators. *Avelut* (mourning) implies "withdrawal," a personal and physical retreat from the community by the mourner, the *avel*. The mandate of our humanity as well as of our religion is an obligation to bring sensitivity and empathy to mourners, that we relieve them of the intolerable burden of intense loneliness and stem their natural rush to withdraw. At no other time are people more in need of such companionship.

The general purpose of consolation, *nichum avelim*, is to relieve the burden of despair and to express affirmation that the world at large is not a hateful and angry place but can be a warm and friendly one. It is a beckoning with open arms for the mourners to return to society with positive expectations. Consoling mourners, Maimonides said, is *gemilut hesed* (a genuine kindness) to both the living and the dead.

As comforters, we must listen to the mourner's story. The primary role of a witness is to listen and to do nothing more, to be human *beings*, not human *doings*. We take this opportunity to be still, not engaging in the familiar stereotypical response. As for the storytellers, the mourners, they are often amazed to realize just how important it is to have real witnesses who will listen in this way.

A condolence call is not a time to persuade mourners of anything at all. Consolation is for the sake of compassion, and compassion does not mix well with convincing, instructing, exhorting, arguing, or debating. This is a time for accompanying people on their very own paths. Even if the mourners themselves want to discuss divisive matters, the principal purpose of consolation visits is to relieve their fears for the future or their guilt for the past. The Sages said it is not proper, indeed it borders on sacrilege, to impress upon mourners the general inevitability of death, as though to doubt the specific purpose and justice of a decree that God issued.

A condolence call is also a time for giving mourners space and "permission" for an intensely personal evaluation of their lives, and they should not be deprived of this indulgence. It is unseemly, even entirely useless, to assure mourners that others have suffered similar tragedies or worse fates, as though by right they should be less despairing. "It could have been worse" is cold consolation.

Dos and Don'ts

The following traditions of condolence are suggested to help comforters make a compassionate visit in fulfillment of Judaism's requirement.

- **Allow mourners to begin the conversation and set the tone at all times.** This is a religious must. Be especially sensitive in situations such as suicide, young deaths, or guilt-ridden grief.
- **Do not to try to fix the problems and fears of the grief-**

stricken. Recognize that we cannot solve the mourners' problems with a random visit, no matter how well equipped we are and how hard we try.

- **Be an open listener.** Allow mourners an opportunity to express all of their feelings in a safe, noncombative, nonthreatening, and nonjudgmental atmosphere so they can break through their loneliness and share their pain and loss for a short time. The grief-stricken need friends to validate their grief, not to interpret it or manipulate their feelings.

- **Listen attentively, not casually.** We should demonstrate concern for mourners' well-being. We should wear a mien of seriousness, not only of sadness.

- **Silence is best.** We are advised to say nothing at all, especially at the outset, rather than to be endlessly talkative.

- **Our conversation should not be distracting but therapeutic.** The small talk of mourners should trigger our interest, even though it may not be of world-shaking significance.

- **Speak of the departed.** This may appear hurtful at first, but in fact helps mourners unburden themselves. We should feel free to recall events in the deceased's life, the departed one's opinions on important matters, and the quality of the deceased's relationships. Whether or not the deceased was an important personality, every individual has redeeming features and has done good things. We should search for these values before visiting.

- **Use humor wisely.** A joke or raucous story brings relief to comforters, but they are entirely inappropriate for mourners. Conversely, light-hearted or humorous anecdotes of the deceased, spoken respectfully, are quite in place. In fact, it is altogether proper to provide for some moments of appropriate levity to relieve the thick, emotion-laden atmosphere—but only if we feel comfortable doing so, and only if we are able to deliver such anecdotes with sensitivity.

- **Do not dwell on your own mourning experiences.** This may appear to belittle the grief of the newly bereaved. Consolation is not about how we suffered or how we experienced grief. Mourners are at the center of concern; everything else should be peripheral.

- **Remind mourners, whenever possible, that their feelings are normal reactions.** Let them know that the seemingly "crazy" symptoms of grief are universal and that the vast majority of people have successfully dealt with loss in the past.

- **Encourage their self-reliance and offer mourners positive feedback on their successful coping or small victories in the progress of their bereavement.** Believe in their ability to recover and grieve successfully. Giving people courage makes them courageous. Phillips Brooks once said: "There is in every man something greater than he had begun to dream of. Men are nobler than they think themselves."

- **Do not offer gratuitous psychological advice.** Even the most talented and capable comforters must be wary of falling into this trap.

- **There is no religious preference for visiting a house of mourning—whether by day or by night.** For nonrelatives, visits may be delayed until the second day after interment. However, if for some reason this delay cannot be arranged, visits may be made even on the very first day. Formally and traditionally, consoling the bereaved begins at the cemetery when mourners leave the grave and pass through parallel rows of friends and relatives as they exit.

- **We do not customarily pay condolence calls on the Sabbath or holidays.** These are days when traditional Jews do not mourn publicly, since mourning would conflict with the joyous spirit of the celebration for the whole Jewish community. However, mourners may receive shiva visitation and condolences on certain special days: *chol ha'mo'ed* (the weekdays of major holidays), Rosh Hodesh (the start of a new Jewish month), Purim, and Hanukkah. Psychologically, of course, grief often reaches crucial and anguishing proportions during holidays. Mourners tend, at these times—as on birthdays and anniversaries—to feel abandoned and alone, truly bereft. So it is well to visit mourners just before and as soon as possible at the end of such a traditionally mandated break in the mourning.

- **Visiting after shiva.** If we were unable to visit during shiva, tradition says that we can continue to express condolences at any time during the subsequent twelve months upon meeting those bereaved of parents and during the next thirty days for those bereaved of other relatives.

- **When mourners return to work.** Sometimes mourners need to conduct business during shiva. Sometimes it is even religiously permissible to do so. In such cases, condolence calls may still be made to mourners.

- **When making condolence calls, offer no words of greeting—neither of welcome nor of farewell.** Mourners should not respond verbally to greetings during the first three days. Traditionally, mourners nod or convey their acknowledgment of the presence of comforters in some other way, such as by repeating a visitor's name.

- **It is not up to us as comforters to remind mourners of their religious duties.** For instance, we should not urge a mourner to sit on the shiva stool (it is not even religiously required that the mourner always be seated), since our innocent remark may imply to the mourner that he or she is acting improperly.

As consolers we should be sensitive to the feelings of the mourners and be especially alert to any signal that we should leave! There is a time for all things and surely there is a time for leaving the house of the bereaved. We should never stay too long, mistakenly believing that our presence brings an unusual degree of relief or mistakenly measuring the value of our compassion by the length of our visit. Upon leaving, we traditionally recite the following phrase in Hebrew or in English or both: *"Ha'makom yenachem etkhem betokh she'ar avelei Tziyon vi'Yerushalayim*" (May God comfort you among the other mourners of Zion and Jerusalem).

We should expect some unusual behavior during a shiva call, but that behavior is motivated by Jewish tradition itself. Mourners traditionally do not rise to greet any guest, no matter what the guest's stature. Mourners—preferably but not necessarily—sit, even as comforters are about to leave. Nevertheless, especially during prolonged visits, mourners need not sit all the time, but may stand and walk as they desire. At mealtime, in the company of guests, mourners may sit at the head of the table but on a lower stool.

Chapter 8

Unconventional Truths of Mourning

If you resist the pain, it intensifies. If you breathe into the pain, slowly pressing into it, the pain diminishes. The flow of grief is similar over time ... by riding the wave, allowing it to be, surrendering to the motion ... this is the stance of receiving the grief. Once truly received, you can choose to be positive or at least neutral toward it.

—M. Fumia

While the Sages of Judaism often applied stringent interpretation to moral and religious questions on most topics, in grief they always mandated leniency. This did not open the doors to random, personal interpretation of the law; rather it said this: Mourners suffer deep anguish and trauma; helping them recover often requires hands-off gentleness as well as certain counterintuitive insights to relieve the human burden.

As we have seen, Jewish bereavement practices embrace contradictory ideas and emotions. The needs of mourners for both solitude and shared grieving, silence and telling their story, being caregivers and care receivers, expanding and contracting times and actions, coping with waves of denial and waves of acceptance seem to defy rationality. Yet, all of these experiences reflect the nature of mourning. The work of grief is suffused with irony, inconsistency, even inversion. Such elasticity is a particular strength of Judaism's mourning traditions.

But in our rational, modern society, we may find such contradictory impulses difficult to accept. How do we come to terms with the apparent irrationality of living with such contradictions?

The Nobel prize-winning physicist Niels Bohr suggested a way of reconciling such apparent logical tensions: "The opposite of a correct statement is a false statement. But the opposite of a profound truth may well be another profound truth." Bohr understood this principle from his work with the physics of light. It can be scientifically proven that light moves in waves. But it can also be scientifically proven that the opposite is true: that light is transmitted as particles. It seems that the two principles are mutually exclusive—light must either function as waves, which are constantly in motion, or as particles, which never move of their own volition. Yet quantum physics is based on the premise that both principles are true—and scientists have proven that this is in fact the case.

A similar process also applies in the study of Torah. When two verses, equally valid, seem to contradict one another, a third relevant verse is cited by the Rabbis to explain how both may nonetheless be true within the logic of the Bible. Likewise, Jewish mourning tradition, seeing beneath the surface and not agitated by logical inconsistency, is able to direct mourners to withdraw to their homes in order to be solitary, yet at the same time it instructs the community to visit the home of mourners to share their grieving. Can we have it both ways? Definitely, because both are equally profound truths of the grieving heart.

Live Your Way into the Answer

Have patience with everything unresolved in your heart and try to love the questions themselves. ... Don't search for the answers, which could not be given now. ... And the point is, to live everything. Live the questions now. Perhaps then, someday far into the future, you will gradually, without even noticing it, live your way into the answer.

—Rainer Maria Rilke

If we cannot solve these inherent contradictions or if we have difficulty understanding a ritual or mitzvah, we need not surrender to despair. My grandfather used to tell me repeatedly, "From a question, you don't die." We can live with contradictions, even in spite of them. And then we need to make the best of the situation, despite the fact that we will not always find satisfying solutions to the perpetual perplexities of death.

The Loss: Accept It, Don't Fight It

What is to give light must endure burning.

—Victor Frankl

In bereavement, people experience different levels of acceptance at different points in the process. Acceptance does not imply that we like what has happened, nor does it mean that we forget our loved one. It means that we appreciate the magnitude of what has happened, that we know that our lives will never be the same, that we must learn to live with our loss, and to accept the reality of the person who has been lost, both the good and the not so good.

To accept means to realize fully that this tragedy has happened to us, unreal as it may seem; that God has decreed it; that it is utterly irreversible; that no amount of imagination or hope can ever bring the dead back to life; that life has changed forever; that rebelling against that change will be of no avail; and that we must allow the pain of absence to flow through us.

Accepting means that we are willing to relearn reality. It means that we understand that at some point we must end our impossible wish that the person we loved will return. It means being ready to clear psychic space in which to continue to love the deceased on a spiritual level.

Unblocking a Path to Healing

As a philosophy for mourners and others learning to live with pain and frustration, the idea of acceptance can be a powerful healing tool. Affirming death in its full terror can be a surprising source of serenity and an antidote to months, perhaps years, of denying, ignoring, and struggling.

The Bible provides an early example of this dynamic. Jacob—although he rends his clothes to indicate the tear in his heart after the death of Joseph—refuses to fully accept that Joseph has died. He takes the news that his sons bring him as news of a loss, not of an irretrievable death. Since he cannot bring himself to accept Joseph's death, he does not heal. In the biblical narrative, this is all to the good because Joseph is in fact not dead, but alive in Egypt, as Jacob finds out later. But Jacob's lifelong, unresolved grieving does demonstrate that there can be no healing without stouthearted acceptance.

The complex notion of acceptance is clearly and profoundly expressed in the well-known prayer attributed to Reinhold Neibuhr: "God, grant me the serenity to accept the things I cannot change, the courage to change the things I can, and the wisdom to know the difference."

Accepting the unchangeable does not require resignation or a refusal to use our talents and abilities to live life to its fullest. Rather, it can liberate us from crippling and counterproductive emotions, such as anxiety, fear, guilt, and remorse. This is the test: We need to ask ourselves—is there anything I can do about this problem today? If there is, I will do it. If there isn't, I will accept the predicament and not dissipate my soul and my stamina in senseless struggle. Out of such acceptance comes true serenity.

Accepting and Denying: Alternating Current

Most people who are considered to be in denial alternate between half-hearted acceptance and halfhearted denial. Herman Feifel, one of America's foremost thanatologists, has reported that his studies consistently demonstrate that people not only have such responses successively; they often have them simultaneously.

We need to accept that some people will always resort to denial, especially if they are terminally ill or in the early stages of the grief process. But we should help such people realize that, although denial is understandable, they should engage in such behavior only in passing. A mourner once said that in grief she experienced both anger and acceptance simultaneously—she discovered that she was afraid to accept her loss fully because such acquiescence might suggest that she had given in to fate and sanctioned the injustice of her loss. To survive, she chose both acceptance and indignation at the same time.

Rebelling against our fate gains us nothing but temporary release. Self-pity leads only to self-victimization. To move through our grief, we need to accept our feelings both as a bundle of possibilities and a bundle of impossibilities, and to make the most of them.

The Best Way Out Is Through

Robert Frost said it eloquently in seven words: "The best way out is always through." Acceptance means bowing to the inevitable—accepting life "as is," and not "as if." We slowly come to recognize that the only aspects of life that we can control at will are not life or death, our own or others', but rather our attitudes and perspectives on what befalls us or bereaves us and how we choose to react to them. We simply cannot blow the shadows away. We cannot renegotiate the past, only commemorate it and then put it into service as the prelude it was meant to be.

Getting "through" is the only way to get to the highest level of grief resolution, which is transcending grief. But that cannot happen unless our grief has been processed rather than skipped over.

To accept is not to succumb; it is to survive with the past intact. It is not what we have lost but what we have left that fashions a future.

The great Harvard philosopher William James summarized the truth of all misfortune: "Be willing to have it so: Acceptance of what has happened is the first step in overcoming the consequences of any misfortune. Don't fight—if you can't beat it—accept it."

Does Accepting Imply Forgetting?

Does acceptance mean forgetting the past, turning away from it, throwing in the towel? Does acceptance not in fact amount to a betrayal?

No, accepting the truth does not lead to forgetting or betraying what and whom we have lost. We need to adopt an attitude that emphasizes that our beloved's relationship with us does not depend on denial, subterfuge, or any other mental contrivance, but on truth. Authentic love that is based on such truth can withstand even the exquisitely painful trauma of separation.

Some people do feel that accepting a death is a kind of betrayal. In a sense, they believe that if they accept it, they are admitting that what was once unthinkable has become reality. They feel that acquiescence suggests that they have finally succumbed like everyone else, that they fully accept the injustice of death. For some, such acceptance may signify that they have stopped mourning by conceding defeat. They may feel that with this acceptance they have said good-bye to their beloved for all time. None of this, of course, is true. Accepting does not mean relinquishing memory, nor does it imply any betrayal.

The Pain: Wasting Afflictions

Sufferings have a greater effect than sacrifices, for sacrifices are performed with one's goods, but sufferings are with one's body.

—Mekhilta Yitro 10

Someday, at the end of the nightmare
    Of knowing,
May I emerge singing praise and
    Jubilation to assenting angels.
May I strike my heart's keys clearly,
    And may none fail
Because of slack, uncertain,
    Or fraying strings.
May the tears that stream down my face
Make me more radiant:
    May my hidden weeping
bloom. How I will cherish you then,
    you grief-torn nights!
had I only received you, inconsolable
    sisters.
On more abject knees, only buried myself
    with more abandon
in your loosened hair. How we waste
    our afflictions!
We study them, stare out beyond them
    into bleak continuance.
hoping to glimpse some end. Whereas
    they're really
our wintering foliage, our dark greens
    of meaning, one
of the seasons of the clandestine year—
    not only
a season—they're site, settlement,
    shelter, soil, abode.

—Rainer Maria Rilke

Ordinarily, we shun the terrifying experience of despair, which literally means hopelessness, from the Latin "*de-spair*"—"*de*," "without," and "*esperare*," "to hope"—to be without hope. But what if despair could become a constructive emotion? What if we could convert it to our benefit? The art of living lies less in eliminating our troubles than in growing with them, said Bernard Baruch, the twentieth-century American financial advisor. And the Greek poet Homer noted that we derive the same strength from despair as we do from hope. How then can we tap into that strength and convert hopelessness into faith in the future?

Our age is a narcissistic one. We have pampered ourselves to such an extreme that many of us can no longer tolerate even a hint of pain, even the most minimal suffering. Of course, neither pain nor suffering is welcome to anyone. But life is sometimes soaked through with it. This is a lesson even children learn as they experience the world. Throughout our lives we must endure crises, tragedies, and problems, even as we experience life's joys, celebrations, and accomplishments. The truth about life is this: We enter it causing pain and we leave it causing suffering. We need to understand that the opposite of life is death, not suffering. Indeed, we can grow and live better as a consequence of suffering.

We can see this truth played out in nature. Rain is a blessing, sometimes rescuing whole populations. But we cannot have rain without dark clouds. Sir Thomas Browne, in 1646, made the same point: "Light that makes some things seen, makes some things invisible. Were it not for darkness and the shadow of the earth, the noblest part of the Creation would remain unseen, and the stars in heaven invisible."

Two medieval rabbinic sages disputed whether prayer is obligatory or only permissible. The crux of their dispute hinged on a biblical verse that says one is to pray during times of trouble. One sage said that it is only during trouble that we must pray. The other said that since all of life has the constant potential of bursting into trouble, one is therefore always obliged to pray. If, then, trouble is always with us, as the second sage contends, knowing how to deal with it becomes one of the most significant tasks facing us during our lifetime.

What distinguishes us from one another is how we endure the agonies of life, and further, whether we can learn to grow from the endurance itself. In this regard, tears are not a sign of weakness but are more often a sign of personal strength. They are the fearless expression of the internal tensions that we have the courage to reveal. Sweetness, as Samson's proverb had it, comes from strength, not from submission. This is not to say that being afraid signals cowardice; everyone is afraid in the face of terror. But how we show our fear, how we endure in its presence, reveals our true character. To learn from and grow from our tears, fears, and suffering makes us fully human.

What is not a sign of growth is allowing ourselves to slip into help-less victimhood, cowering under the burden of endless bereavement. Some mourners suffer so much that they require emotional support from trained professionals. Psychologists tell us that such severe neurotic behavior can usually be traced back to an earlier unresolved grief. For-tunately, most of us have the resources we need to endure such troubled times and to grow.

What is truly strange about the common assumption that life ought to be easy and secure, that suffering is to be avoided whenever possible, and that grief should be denied rather than transcended, is that it does not correspond with our experience. Ironically, parents who desperately seek to protect their children from hardship and to insure their success look back on their own childhood struggles with a sense of triumph. The precious moments in their own lives, the ones that hold for them the deepest meaning and from which they have learned the most, are those in which they came face-to-face with adversities and overcame them—a lost job, a poor education, a debilitating illness, a parent's death, and so on.

Nothing is born without sacrifice; everything has a cost. The liter-ary critic Edmund Wilson penned *The Wound and the Bow* to teach that out of suffering may grow creativity, and Thomas Mann pointed out that Dostoevsky's epilepsy did not hinder his genius but contributed to it. Every human life replays the burden of Adam and Eve: When they were exiled from the Garden of Eden, God's curse was "In pain shall you bear children" (Gen. 3:16), but only then did they bear children. Out of curses blessings grow.

Growing Through Pain: Tough Love

Why should it be necessary for people to experience pain? Joshua Weinstein has argued that there is much evidence to suggest that the very existence of pain is to teach sufferers where to focus their energies and how much effort to expend. The central nervous system is responsible for action and initiative and has control over the movements of the body. As such, it is prone to disastrous error, to self-destructive action, and harmful motion. Were it not for pain, the nervous system could instruct a hand to go directly into a fire to retrieve a potato. Pain overwhelms the nervous system with its demands so that all other considerations and plans are momentarily shunted aside. Only pain inhibits our destructive actions in time to avert catastrophes. Should we, then, pray to be rid of pain?

Pain, in a word, protects us from harming ourselves; it coordinates and constrains the subjective feelings of the mind at the center of our being, aligning them with the reality at the periphery of our being. It is a further wonder that the body also contains an antidote to pain. In extreme cases, the body can achieve a deliberate numbness. Under the influence of adrenaline, the brain can produce its own painkillers, more effective than codeine or heroin.

As a further protection, pain expresses itself in degrees. This is crucial because it tells the central nervous system the exact degree of urgency required in a particular danger. The center has to find balance in the competing demands of pain made on the body: hunger and thirst, an infected tooth, a fractured arm. Without proportionality in the degrees of pain there would be no way to distinguish a minor irritation from a life-threatening emergency.

Pain is a gift of divine love, but it is tough love. The pain of grief is often, as I noted at the very beginning, a divine gift that enables us to grapple with our loss out of the depths of our humanity.

Saying Yes to Truth

The first and most dramatic benefit of adversity is that it opens our eyes. Despair can be constructive because it forces us, at long last, to look unflinchingly into a mirror of truth. When we hit bottom with a psychological thud, we have no place left to go. We have no option but to confront reality without distortion and to evaluate it. In an instant, we are able to glimpse beyond our illusions and relinquish our neurotic poses. This is the time to let go of old, failed, and probably inappropriate hopes; of imagined, frustrating loves; of dependencies that surreptitiously infantilize us; of self-deceptions that shore up our ego while masking truths about who we are. Hitting the bottom in despair produces what educators call a "teachable moment."

Alcoholics Anonymous is enormously successful for one reason. It is based on the simple but uncompromising proposition that alcoholics cannot begin to extricate themselves from their dependency until they are in a state of such despair that they have no more illusions and preposterous hopes. They realize they are beyond the possibility of self-healing. When they hit bottom and reach ultimate despair, there is no choice but to seek help.

The psychiatrist Rollo May, a pioneer in existential psychology, described a young patient who was struggling fiercely to clamber up out of despair but was unable to gain a foothold. Instead, the patient was pressed farther down into the pit, where he hit bottom. Within a brief period, his fiancée deserted him, his mother died, and other catastrophes piled up on him. One would have expected him to be paralyzed in a swamp of self-pity. But, instead, his despair elicited a shock of revelation, electrifying him to the realization that since he could not change his miserable existence, he would have to change himself. He was stunned into seeing the truth as it was. And he began then to discard his futile and fantastic hopes and slowly started to map new plans for himself.

A free fall into the pit of hopelessness can shock us into searching for a new hope. At the very moment when we would rather just disappear from the face of the earth, we suddenly know that it is up to us to strive and succeed. The existentialist philosopher Jean Paul Sartre noted profoundly: "Human life begins on the far side of despair."

Trouble Expands the Human Capacity

Sweet are the uses of adversity; which, like the toad, ugly and venomous, wears yet a precious jewel in his head.

—William Shakespeare

Life is not life without calamities. Trouble is inherent in the human condition. Everyone experiences the death of a close relative or friend; everyone confronts pain; everyone faces injustice. Even though we all strive for a trouble-free life, we need to accept the fact that life is never this way.

Despair often does this dirty job for us. We learn not to expect justice just because we believe it is our due, and we learn that we will not always be repaid in kind for a kindness. This is not cynicism; we must not confuse cynicism with realism. If despair teaches us this truth— though it may be a truth that never receives good press—we must factor it into our lives. Despair teaches us to deal with reality rather than to live in some imagined paradise.

Despair teaches us about our inner strength, too. We often squeeze out of ourselves what a situation demands; we do what we have to do. When the demands on us are more than we anticipate, we respond with more of ourselves: more patience, more endurance, more courage, more concentration, and more energy. And when we think we've finally come to the last ounce of our strength, miraculously we find more strength to meet still greater demands, and we're astonished at our own resources.

Our own despair also helps us appreciate other people's adversity. When the Israelites were trekking to the Holy Land, they were told by God to recall the slavery they endured in Egypt; to practice compassion, empathy, and neighborliness; and to learn to understand how to treat others in bondage. Similarly, victims of modern disasters reach out to others in comparable straits. Victims of a North Carolina hurricane have helped Miami hurricane victims. In turn, Miami victims have helped Oahu hurricane victims, even while they were still helping themselves. When homeless people succeed, they often turn to help other homeless. So those who have once despaired become more sensitive to the desperate; and those who need to be consoled are better equipped to console others.

Good fortune rarely leads us to God. Most people are grateful, but gratitude rarely causes us to question why we deserved such good fortune. Distress, on the other hand, often leads us directly to God. We may blame our misfortune on some unseen power or appeal to that power for help. How we relate to that higher power varies with each individual, but this remains true: Our despair goads us to seek a higher promise.

The Chinese ideogram for "crisis" consists of two symbols: "danger" and "opportunity." Every danger has hidden inside it an unexpected opportunity. Every new chance, on the other hand, holds inside its burnished shell a lurking danger. That is why a great opportunity is also our greatest burden. And why adversity can be turned to our advantage. If this is all true, then trouble becomes one of the most valuable trusts committed to our care. Of course, we don't want the trouble, no matter what it teaches. But once it has found us, we should seize it as an opportunity.

Simply put: No hardship, no hardihood; no fight, no fortitude; no suffering, no sympathy; and no pain, no patience. As George Eliot once whimsically observed: "Worldly faces never look so worldly as at a funeral."

Enlarge the Picture

As mourners, we are frequently so electrified by the misfortune that has befallen us that we act as though we were specifically targeted. Not infrequently we cry, "Why me?" "What will happen to me now?" Judaism reminds comforters that it is inappropriate to use a charged moment such as this to deride mourners' self-centeredness, to remind mourners that they are neither personally victimized nor the only ones suffering loss. Tradition provides a more subtle alternative in the traditional greeting, "May God comfort you among the other mourners of Zion and Jerusalem." Mourners and comforters both need to enlarge the picture and see beyond themselves.

Let me share an apt anecdote here: Napoleon's lieutenants in the French army were astonished when they realized that an enemy regiment was camped virtually at the entrance to their fort. They rushed to alert the general. He reacted to their hysteria with unusual calm and simply told them to get larger maps.

Death, horrible as it is, is not a local event but the way of the world.

The Past: Remember It, Don't Forget It

Memory nourishes the heart, and grief abates.

—Marcel Proust

"Forget it" is the single worst suggestion we can offer mourners. First of all, we cannot forget just by willing it. Second, only by remembering can we process our loss and achieve tranquility. Healing comes as a result of confronting and resolving, not from escaping and avoiding. Remembering allows us to relive cherished times, until memory is second nature, until acute awareness of our loss becomes latent, receding farther back in consciousness with every recollection. Remembering affirms the presence of our love and keeps that memory alive, and this by itself cushions the sting of invisibility. When loss is felt without any great hurry to push it into the past, the heart will mend.

To underscore this insight, the Sages added the *Yizkor* (Remembrance) prayer to the holiday services four times every year. *Yizkor* summons anew the image of a cherished life. Thus tradition makes it clear that there is harm in brushing memory aside. It is better to hold on to the image of our lost one as long as need be, releasing it only naturally and gradually, without conscious effort.

It is only in rare, extreme cases that remembering is counterproductive: when it leads to denying the reality of death. World-famous neurologist Oliver Sachs noted that the memory modules inside our brains can get stuck in one episode of the past, causing a convulsive upsurge of scenes and melodies that are stored away, resulting in abnormal reactions, such as hearing over and over a series of hated songs from childhood without stop. But that surely is atypical. In nonpathological circumstances, the best advice is to trust the natural mourning process, to assume that the mourner's mental health is sound, and to be confident that the mourner's reactions are normal.

Remembering Stimulates Closure

Memory can serve mourners as a very satisfying safe passage from grief to recovery. Most often it enables us to relive cherished moments, and also difficult moments, harmlessly.

Think of a molecular tape recorder located at a point in the cortex, at the base of the brain, that is stacked with an infinite number of dormant memories, subcortical imprints of remote events well below the horizon of everyday consciousness. Throughout our lives, the tape gets imprinted with what pioneering neurophysiologists Wilder Penfield and Phanor Perot called "the brain's record of all visual and auditory experiences," keeping forever all our memories, every single impression—cognitive and sensory—of everything that ever happened to us, waiting to be called up when the brain decides to turn on the recorder.

However, the mechanism of memory is far from objective; rather, it is an impression of the past that is not always accurate. We tend to remember selectively: matters cherished or hated; matters that put us at the center of an event, though we may not have been either at the center or present at the time; even completely invented "objective" memories of matters we heard about or witnessed only in a photograph or movie. Nevertheless, our memories are effectively therapeutic in times of trauma.

When we consciously remember, we spark an "episodic recall" rather than a mere fleeting memory that comes unbidden. Episodic recall works like an iconic replay of our life's most salient events: a wedding, a gift, an honor, a birth, a party, a surprise, and an ego inflator. It is enormously satisfying, is 99 percent safe, is not habit forming, and can become a channel that leads circuitously to the ultimate goal of recovery from severe grief.

Instinctively we seek to remember the good old days, even if they weren't good, only old. And we do this, often in the face of those who strongly discourage such remembering. We devise schemes and invent structures that purposely stir our recollections. For example, we look for ways to retain our parents' presence in our daily lives—in thoughts, prayers, pictures, inherited artifacts, symbolic objects, and customary practices.

Sigmund Freud called this process "grief work," and this was also the original title of his essay on mourning: *"Treuer Arbeit."* The "work" is a process of closing the gaping emotional wound left by the departure of a friend or relative. One of the successful outcomes of grief work is discovering that we can actually retain the memories and re-envision the intimate experience of knowing and loving the deceased, even as we form new love relationships or enrich existing ones. Paradoxically, we can experience the sense of being bereft at the very same time that we resume active participation in life. It can be hard work, but it can be done.

On one level of consciousness, doing such grief work allows us finally and completely to say good-bye to the deceased. And on another level, we can bring a new loved one into the hidden chambers of our heart. We can enjoy our recovery while bewailing our loss, because the human heart is large enough for both.

The Present: A Time to Heal, Not Cure

It does seem awkward, even a bit absurd, to speak of "healing" to mourners who have been wounded to the quick. What healing can come when someone close is gone for good?

To understand this paradox, we must realize that curing and healing are not the same. Mourning is not a medical problem (unless it triggers physiological or psychological pathology), and it should not be treated as such. Mourning is an existential component of living. The end goal we seek for mourners is not to be cured of untoward symptoms, but to be *healed*.

Healing vs. Curing

"Healing" and "curing" reflect two quite different perspectives concerning human health and illness. Cure strives to make well the heart damaged in a heart attack; healing strives to make well the person who had the heart attack. Curing does combat with a medical armamentarium: blood counts, CT scans, and electrolyte levels; healing seeks to clarify emotional burdens and resolve conflicts. Curing finds its modality in external sources: pharmaceuticals, radiation, and surgery. Healing draws only from inner resources: experience, faith, strength of character, and the power of the soul. The person who delivers a cure has to be proficient in scientific, technical, and intellectual matters. The person who wants to heal need not have technical know-how but must be demonstrably empathic and deeply concerned with the well-being of others.

To achieve these disparate goals, healing and curing employ different modes of thinking. Curing uses analytic thinking; healing uses synthetic thinking. Analytic thinking reduces every problem to its constituent parts and divides these parts into identifiable, manageable proportions. For example, curing finds disease not in the person as a whole (as was true in ancient medicine and is still true in eastern and holistic medical traditions) but in the kidney or prostate, where the disease is localized, and then treats it. The health professional only *delivers* the cure but does not actually activate it; the treatment or medication does that. And since it is the chemicals or therapy actually effecting the cure, any health professional—an associate, a resident, or a nurse—can substitute for the doctor. The healer, on the other hand, serves as the personal interface between the world of the sick and the world of the well. The healer helps control the life that the patient cannot manage alone. No substitute agent can supplant the healer in that pivotal healing position.

The goal of curing is to return the diseased part to functional integrity. But healing seeks to return the whole person to health or fitness. For example, amputees return to health when they feel strong, positive, ready—actually healthy—despite the fact that they will never return to complete physical intactness. Stroke victims may limp for the rest of their lives, but they are healthy when they feel that they are whole again—when they are wholesome, they are healed. Conversely, if because of their limp, they feel vulnerable, victimized, threatened, bent, and stared at, they are not healed at all, even though they may be medically sound.

When God Heals; When People Heal

Rabbenu Bachya, a tenth-century sage, noted that the Torah uses precise words—down to a single punctuation dot—to distinguish between human and divine healing. The Hebrew word used in the Torah for "to cure" is *ve'rapo;* the hard "P" is used for curing done by human beings, since such cures invariably cause pain as they work their miracles. But when describing healing, the Torah introduces a subtle change by removing the dot from the center of the Hebrew letter "P," thereby changing the pronunciation from a hard "P" to a pillowed "F"—*"rofeh"*—as evidenced in the verse, "For I God will heal you" (Exod. 21:19). Thus, the Bible defangs the pain caused by the human process of curing by eliminating a single dot! This is designed to teach that God heals; human beings cure—which often proves a hard remedy for those afflicted. Indeed, the Jerusalem Bible translates *"refu'ah"* as "F", written without a hard dot, to mean "heal," as opposed to "cure." Ecclesiastes describes the human conundrum: There is a time to kill and a time to heal (Eccl. 3:3). Using the explosive "P," Moses pleads with God for his sister who is diseased: "Please God, heal her"—using the soft "F"—"heal her softly" (Num. 12:13).

Would that all people could achieve divine healing and experience a soft landing after pain and tragedy. We pray that all those who suffer will be healed, even if the medium for such healing is another human being and even if the only path to such wholeness has to be a hard landing.

PART III

MAKING WHOLE THE FRAGMENTED SOUL

Chapter 9

A Cosmic Specialness

I should like to call attention to the following facts. During the past thirty years, people from all civilized countries of the earth have consulted me. I have treated many hundreds of patients ... Protestants ... Jews (and a small number of Catholics). Among all my patients ... there has not been one whose problem in the last resort was not that of finding a religious outlook on life. It is safe to say that every one of them fell ill because he had lost that which the living religions of every age have given to their followers, and none of them has really been healed who did not regain his religious outlook.

—Carl Jung

Without an inner transcendent experience humans lack the resources to withstand the blandishments of the world.

—Carl Jung

Two Geographies

We live in two geographies. One is the tangible world that demands practical solutions to complex daily problems. That is why psychiatrists often look for some pathological abnormality in a severe grief reaction and why 85 percent of doctors impulsively prescribe

139

pills for tears. In this geography, we need to understand why such and such is happening. The philosopher Friedrich Nietzsche once said, "He who has a why to live can bear with almost any how." Mourning is a litany of "whys."

On this level, we deal with the "real" world of cause and effect, of seeking instantaneous resolutions to complicated problems, of doing whatever needs to be done for the job at hand. We look for explanations for every disturbing event—and even when this seeking does not result in an effective solution, we feel that "understanding" a problem some-how makes the incomprehensible excusable, or at least bearable. Carl Jung noted: "Understanding does not cure evil, but it is a definite help, inasmuch as one can cope with a comprehensible darkness." We spend most of our workaday lives on this very real world level.

But there is a problem with living just on this level. Such a practi-cal approach to life's ups and downs lacks ultimate meaning. It fails to provide perspective on the larger shape of our actions.

Fortunately, we also live in another world: the geography of the spirit. On this level, every human being has a transcendent dimension. We sense that there is "something out there," a power beyond our cor-poreal reality that relates to us as persons, as souls, and as sentient hu-man beings, and that ultimately controls our destiny. What eats away at our hearts in mourning is primarily a crisis of spirituality. Among the first expressions that bursts forth from our lips upon hearing of a death is sheer spiritual agony: "Oh, my God! Why? Why her? Why this ter-rible death? What did she ever do to deserve this?"

This terrifying moment is not a time for persuasion or justification or apologetics, theology, or philosophy. In this spiritual landscape we are not interested in a reasoned answer to these types of questions. We want only a look of understanding and empathy from another human being, together with that person's willingness to share our burden. Spiritually attuned people do not need to be cured as much as to be healed; they need consolers to comfort them, not a pill to sedate to them; a listen-ing ear and a warm smile rather than a medical concoction. Similarly, our agony is a cry of the heart, not a body blow to our reason; and that is not going to be assuaged by sophisticated ideas and philosophical abstractions.

In spiritual discourse, we do not find answers in deductive logic or in statistics that make sense to the mind but ignore the soul. Rather, we proceed by metaphor, poetry, images, narrative, and especially by parable, which conceals more than it reveals. In such a framework, words are not mere words, and meanings are not only definitions. In spiritual struggle, death is not primarily a biological fact; it is the irreversible breaking of an intimate bond.

Words have special power in the stories that shape us. Great narratives are not to be judged by their logic but by the emotions and ideas they inspire. They are the profound touchstones of our tradition—Abraham on Mount Moriah preparing to sacrifice Isaac, Moses on Mount Sinai, Elijah facing down Ahab, Odysseus lashed to the mast, even Huck's friendship with Jim.

Matters of the soul—hope and empathy, meaning and memory, religion and idealism—trickle into our innards gradually, by osmosis and intuition. A wound inflicted by the breach of death does not cause pain that is mitigated by chemicals; it causes suffering that needs to be healed by the spiritual insights unlocked by our tradition, which address the anguished moments of the bereft. It is on the spiritual landscape that we engage the process of mourning.

Everyone Has a Transcendent Dimension

Most of us have an innate sense of a hidden, transcendent force that governs the universe. This force has cosmic significance—beyond nature, beyond reason, beyond normal life, beyond human striving. It is greater than ourselves and transcends our everyday needs. Most of us, then, consider ourselves part of a grand plan that we cannot grasp, a cosmic design we cannot comprehend. We experience a sense of awe when contemplating the universe, and we are intuitively attracted to the sacred.

Spirituality generates openness to mystery, to paradoxes such as why bad things happen to good people, and to the ambiguities of our daily lives and its absurdities. Spirituality helps stabilize us and at the same time stimulates our hopes and our thoughts. Sometimes quite ordinary people experience an oceanic mystical encounter and, in astonishment, they gasp: "There must be a God"—and find that it is a replenishing experience, reinvigorating their souls. Blaise Pascal, the great French philosopher, said it well: "It is the heart which perceives God and not the reason." The heart is captured by the spiritual experience and knows it as a fact, a part of reality, though it is immeasurable, unprovable, in any scientific laboratory.

This sense of transcendence significantly shapes our outlook on many earthly matters. It prompts us to intuit such vital ideas as a life after death, and thrusts our mystical imaginings into flights of theological fancy (for example, projecting a celestial reunion of our relatives in the afterlife). Ralph Waldo Emerson once mused: "I suppose you could never prove to the mind of the most ingenious mollusk that such a creature as a whale was possible." Curiously, many of these "wild" intuitions are being re-examined today, as scientists analyze a vast array of end-of-life experiences, although this is an area in which science may never gain absolute certainty.

Each of us is composed of unique psychological and genetic elements, of unique environmental and spiritual qualities. We address this awesome spiritual power on all these levels and by a variety of names (God, the Force, a Higher Power). Or we use no name at all, addressing what we perceive as a diffused presence, hovering over the heights of nature and crouching in the crevices beneath our feet. This perception of a nameless transcendence is perhaps the most glorious tribute possible to the omniscient, omnipotent, dominant force in existence.

The Heightened Spiritual Sensitivity of Mourners

Confrontation with death intuitively triggers within us a dialogue with a spiritual power. And even in extreme cases of murder or death through negligence, we sense that the ultimate source of this terrible act must be the transcendent God. Even if we ascribe death to anonymous Fates, we know that it nonetheless represents a power beyond the reach of our human minds.

We see this understanding expressed routinely, even if not specifically articulated, in the mourner's characteristic question, "Why me?" This question clearly presumes that someone or something is listening to our plaint and is not simply another person but something greater. "Why me?" is a natural human cry to this unknown transcendent Providence.

Further evidence of our spiritual proclivity in the face of death has been given creative form in the ancient prose poem *Kaddish*, recited by Jewish mourners, which I discussed at some length in Chapter 6. Significantly, the words of this poem are unrelated in any explicit way to grief or to the deceased; its words in praise of God are recited with enthusiasm like an article of faith, spiritually, even ecstatically, with the mourner concentrating on the recently deceased. It is probably the most intent-intense of all Jewish communal prayers, a veritable light and sound dream fantasy, consisting of piercing words, staccato verbal flashes, mind-numbing noun endings (*tushbechata, nechemata*), the mesmerizing repetition of simple words (*alam, almei, almaya,* and *chayeikhon, yomeikhon*), then the rocking, moaning, swaying tunes interrupted after every sentence with communal responses of "amen," "amen," "amen." Its very recital elicits overtones of another world, the spellbinding music of the spheres that softly caresses the inner sadness of the mourner who recites it.

With every repetition of the *Kaddish,* mourners gain a renewed connection to the transcendent that binds them tightly to their people, both in their immediate environment and in history. *Kaddish* is the DNA of Jewish spirituality—a transcendental double-spiraled helix that intertwines the spiritual cores of heaven and earth, linking them eternally. The climax of this spiritual linkage is in the prayer's crescendo: *"Oseh shalom bimromav—hu ya'aseh shalom aleinu"* (The One who makes peace in the heavenly heights—that One will make peace for us and for all Israel). Though we are earth-bound dwarfs, we hereby contract our futures with God in the heights of God's universe.

Kaddish is the celestial platform from which our Sages launched that eternal spiritual unity between God and the Jewish people. This connection with God was considered so crucial that, legend has it, Rabbi Israel Isserlein, chief rabbi of Vienna in the early 1400s, allowed a woman mourning her deceased parent to hold a *mincha* (afternoon) service, preceded by a talmudic study session at the deceased's home, specifically so that she could recite the *Kaddish* after the learning, an observance not practiced at the community synagogue, where only men recited it. This is another reason why the tradition prefers we hold religious services in the home of the deceased—to nurture the spiritual union between mourners and God.

Tradition has it that the second-century C.E. scholar Rabbi Akiva wrote the *Kaddish* prayer—originally for an ignorant child whose wayward parent had died, packing into it words such as "purity," "holiness," "heaven," and "peace," the jewels of the holy language. Furthermore, he composed the prayer in Aramaic, the mother tongue of his time, a language that Midrash says the holy angels can't understand! The words were meant for God's ears only, an intimate conversation between the mourner and the Divine.

The Reach Is Galactic; The Roots Subterranean

The roots of human spirituality are obscure. We have no authorized cartography of this invisible world. The Sages described authentic spirituality that inhabits our earth-bound minds as "fire inside water"—an otherworldly pure spirit hiding inside a thoroughly material existence. At bottom, it is simply impossible to fully understand the existence of this mysterious presence.

The most appropriate biblical metaphor for this that I can think of is Jacob's ladder. The Bible tells us that this ladder had feet deep into the ground and its top nestled in the divine heights of the heavens. Strangely, the angels that traversed this mystical ladder first went up and then came down, although we would expect the opposite of God's messengers, who presumably are sent down from heaven. But Jacob's angels arise from the earth because that is where they have been lodging, as it were, and they scramble up the ladder into the spiritual stratosphere. As I see it, these homeward-bound angels returning to heaven are the "angels" of human beings, our good qualities; the spirit that emanates from each of our souls receives its goal and mission from the heavens but has its roots planted in the ground. Jacob's ladder is thus a stunning graphic portrayal of the spirituality of human striving. The Bible portrays this spiritual striving in precisely the kind of transcendent framework we sense when we connect most intimately with the Divine.

The signposts leading us to spiritual understanding are symbol, ritual, narrative, allegory, parable, and metaphor—imaginative devices that lead to insights that soar beyond all understanding in the conventional sense. Such transcendental insights and experiences have been verified by profoundly spiritual people, by historically validated anecdotal evidence recorded in most of the major religions, and by the universally acknowledged fact that they have riveted the attention of masses of people from all civilizations since the dawn of history. The mystical teachings giving rise to these experiences surely should not be dismissed as the products of exuberant imagination and superstition. Rather, we need to acknowledge that spirituality represents an experiential dimension of human consciousness, a reality that we can productively apply, using both our intuition and rational mind, to our own lives.

Spirituality affords mourners a source of trust, even after the violation of trust caused by death. The Almighty is the only place where we can find succor from our troubles; it is this transcendental power we must address in our grief. Study after study confirms that those who have faith fare better in coping with immediate post-traumatic stress as well as with accepting death as the natural consequence of life.

In Jewish literature, spiritual experiences are often portrayed as providing intimations of the future life, *olam ha'ba* (the world to come), in a distant universe beyond time and space. Even simple Jews in the shtetl, in light-hearted Yiddish conversation, took the idea of this other world so much for granted that they casually referred to it as *yener velt* (that [other] world). In fact, to the Jewish mind throughout history, the spiritual universe was always a familiar piece of religious real estate, not the exclusive province of scholars or theologians.

The Deaf Don't Dance

Israel Baal Shem Tov, the eighteenth-century founder of Hasidism, once told a story about a deaf man who came upon a house in which people were dancing. Their contortions, their frenzy, and their joy were puzzling to him. Their wild motions and gestures, raised arms, kicking feet, smiling faces, and trance-like looks seemed to him unequivocal signs that they had gone insane. But, the Baal Shem Tov explained, the truth was that they were dancing in harmony to music that he could not imagine, let alone hear, because he was deaf.

There are those who, though not stone deaf to spirituality, still cannot quite make out the "harmony of the spheres," as Anatole France called spirituality. And then there are those who, though hard of hearing to spiritual concerns, may sometimes become sensitized to the supernatural by an alarming personal incident that grabs their ears and compels them—by radical awe, sheer terror, dramatic irony, or striking coincidence—to turn to the transcendent as the *prima facie* controlling power behind otherwise inexplicable events. They hear the music and may even learn to dance to its beat.

Mourning is a striking example of such a sensitizing event. We are suddenly bereft of a loved one in a manner that may fly in the face of our sense of justice and reason, at a time that may be shockingly untimely, by a force that seems oblivious to human effort and yearning. At first we assume that the deceased was summarily torn out of the human scene by a perverse power outside the universe. Who can do such a thing? What is that power? Such questions cascade, threatening to overwhelm us. Instinctively, our first reaction is to rage against that power.

But underneath this reaction is our implicit belief that a spiritual entity in fact superintends humanity and nature. Indeed, that alarming event can transform itself into a defining moment in our religious life.

There's a Plan for Everything

The spiritually gifted create a special relationship with the Almighty. They know in their heart of hearts that only God determines life and death, and they accept implicitly that, in wisdom, God does what is just—even though it may defy our comprehension. Since they believe that there is a superintending, controlling power, they accept that whatever may happen, there is a plan, although we do not know what it is. When things happen, they happen according to design, not in random strikes.

A young couple I know in Palm Springs, California, suffered the death of their four-year-old, who walked into a swimming pool and drowned. Their entire community and all its clergymen were shocked into speechlessness. Remarkably, the mother of the boy herself provided the only consoling words. "It is not mine to question God. God gave and God took back." Those whose beliefs are founded in this sense of destiny or fate, and have such a profound, unshakable trust in God, believe that God's decision is not arguable, that it must be accepted. For them, there is no other way. Such people demonstrate supreme trust in Providence; theirs is the very peak of religious faith. Indeed, such moments serve as the litmus test of a person's faith.

Since that unforgettable moment in Palm Springs, I have met other victims of horrendous fortune. They too have said, calmly and quite sincerely, "This is God's will. I trust in God. I don't understand, but whatever God does I accept. I can't change God's will. It's out of my hands." Such heartfelt declarations represent the apex of human spirituality. I am in awe of such trust. To me, it is one of the "rumors of angels."

When God Hides, Who Seeks?

When we are drowning in sadness, we scream at the heavens, demanding to know how God could have permitted such a terrible end to befall someone who has done so much good, who is undeserving of such punishment, somebody we hold dear. Where were you, God? In the ninth century C.E., the great scholar Saadia Gaon was succinct in expressing such sentiments, speaking for all ages: "We called you, Eternal our God, and you distanced yourself from us" (*Keranukha, Adonai Eloheinu: rachakta mimenu*). Where were you when we needed you? Were you hidden from your people? In Hebrew, the expression used for this is "*hester panim,*" literally, the "hiding of God's face."

It is told that the grandson of a great rabbi once ran crying into his grandfather's study. "What's the matter?" asked the rabbi. The child replied, "I was playing hide-and-seek with my friend, and I hid, and now my friend isn't even looking for me!" The grandfather commiserated with his grandson's frustration. Then he said , "You know, God weeps for the very same reason. God's face is sometimes hidden from people, and He implores them to look for Him—but no one comes looking for God! God, too, weeps in despair."

The rabbi understood that what we perceive as God's hiding is actually our hiding from God! It is the replay in every person's life of that defining moment in Paradise. After Adam sinned, he crouched in fear and hid from God. The Bible recounts, in human terms, that God then called to Adam: *Ayekah* (Where are you hiding)? The Sages pounced on the hint in the text. With a slight vowel change, "*Ayekah*" became "*Eikhah*" (Woe betide us!). When Adam hides, God's face is hidden in response. When Adam hides, the word "*Ayekah*" leads us to *Eikhah*, lamentations. We hide so often from God's demands, God's moral standards, God's insistence on our kindness and charity and spirituality; but we avoid Him when we discover He is hidden.

But of course, God sometimes is hidden, not because we don't look for God, but because that is what God chooses to do for reasons we will never be able to divine. We need to hope that God, in the words of the Torah, will make God's face to shine upon us, and grant us peace.

Death that is "unnatural," untimely, undeserved, and unexpected often stirs questions and resentment, even in those who faithfully trust in God. During such times, these mourners generally do not conclude that there is no God but rather that God's "face is hidden," which means that they accept that God is relinquishing supervision during this time, and as a consequence the world freezes in God's shadow. The concept of "*hester panim*," which in Hebrew means "the hiding of God's face," the metaphoric eclipse of the divine sun that warms us and shines upon us.

It is precisely at this dark moment, when God seems to be hiding, when we need God and cry out to God but hear no answer, when we assume that God doesn't care or can't hear—that we must make our most concerted effort to find God. Perhaps, in grief, when we so desperately seek God, we will be successful. Indeed, in finding God we may even find ourselves.

Chapter 10

The Promise of Jewish Spirituality

Spirituality is, in the end, a path of great consolation, great strength, and great comfort. For there is a healing force—a spiritual force, an energy greater than the self—that can, if you let it in, mend the broken places in your soul and replenish your depleted waters like an internal reservoir.

—Ashley Davis Prend

There are mechanisms through which spirituality contributes to down-to-earth healing, empowering mourners to reintegrate themselves into society after their loss, to regenerate their intactness, to reset their orientation, and to rediscover the meaning of their lives.

—Charlene Westgate

Mourners—whose lives have been shattered, disoriented, and vacuumed of all meaning—need to adapt to a newly arranged environment. Clearly, however, mourners need much more, not in terms of strategic behavioral and attitudinal maneuvers but in spiritual terms. Belief in one God implies a unified universe, coherence in nature and in society. Most casualties that befall mourners in severe grief are anti-thetical to coherence. Yet, the idea of coherence, of underlying unity, is the first fruit of spirituality. This contributes positively to healing in three distinct ways:

- Coherence is a means of making sense of a traumatic life event and enables us to reframe that event in a positive way. God is the power at the center of the universe, imposing a structure of meaning on all events. Coherence assumes that death is not a random malevolence.
- Coherence provides emotional support and enhances our self-esteem, which has been badly battered by our loss. It reassures us that we are valued, singled out, and cared for by God, in what is otherwise a cold and friendless world.
- As mourners our instinctive view of the community is that it has been fractured, broken, and scattered. Our sense of coher-ence can reassure us that our community is still vital, easing our re-entry into society.

Standard dictionaries list three disciplines in which "coherence" dominates:

- *Physics: exhibiting coherence.* The force by which the molecules of a substance are held together. The act or condition of coher-ing; a tendency to stick together; having cohesion.
- *Logic: being coherent.* To be connected naturally or rationally by a central theme. The quality of congruity, being logically inte-grated, consistent, and intelligible; clearly articulated.
- *Social work: having cultural cohesion.* Populations and individu-als who have intellectual and moral affinity with one another.

During times of mourning, we need to recoup our sense of the world's coherence, to regain an integrated worldview, a satisfying grand explanation, a larger design in which mourners are included. We need to find a sense of meaning that can account for our new circumstances and to regain our sense of belonging to a community. Spirituality gives birth to such coherence in all its connotations, providing coherent meaning, a cohesive sense of self, and social cohesion as the mourner rejoins the community from which he or she has been separated by grief.

Cohesiveness: A Sense of Wholeness

As it is used in physics, coherence refers to the quality of being bound together. In spiritual terms, we can understand this to refer to the cohesiveness of the world and the unity of one's inner life. In Judaism, this idea of one world and one humanity derives from monotheism, the oneness of God. A report on spiritual wellness noted "that the spiritual dimension is an innate component of human functioning that acts to integrate all other components." This spiritual idea is what imposes pattern, structure, and harmony on the world. Most important for us, the spiritual cohesiveness of the oneness of God helps make our fragmented souls whole again—it empowers us as mourners to recover our inner coherence, our sanity.

For a mind in pieces, disorganized by the uprooting of a death, spirituality can tame and organize wild thoughts, link disparate imaginings, hopes, and widespread fears. It enables the unfolding of wholeness, a sense of living in interconnection with all humanity. It also fosters a seamless togetherness of our personal lives—the mind, body, psyche, and soul—and the interconnectedness of brain with immune system, endocrine system, and neural system. This inner sense of unity binds together the shattered pieces of a broken heart.

In a universal sense, everything in the physical world follows a special pattern called the "laws of nature." In a personal sense, every aspect of our lives—at home, work, and play—is a variation on one grand theme.

The disorientation that in grief desperately cries out for a permanent, immovable framework stimulates the oldest consolation in the religious catalog, the phrase that Jewish people traditionally recite as they leave the house of shiva: *"Ha'makom yenachem etkhem betokh she'ar avelei Tziyon vi'Yerushalayim"* (May God [literally, called "the Place"] console you among all the mourners of Zion and Jerusalem). It is the unity and certainty of a central spiritual "place" that comforts. This idea of coherence is essential to living, and serves as an effective metaphor of healing from grief.

Coherence: Meaning in Life

In a second sense, "coherence" means making sense, giving meaning. As specks in the galactic universe, we draw our primary significance from our connection with a transcendent power—the eternal, omnipotent, ever-present power of the Creator. The idea of coherence allows us to be comfortable and to fit into the universe knowing that we belong there.

The structure of meaning guiding our lives needs to originate outside ourselves, from a transcendent Being that says, "This is good, this is evil. Do this, don't do that." "Good ultimately is rewarded, evil ultimately is punished." "To be honorable is a goal in life." "To raise children is to contribute to society." These ethical imperatives form the order, the coherence of life on earth, and they are derived from a supernatural being. Gordon Allport, an authority on the psychology of personality, asks whether a person can ever really attain integration in the cosmos, within the scheme of life itself, until he or she has entered into a treaty with the cosmos. Although we may not listen to God and may even deny God's existence, we intuitively contract with a transcendent entity, and within this contract we derive a structure of meaning by which we live our lives.

The opposite of "coherent" is "incoherent." That which is incoherent cannot satisfy the hunger of the human soul. Victor Frankl, a psychologist, dedicated his life to the study of "meaning" through a therapeutic method, called logotherapy, noted that in ancient legends a hero leaves home to search for the meaning of life or the secret of eternal youth. But meaning is not always to be found far from home. Too many of us spend too many years looking for answers "out there," only to discover that meaning is not found by the wandering soul but is grasped in the crucible of our own transcendent soul.

Sigmund Freud had a picture of the sphinx and the pyramids displayed prominently in his consulting room. To him, these objects represented permanence, an antidote to the "passing shadow" of the frail human life. One day, Freud fainted, and as he awakened, he said, "How sweet it must be to die." He continued in most un-Freudian terms: "What joy there is in such yielding. The comfort, the trust, the relief in one's chest and shoulders, the lightness in one's heart, the sense of being sustained by something larger, less fallible. In that way we are able to melt ourselves trustingly into the arms of the Great Father."

Meaning has to be larger than an individual, a part of the very texture of creation. That is why a dominant motif of Jewish sacred literature is not Ecclesiastes' shocking "utter futility!" (1:2) but Genesis' whisper: "in the image of God He created him; male and female" (1:27), and the quiet observation of Psalms: "You have made [the human] little less than divine [the angels]" (8:6).

The Reverse Tapestry

But what happens when this magnificent sense of coherence goes topsy-turvy, when our structure of meaning collapses in the face of a sudden crash, when one of our expectations is dashed, when life "signifies nothing at all"? Often, we turn cynical: "Who needs this?" "It's all random; there is no God; and if there is one, it's a God who doesn't care."

Rabbi Joseph B. Soloveitchik used an ancient, unforgettable metaphor to respond to this plaint:

Imagine you are looking at the back of a magnificent unlined tapestry hanging in a museum. You see a profusion of threads strung wildly in every direction, a riot of colors with no apparent purposeful arrangement; no fine embroidery, only stitching—an appalling mess. But then you realize that you are looking at only the underside of a brilliant work of art and, after staring at it, the picture begins to fall into place. You begin to detect a motif, a hint of a grand design, a trace of a pattern, a fragment of a human figure. Now you sense hints of the tapestry's coherence and harmony. You know that if you could see its front side you would find it breathtakingly beautiful.

———

From the earth, we contemplate God's universe from its reverse side, as it were. If we believe God is a divine designer, we will discover a coherent meaning from the clues we find, a grand design in the seemingly wild threads and colors of this world. Though we will never get to see it from God's perspective, we intuit that it is magnificent. We may be confused about the patterns of life, and on the surface it often makes no sense, but we feel certain that behind it all, beyond the reach of our senses there is justice and fairness—reward for good and punishment for evil.

If you believe that creation is divine and that the world is created with purpose, then even if the threads of life are bewildering, you can be confident that the universe has a system and plan and pattern, and you can return from mourning to living an orderly life once again.

For What Shall We Live?

We often find no answers to the "whys" of our life. Life is not an intellectual puzzle. We do not grow by solving paradoxes; we grow by finding new meaning in what seems at first glance to lack purpose or sense.

"For what shall we live?" I don't remember where or when I first heard this question, but I do remember the answer. "For that for which we would die." If we would die for our children, we should live for them; if we would die for our country, we should get involved in our country's welfare; if we would die for our faith, then our faith is worth believing in, struggling for, and adhering to. But I know of no one who would willingly die for even the most lucrative success in business or an exalted political position. As we get closer to our own deaths, it is fitting that we shuck the old code words that once stirred our passions and blinded our sight—those things that rank in the "not-to-die-for" category—and spend more time on the "what-to-live-for" concerns.

Finding meaning in life is not only a result of being religious, it can also be a precondition for being religious. If we cannot sense meaning in our lives, we may never discover spirituality. But when life does hold meaning for us, we view it through different eyes. We may be racked with unbearable suffering yet we want to go on and on living, investing hope in tomorrow. We may be upset, frustrated, despairing, depressed—but our connection with God, the Ultimate Power, source of our spirituality and the meaning of our lives, keeps us steady and strong and alive. How else could we account for the miraculous persistence of tens of thousands of Holocaust survivors who did not commit suicide?

The Old Man and the Angel of Death

In Poland there once was a desperately poor man, Yosef, who struggled every day to earn a few *kopecks* gathering loose twigs and scraps of wood. He painfully picked up each scrap and threw it into a canvas bag over his shoulder, and at the end of the day sold it for firewood. He hated every minute of this work. He had grown too old; he moved too slowly, his back ached too much to do it anymore. "Oh God, who needs this life?" he complained over and over. "I'm tired of it, take me out of here."

One day, as he was gathering his wood, his full sack split wide open and the wood fell all over the cobblestones. He looked at the shambles and shrieked with a head-splitting cry, "God, I told you I had enough. Take me away from this terrible place. Let me die."

At that moment, the Angel of Death appeared in front of him. "You called for me?" he asked.

Yosef gulped. "Yes, yes, I'm glad you came," he said after a minute. "Could you help me pick up these sticks?"

———

In spite of everything, our will to live stubbornly keeps us alive. Finding meaning in life teaches us not to surrender to death. No matter the severity of what happens, when life has meaning, such meaning overrides any desire to abandon it. This is the spiritual drive that keeps people from losing hope or committing suicide through frustration, depression, hopelessness, debilitating disease, terminal illness, and, yes, even in the face of the Holocaust.

Cohesion: The Glue of Community

The third way of thinking about coherence is as the connectedness of individuals to one another. We live and share values with others of like minds—through singing, praying, chanting, dancing, studying—and also through the common fears and mutual defenses that make us circle the wagons. Through suffering we also experience a sense of togetherness. Mourning belongs to a spiritual fellowship of shared values to which we naturally relate. We call this connectedness "community," and it is particularly relevant to us when we are depressed and grieving.

The mapping of the human genome at the beginning of the twenty-first century, one of the most astonishing scientific projects in human history, confirmed what geneticists have known for decades: just how connected we all are. Genetically, we humans are all extraordinarily alike. There are far fewer genetic differences among humans—from professors to cannibals—than among many other species that have been studied. Infinitesimal discrepancies in single genes account for most of the variations we see in skin color, hair texture, and other superficial traits.

But our similarities go far beyond the physical. The Sages, thousands of years ago, sensed this when they noted that there is an invisible but unmistakable interconnectedness in all human suffering. We detect, sympathize, and act to relieve suffering in others precisely because we know the feeling in our own bones. And this is why the highly structured Jewish bereavement practices include the community as an essential component of healing. Individuals are not left to fend for themselves but have the community to comfort and console them, according to precise ritual patterns. Mourners who attend synagogue regularly recite the *Kaddish* as a sacred portion specifically devoted to their own loss, but they are responded to by their neighbor's "amens."

Chapter 11

The World Beyond
the Grave

Science has a real surprise for the skeptics. Science, for instance, tells us that nothing in nature, not even the tiniest particle, can disappear without a trace. Nature does not know extinction. All it knows is transformation. Now if God applies this fundamental principle to the most minute and insignificant parts of His universe, doesn't it make sense to assume He applies it also to the human soul? I think it does. And everything science has taught me and continues to teach me strengthens my belief in the continuity of our spiritual existence after death. Nothing disappears without a trace.

—Wernher von Braun

Is there anything at all beyond the grave? We ask ourselves this question, but only in a whisper. Heaven is not a public agenda item; dealing with ultimately unknowable matters makes even the most spiritual mourners uneasy. But it is a subtext, especially to mourners; we do think about this question, and we know that our forebears thought about it

---

Please note: Because of the historic complexity of the eschatological themes discussed in this chapter, the terms I use are necessarily imprecise and reflect popular rather than academic or philosphic meaning.

as well. We also know that there were sages who devoted much of their lives thinking about life and death in profound ways. We sense that the logic of life implies that living does not simply stop when we die; we feel that there must be answers somewhere. It just sometimes seems childish to ask.

In the summer of 2000, newspapers reported on a young teenager who solicited letters from grieving children and adolescents from all over the world. The predominant theme of those letters, by far, was heaven. A child, unencumbered by adult "sophistication," asks such questions straightforwardly: "Where is heaven?" "What happened to my grandmother?" "Will Uncle Bill come back from heaven?" Of course, "heaven" is a common term used by parents as a catchall answer to the probing questions children ask about death. Children's questions, so innocently posed, should make us adults think these matters through for ourselves as well. If "heaven" is such a useful answer for the simple questions of children, perhaps it can also serve as shorthand for us adults, too. There is as much truth in simplicity as there is in complexity—perhaps even more.

When It's Over, Is It All Over?

Is there another life? Shall I awake and find all this a dream? There must be, we cannot be created for this sort of suffering.

—John Keats

Historically, we have always had an abiding faith in a world beyond the grave. Beyond proof, but unshakable, this idea has been cherished since the beginning of thought. It first makes its appearance in religious literature not as fiat, commanded irrevocably by an absolute God, but rather plantlike, growing and developing naturally in human culture. It then sprouts forth as sublime prayer and sacred hymn. Only later does it become entangled in complex metaphysical speculation, emerging in the philosophical traditions of the past few centuries and continuing into our own day.

The afterlife is not just a rational construct of a religious philosophy imposed on believers. It springs from within the hearts of the masses, a sort of *consensus gentium*, inside out, a hope beyond and above the rational, a longing for the warm sun of eternity. The afterlife is not a theory to be proven logically or demonstrated by rational analysis. It is axiomatic. It is to the soul what oxygen is to the lungs. There is little meaning to life, to God, to our constant strivings, and to all of our achievements, unless there is a world beyond the grave.

The Bible, so concerned with human actions in this world and agonizing over our day-to-day morals, is relatively silent about the world to come. This very silence is a testimony to this awesome concept, which the Bible takes for granted as we take for granted the biosphere in which we live. No elaborate apologia, no complex abstractions are necessary. The Bible, which records the sacred dialogue between God and human beings, surely must be predicated on the soul's eternal existence. In its own time and on its own terms, this premise was not a matter of debate. But it certainly was later in history, when whole movements interpreted Scripture with such slavish literalism that they dismissed the concept of an afterlife because they could not find it crystallized in letter and verse; or later yet, when philosophers began to apply the yardstick of rationalism to every hope and idea, seeking empirical proof for this conviction of the soul. No, in the world of Torah, the idea of the eternal soul was a fundamental creed, always present, unnecessary to articulate.

If the soul is immortal, then death cannot be considered the final act. If the life of the soul is to be continued, then death, however bitter, is deprived of its treacherous power of casting mourners into a lifetime of agonizing hopelessness over an irretrievable loss. Terrible though it is, death is clearly a threshold to a new world, the world to come.

A Parable

In a handful of sparse Hebrew sentences on which I have elaborated, a prominent Israeli scholar, Rabbi Yecheil Michael Tuckachinsky, pro-

vides a telling analogy that conveys hope and confidence in a life after life, although it must be refracted through the prism of death:

Imagine twin boys growing peacefully in the warmth of the womb.
Their mouths are closed, and they are being nourished via the umbili-
cal cord. Their lives are serene. The whole world, to these brothers, is
the interior of the womb. Who could conceive anything larger, better,
more comfortable? They begin to wonder: "We are getting lower and
lower. Surely if this continues, we will exit one day. What will happen
after we exit?"

Now, the first boy is a believer. He is heir to a religious tradition that
tells him there will be a new life after this wet and warm existence of
the womb. A strange belief, seemingly without foundation, but one to
which he holds fast. The second boy is a thoroughgoing skeptic. Legends do not deceive him. He believes only in that which can be demonstrated. He is enlightened and tolerates no idle conjecture. What is
not within one's experience can have no basis in one's imagination.

Says the faithful brother, "After our death here, there will be a new
great world. We will eat through the mouth. We will see great distances,
and we will hear through the ears on the sides of our heads. Why, our
feet will be straightened! And our heads—up and free, rather than
down and boxed in."

Replies the skeptic, "Nonsense. You're straining your imagination
again. There is no foundation for this belief. It is only your survival
instinct, an elaborate defense mechanism, and a historically condi-
tioned subterfuge. You are looking for something to calm your fear of
death. There is only this world. There is no world to come!"

"Well then," asks the first, "what do you say it will be like?"

The second brother snappily replies with all the assurance of the
slightly knowledgeable, "We will go out with a bang. Our world will
collapse, and we will sink into oblivion. No more. Nothing. Black void.
An end to consciousness. Forgotten. This may not be a comforting
thought, but it is logical."

Suddenly, the membrane holding the water inside the womb bursts. The womb convulses. Upheaval! Turmoil! Writhing! Everything lets loose. Then, a mysterious pounding—a crushing, staccato pounding. Faster, faster, lower, lower.

The believing brother exits. Tearing himself from the womb, he falls outward. The second brother shrieks, startled by the "accident" that has befallen his brother. He bewails and bemoans the tragedy—the death of a perfectly fine fellow. "Why? Why? Why didn't he take better care? Why did he fall into that terrible abyss?"

As he thus laments, he hears a head-splitting cry and a great tumult from the black abyss, and he trembles, "Oh my! What a horrible end! As I predicted!"

Meanwhile as the skeptic brother mourns, his dead brother has been born into the new world. The head-splitting cry is a sign of health and vigor, and the tumult is really a chorus of *Mazal tov!* from the waiting family who is thanking God for the birth of a healthy child.

————

Indeed, in words I used in *The Jewish Way in Death and Mourning*, we come from the darkness of the "not yet" and proceed to the darkness of the "no more." While it is difficult to imagine the "not yet," it is more difficult to picture the "no more." As we separate and "die" from the womb, only to be born to life, so we separate and die from our world, only to be reborn to life eternal. The exit from the womb is the birth of the body. The exit from the body is the birth of the soul. As the womb requires a gestation period of nine months, the world requires a residence of decades. As the womb is *"prozdor"* (an anteroom) for the preparation for life, so our present existence is *prozdor* to the world beyond.

Will God Vanquish Death?

The Jewish burial service ends with this shocking phrase: "May death be swallowed forever" (*Bila ha'mavet la'netzach*). Is it at all conceivable that we, stalked by death every day of our lives and ultimately vanquished by death at every encounter, can ever experience the death of death? Think of it this way: If fear of death is the greatest enemy, then the cure must be to abolish death. How in the world can anyone possibly propose such a fantasy?

But is the phrase that ends the funeral service just a placating fantasy in the face of reality's worst fear? No, Judaism would not deceive mourners with playful words meant to becalm but concealing a cruel reality. And scientists would not be feverishly working on this problem at this very moment if it were merely pie in the sky.

Truth is stranger than fiction. Very soon we may be able to abolish death at least from our imaginations and allay our anxieties about it. Indeed, we may one day be able to prolong life to such a great extent that the fear of death will be out of sight. And with that triumph will vanish that fiendish sense of being driven that has so haunted us—humiliatingly and destructively—all through our history. Already in 1794, the philosopher Condorcet said: "The interval between the birth of man and his decay will have no assignable limit." Potentially we will be able to become the foreshadowers of the truly God-like creatures who would seek eternal life, and whom God warned us about in the first chapter of Genesis. We will conquer death. Only now it will be not by an act of rebellion but as a fulfillment for our striving, rewarded by God.

Did science ever expect this? Not until the last decade of the nineteenth century. Did religion know this? As fact, of course not. As hope, yes—from the day after Adam and Eve were expelled from the Garden of Eden.

Will Simple People Achieve Immortality?

To have lived at all is a measure of immortality; for a baby to be born, to become a man, a woman, to beget others like himself, is an act of faith in itself, even an act of defiance. It is as though every human being born into this world burns, for a brief moment, like a star, and be-

cause its pinpoint of light shines in the darkness, so there is glory, so there is life.

—Daphne Du Maurier

The concept of an afterlife is fundamental even to many who are otherwise not observant. It is an article of faith in the Jews' creed, although it is not the view of most Jews. This concept is not merely an added detail that might lose its significance in some later age. It is an essential and enduring principle. Indeed, the Mishnah expressly excludes from the reward of the world beyond anyone who denies that the resurrection of the dead has biblical warrant. Maimonides considered this belief one of the thirteen basic truths that every Jew is commanded to hold.

The concept of resurrection entered the prayer book as a declaration in the philosophic hymns of "Yigdal" and "Ani Ma'amin." Centuries later, hundreds of thousands of Jews, packed in cattle cars, en route to the crematoria, sang "Ani Ma'amin," affirming the coming of the Messiah and the resurrection of the Jews in the face of death.

Although Jewish philosophers changed the formulation and counting of Maimonides' Thirteen Principles, they still retained resurrection as a fundamental principle without which the Jewish religion is inconceivable. In the early fifteenth century, the philosopher Simeon Ben Zemah Duran reduced the fundamentals to three, but among them resurrection was included. Joseph Albo, in the same era, revised the structure of dogmas, but even in his system immortality remained a universally binding belief.

No matter how the basic principles were reduced or revised, the next life remained a major tenet of Judaism. Indeed, we may say of it what Hermann Cohen, the German Jewish philosopher, is said to have noted about the Messiah: If the Jewish religion had done nothing more for humanity than introduce the messianic idea of the Old Testament prophets, it still could have claimed to be the bedrock of all the world's ethical culture.

Strange as it may appear and despite the historic near-unanimity of scholarly opinion on this fundamental belief, the practical details of immortality are ambiguous and vague. There is no formal eschatology in Judaism, only a traditional consensus that illuminates the way. The veil has never been pierced, and only shadowy structures can be discerned. But the beauty of the concept of immortality and its colossal religious significance do not lie in its details.

Maimonides denied that anyone can have a clear picture of the afterlife. He compared earthbound creatures with the blind who cannot learn to appreciate colors merely by being given a verbal description. Flesh-and-blood mortals cannot have any precise conception of the pure, spiritual bliss of the world beyond. Thus, said Maimonides, the precise sequence in which the afterlife will finally unravel is not a cardinal article of the faith, and the faithful should not concern themselves with the details. So it is often in Judaism that abstract principles must be held in the larger, conceptual sense, while the formal philosophic details are blurred. Precisely the reverse is true about pragmatic religious behaviors—the observances of the faith are worked out to their most minute detail, although the basic concept behind them may remain unknown forever. For all that, there is a consensus of belief concerning the afterlife, based on talmudic derivations from the Torah and philosophic analysis of statements uttered by the Sages.

Will the Dead Be Resurrected?

The body returns to the earth, dust to dust, but the soul returns to God who gave it. This doctrine of the immortality of the soul is affirmed not only by Judaism and other religions but by many noted secular philosophers as well. Traditional Judaism, however, also believes in the eventual resurrection of the physical body, which will be reunited with the soul at a later time, on a "great and awesome day of the Eternal." The human form of the righteous of all ages, buried and long since thoroughly decomposed, will be resurrected at God's will. Jews have believed this for centuries, despite the facts of science.

The most dramatic portrayal of bodily resurrection can be found in the Valley of Dry Bones prophecy in Ezekiel 37. It recalls past deliverances and envisions the future redemption of Israel and the eventual quickening of the dead. The belief in a bodily resurrection of the dead appears, at first, to the contemporary mind to be incredible. But when approached from God's-eye view, why should rebirth be more miraculous than birth itself? The attraction of sperm and egg; the subsequent fertilization and development in the womb, culminating in the birth of the astoundingly complex network of tubes and glands, bones, and organs: their incredibly precise functioning and the unbelievably intricate human brain that guides them is surely a miracle of the first magnitude.

Curiously, the miraculous object itself, the human being, takes this for granted. In our preoccupation with daily trivia, we ignore the miracle of our own existence. The idea of rebirth may appear strange because no one has ever experienced a similar occurrence and we cannot put together the stuff of imagination. Perhaps it is because we can be active in creating life but cannot participate with God in the re-creation of life. Perhaps it is because, scientifically, re-creation flies against biological theory, even while we are coming to know how life is developed and our researchers are able to clone individual organisms in the laboratory test tube. But who created the researching biologist? And can we not postulate an omnipotent divine biologist who created us all? Surely resurrection is not beyond the capacity of an omnipotent God.

The Sages simplified the concept of bodily resurrection by posing an analogy that brings it within our experience. A tree, once alive with blossoms and fruit, full of the sap of life, stands cold and still in the winter. Its leaves have turned brown and fallen; its fruit rots on the ground. But the warm rains come and the sun shines. Buds sprout. Green leaves appear. Colorful fruits burst from their seed. With the coming of spring, God resurrects nature. For this reason, the blessing of God for reviving the dead, which is recited in every daily *Amidah* prayer, the central "standing" prayer, incorporates also the seasonal requests for rain. When praying for human redemption, the prayer book uses the phrase "*matzmi'ach yeshu'ah*" (planting salvation). Indeed, the Talmud compares the day of resurrection with the rainy season and says that the rainy season is the more significant of the two because resurrection serves only the righteous, whereas the rain falls indiscriminately on us all.

"I Believe"

This sentiment is encapsulated by the lyrics of the popular song "I Believe":

> I believe for every drop of rain that falls a flower grows
> I believe that somewhere in the darkest night a candle glows
> I believe for every one who goes astray someone will come to show the way
> I believe, I believe …
>
> I believe, above the storm the smallest prayer will still be heard
> And I believe that someone in the great somewhere hears every word
> Every time I hear a newborn baby cry or touch a leaf or see the sky
> Then I know why I believe.

Who Is the Messiah?

The generic term "messiah" means "anointed one." Kings and priests were anointed in ancient times to set them apart as leaders. At the end of days, the Messiah will bring redemption to this world. It will be a time of true bliss, unparalleled in our own existence. It will not be a new world, a qualitatively different world. Rather, it will be this world brought to perfection. Universal peace, tranquility, lawfulness, and goodness will prevail, and all will acknowledge the unity and sovereignty of God.

Will the Messiah be a specific person or only a representation of this era of perfection: the "days of Messiah"? Traditional Judaism believes, without equivocation, in the coming of a great hero, anointed for leadership—a descendant of the House of David, who will lead the world out of chaos. He will be flesh and blood, a mortal sent expressly by God to fulfill the glory of God's people.

The traditional belief is that we must work to better the world and help bring the Messiah. It is unfoundedly optimistic to believe that humanity by itself will inevitably progress to such an era. A supernatural gift to us, in the person of the Messiah, will be required to bring the world to this pinnacle of glory. God will directly intervene to prevent the world from rushing headlong into darkness and will bring the redemption through a human personality. The personal Messiah will not, however, be a part of a godhead, as in Judaism's daughter religion, Christianity. He will have no ability to bring redemption himself; he will only deliver the redemption granted by Almighty God. He will have no miraculous powers and will not be able to atone for the sins of others. The Messiah will have no superhuman relationship to God. He will be an exalted personality, of incomparable ability, who will usher in the rehabilitation of the Jewish people and the subsequent regeneration of all humankind.

How the Messiah will come and how we will be able to identify him has aroused the imagination of Jews in every age. Many of these ruminations are contradictory. Some are founded in biblical interpretation, some on traditional beliefs handed down from generation to generation, while others are flights of folkloristic fancy.

The time of the coming of the Messiah has aroused such fantastic conjecture by many who predicted specific dates and signs, causing so much anxiety and unreasonable anticipation and culminating in such heartbreaking and spiritually shattering frustration that the Sages and other Jewish notables through the ages have repeatedly chastised those who "count the days" to "bring near the end" of redemption.

While some theologians have sought to dispute the supernatural introduction of the Messiah or to denigrate the idea of a personal Messiah, there is no *a priori* reason to deny either. On the contrary, there stand three millennia of unwavering conviction on the part of the most profound scholars and the great masses of Jews to affirm it.

When Dream Becomes History

You would not normally expect a Roman general to believe in a mystical vision of immortality or resurrection, and generally they did not (although some pagan beliefs endorsed the idea of resurrection). But the belief of the Jews was so powerful that this idea struck fear into the pagan heart. The historical incident related below demonstrates an earthly embodiment of spirituality—and even more dramatically, the ethereal hope of a life after life. Nowhere in the archives of civilized history can one find more telling testimony to the raw power of spirituality than in Jewish survival in the face of the Roman conquest of Jerusalem in the year 70 C.E.

Rome's brilliant military victory has been immortalized in a magnificent monument that still stands in Rome as a centerpiece of the mighty Roman Empire, the Arch of Titus. Titus was the Roman general who set ablaze the ancient Jewish Temple, reduced Jerusalem to rock, and disemboweled all the Jews—men, women, and children—who stood in his path. Jewish resistance to Titus was brave but feeble. The general did what he was sent to do, and he strode home triumphant, a hero by every standard of warfare. Throngs of Romans welcomed him and his famous regiments as he carried home the spoils he plundered from the Temple. But the whole of his army did not return with him. He was asked why the crack Roman Tenth Legion didn't come back. Had they been killed by the Israelites? Did they succumb to plague?

Nothing of the sort. Titus assured them they were alive and in uniform, and that they were well. Soon they would return home. But why did they not return with him as they always had done?

Titus's response echoes through the centuries. The mightiest Roman conqueror of his day ordered his Tenth Legion to stand armed guard over the corpses of Jews that pockmarked the blood-drenched battlefield because, Titus declared, the people had an insane hope that they would be physically resurrected and ultimately rise from the grave and try to defeat the Roman Legions. Hope took mortality by the throat and forced it to become immortality!

I have made it a mission in all my writing—even in this work on grief—to promote hope. But I would be severely remiss if I gave the impression that hope comes easily—even to someone who has studied it for years and who believes in its mystifying effectiveness. Experience is somewhat like flying at thirty thousand feet. You go up and up, above the clouds, and the flight is smooth, when suddenly you hit turbulence. Abruptly you sink, and you imagine your whole life falling into a black hole in the sky, out of control, and you are holding on. But after some moments, you pass through the violence and begin to fly smoothly again.

We cannot be guaranteed that we will not hit turbulence in our lives. Just the reverse. Storms and squalls will becloud our days. With faith, we can make it through the turbulence and rise again and stride under Titus' Arch in defiance of his disbelief.

Can the Living Relate to the Dead?

Any attempt to describe life after death, given its mystical nature, is only conjectural. My purpose is not to espouse any particular belief so much as to encourage people to take more seriously the idea of life after death and its meaning in the face of grief. By using not only your rational but also your intuitive mind, you can judge for yourself the personal applicability of the kabbalistic-psychological view of the afterlife I present here.

The Bible is filled with phrases such as "gathered unto one's ancestors" and "sleeping with one's Fathers." It is entirely possible that such terms are not only metaphoric but actually allude to the anticipation of encountering our deceased relatives and friends after we die, and are direct references to the "real" world as the wisest of the ancients conceived it. Thousands of years before Raymond Moody and Elisabeth

Kubler-Ross, Jewish tradition sensed a link between the dying and the dead.

The subject evoked mystic conjectures in much of the kabbalistic literature:

> At the hour of a man's departure from the world, his father and his relatives gather round him ... and they accompany his soul to the place where it is to abide.

and

> Rabbi Yochanan ben Zakkai saw King Hezekiah meeting him.

A variety of rabbinic sources claim that at the time of death the dying person is not alone. Either an angel or parent will assist the deceased in the transition from the world of the living to the next world. These guides have a very specific function: to initiate the neophyte into the realm of postmortem consciousness. Texts from many religious traditions point to the fact that there are two types of encounters—one with an angelic or divine being, another with family members or dear friends. Jewish tradition speaks of both types of experience.

In our own time, countless reports exist of people who, just prior to death, have a dream in which a deceased spouse, parent, or sibling informs them they will soon be reunited. It is also commonly reported that at the moment of death people see before their eyes the spirit of a deceased loved one. Those who undergo such near-death experiences report seeing a loving family member who, arriving at just the right time, is prepared to assist them in making the transition from the physical plane.

I realize that these beliefs are ultimately a matter of faith, but they do provide a source of comfort to mourners. I have noticed this time and again in imparting such beliefs, however tentatively I had done so. After writing *The Jewish Way in Death and Mourning*, I discovered that the most enthusiastic responses to that book were for the eighteen pages in which I treated the question of life after death. I have repeatedly issued qualifiers assuring those who could not in good conscience hold these beliefs, that their decisions, integrity, and Jewish faith remain unimpugned. As a matter of personal conviction, I attest that these are indeed my own warmly held beliefs.

The High Heavens

The heavens belong to the Lord, but the earth He gave to man.

—Ps. 115:16

This verse from the Psalms must surely reflect the most primal religious experience. This most sacred space—the heavens that are the heavens of God, that are the symbols of God's abode—why are they nearest the sky?

Infinite and transcendent, the sky is clearly quite apart from puny human beings and our brief span of life. It is understandable that the sky has come to symbolize transcendence because of its infinite height. The "Most High" naturally has become an attribute of divinity; so high, the heavens are a symbol of unreachability, so unchanging, they symbolize the everlasting. Despite our meanderings in space, we still see with the eyes of our earliest ancestors, and our hearts still quicken to the same things theirs did. The sky is still our principal metaphor for limitlessness and eternity, for unchanging, absolute reality.

That is why heaven and earth are the eternal prototypes for eternal and mortal life. And the great gulf between them characterizes our relationship with God: Whereas the life of the heavens is immortal and everlasting, our own life in the earthly sphere is mortal, always ending in death. This paradox is at the heart of our spiritual universe: The earth we inhabit during our lifetime is forever coupled with the unattainable and limitless heaven, two divine opposites eternally joined. It is a cosmic drama, breathtaking in its clash of eternal order with transience and transformation played out in the universe of our souls.

For mourners, death is the intersection of time and eternity, of materiality and spirituality, of certainty and contradiction, of this world and the next. Earth serves as a metaphor of unshakable certainty: The word "*adam*" (human) derives from the word "*adamah*" (soil), the firm and constant ground of existence. The word "*shamayim*" (heaven) derives from the fusion of the words "*esh*" (fire) and "*mayim*" (water)—two mutually exclusive qualities—gravity and antigravity, implosion and explosion, the contracting planets and the expanding universe, symbols of volatility, collision, and change.

Mourners are rooted in the earth; during shiva we even sit on stools that are nearer to the earth. But those who have departed have risen to a place of infinite potential and eternal spirituality, which enables them to transcend our earth-bound lives.

Parallel Lines Meet in Infinity

Mathematicians say that parallel lines meet in infinity. Patently this appears to be a contradiction in terms. If lines are parallel, by definition they cannot meet; if they do, by definition they are not parallel. But this is only if we deal with Euclidian "plane" geometry, the flat geometry of only two dimensions. In a "spherical" geometry that is based on a three-dimensional system (called non-Euclidian geometry), all lines are really curves and "parallel" lines do indeed meet if they continue to infinity.

If the exact science of mathematics, which glories in precise measurement, can project immeasurable infinite space, and imagine the incomprehensible taking place within it, then a religious perspective, which views us in all our three-dimensional complexity, can certainly project an eternal time defined by a fourth dimension when parallel lives—lived by two close individuals on earth—may cross again in eternity. In admittedly metaphoric terms, what is true in astrophysics can certainly apply to the world of heavenly spheres:

Two worlds kiss each other as this world departs and the world-to-come enters.

From the moment of our creation we have been yearning to bridge that eternal divide. Patriarchs and prophets, psalmists and poets, and even the unlettered have been searching the heavens, seeking to know God, just as the astronomer is driven to chart and measure the heavens, feverishly tracking a supernova to find the origins of the universe.

The heaven–earth nexus reached the pinnacle of its expression early in ancient history. Jacob's dream of discovering the gateway to heaven with its staircase bridging the two spheres, angels busily ascending and descending it, creating an endless chain from bottom to top, symbolized a hope for the ages. Jacob was emphatically earth-bound; the angels, emphatically heaven-bound. Jacob discovered the gateway not while standing atop a mountain, nearer the sky, nor while reverently genuflecting, nearer to God, but while lying flat on the ground, with his head smack up against a rock, embedded in the earth, his soul streaking from ground zero to the height of heights. And the angels, as I noted earlier, were first going upward to the sky that was their limit. This is the dream most often portrayed in the history of art, the most psychologically analyzed and the most spiritually interpreted. It is spiritual linkage that was soldered to last for all time.

For all of us, this spiritual connection reaches its climax in death, when earth and heaven kiss. Mourners address God most profoundly during this time, and their souls are more naturally tilted upward at this moment than at times of gratitude or celebration. To symbolize this upward focus, religious traditions often depict the human body as a candle, the soul as its flaming wick, which in death soars skyward, leaving behind the residue of ash that is the body returning to its origin.

I ask myself: Cannot infinite God and finite human being share a spiritual linkage, forever outside our limited capacity to understand, not ever measured by our sophisticated instruments, yet nonetheless true, as it appears as we stare at the horizon?

Parallel Lives Meet in Eternity

I believe, I trust, I know, that these opposite divine realms of heaven and earth exist as parallel lines that meet in eternity as they do in infinity; that the "worlds kiss" at the end of a life, that just as the body (*adam*) is interred into the soil (*adamah*) from which it came, so the nebulous soul (*neshamah*) returns to the *esh* and *mayim*—the fire inside the water that is heaven. I feel in my bones, if not in my reason, as did my ancestors, that there is a mystical dialogue between heaven and earth, as there is a dialogue between us and God, and that two people who were together on earth are not separated after death. They are the parallel lives that meet in eternity.

This vague, abstruse, and ultimately paradoxical idea has resolved itself within my imagination into an image that I have always cherished:

I am standing on the beach in Santa Barbara, California, on a day awash in azure—a blue Pacific and a bluer sky. I squint as I scan the farthest horizon, where the ocean and the sky blend in seamless harmony, with only a faint pencil line to mark the hem. Virginia Woolf once described it this way: "the sea and sky looked all one fabric, as if sails were stuck high up in the sky, or the clouds had dropped down into the sea." Upon the retina of my eye, the infinite distance from the sea to the sky has compressed itself, and—symbolically, mystically, romantically perhaps—it remains lodged in my mind's eye. Cannot this vision be a reflection of a spiritual reality as well as an optical illusion?

Adieu: Till We Meet Again

Mourners often whisper "Till we meet again" when they bury people they love. Many, perhaps even most, picture some shadowy, out-of-focus preview of such a meeting—a reunion in the next life. Over and over again, I hear grievers say they are comforted and nourished by that idea more than by any other. One griever told me: "It radiates comfort to the bottom of my soul to think that my relatives are all together. Now death is beginning to make some sense."

From a variety of other traditional sources, it is evident that the dominant belief has long been that the recently dead communicate with both the heavenly and the earthly realms specifically to pray on behalf of a living person. Before making a critical life decision, Jews have traditionally prayed at a graveside or at home that the dead may serve as *melitz yosher*, a sort of advocate, before God on their behalf or on behalf of other living persons who are vulnerable. Of course, it need not be emphasized that speaking in the "hearing" of the dead is traditionally done with the full realization that no one, not even the dead, can serve as a medium, that prayer must be addressed directly to God.

The mother of a friend of mine assured her children before she died that she was not at all afraid of dying because she "saw" her parents waiting for her in heaven. So real was this image in her mind that when she awakened one morning shortly before she died she asked, "Am I already dead?" When she was told, "No, look, the television is on," she quickly answered, "Turn it off. Don't you see there are dead people here?" To her, she was in the world of the dead, the "next world," and that demanded a silent reverence far from the tumult of everyday earthly life.

People have always felt a linkage between this world and the world to come at this awesome juncture of earth and heaven. In the literature of near-death experiences, ample testimony exists of people who have had a brilliantly clear vision in which a deceased spouse, parent, sibling, or child informed them that their reunion was at hand.

By chance, I came across these profound words by William Penn that someone quoted in an obituary: "They that love beyond the world cannot be separated by it. Death is but crossing the world, as friends do the seas; they live in one another still."

What on Earth Can We Do for Him in Heaven?

Hasidism espoused a sort of after-death care program for departed souls. The movement's founder, the Baal Shem Tov, used to speak of "*tikun ha'neshamot*," the "fixing" or "mending of souls." Before the Sabbath he would help all those souls that had passed during the week peacefully make their entry into the world beyond. It was known that at the *Mincha* service on Friday afternoons he would recite an extra-long *Amidah*, and through his deeply concentrated devotions would act as a guide on behalf of the souls of the dead.

Similarly, in the premodern Jewish world there were lay societies—the *chevrah Tehillim* (Psalms Society) and *chevrah Mishnayot* (Mishnah Society)—that took upon themselves the task of providing after-death care for departed souls by reciting Psalms, the *Kaddish*, and selected texts of the Mishnah.

Are the Dead Aware of the Living?

Many sources in the Talmud and Midrash affirm, in an off-hand, natural way, that the dead are somehow aware of the living. In fact, the classical Rabbis discussed the extent of that awareness. The Babylonian Sage Rav, who was concerned about people's sorrow at funerals, told his colleagues: "Be fervent in my funeral eulogy, because I will be standing right there." As he was dying, Rabbi Yochanan ben Zakkai said that King Hezekiah of Judah was coming to greet him. Simcha Paull Raphael, who has written about the afterlife, affirmed that a rabbinic belief is that the dead communicate with both the human realm and with the heavenly realm, wherein they petition for mercy on behalf of the living.

At the time of death or shortly before, individuals experience an instantaneous recall of all life events. This phenomenon seems to be a spontaneous replay of a person's life experience in its entirety and is documented extensively, both in religious traditions around the world and in contemporary research on near-death experiences. This, too, is in keeping with our understanding of the unity of life and death.

Excellence Resonates

The living are linked to the dead in yet another way. Just as parents spend their lives transmitting their learning and values to their children and grandchildren, so these children in turn reflect back upon their parents the merit the latter have earned in leaving the world a better place than before they walked upon it. In a reversal of the common wisdom that everything that goes up must come down, Judaism teaches that what goes down also comes back up. This concept is known as *"bera mezakeh abba"*—that "a child can reflect merit on the parent," especially after the parent's death. This reflection of merit from children to their forebears testifies to an ongoing connection between the generations, even beyond the grave. In this notion, we find the mirror image of the time-honored idea that children are simply the creation of their parents, the apples that do not fall far from the tree. Rather, Judaism claims that creation actually works both ways: that the generations help develop each other.

In the Talmud, Rav Huna noted that "the love of a parent is for the children, and the love of children is for their children." Here Rav Huna is referring to the machinery of intergenerational dynamics, which always points us to the future. Even though most of us sincerely care for our parents' welfare, the ultimate form of care we engage in is protecting our progeny, for the security of our future. We find this idea memorably expressed in the rabbinic story of the old man who plants a carob tree that will take decades to bear its best fruit:

> "Why is he doing this?" those of the "Me" generation ask. The old man will not live to enjoy the fruits of his labor. "Just as I found mature carob trees when I came into this world," the old man explains in the story, "so I wish to leave more trees to those who come after me."

How well the Sages understood human beings' instinctive unswerving loyalty to children. They took fully to heart their inheritance of the Ten Commandments, the fifth of which speaks of children honoring their parents. They had no doubt in their minds that the merit of a parent is clearly inherited by his or her children.

Today, in the era of genetic sequencing, we understand even better than the Sages that we inherit so much from our parents and previous generations—psychological as well as physical qualities. And we inherit from them not only our genes and our approach to life, but also our spiritual essence, which in a very real sense also contains assimilated elements from past lives as well as the unspoken assumptions by which we live. When these spiritual elements inhabit us for the duration of our corporeal lives, they fashion our faith, our spirituality, our grasp of the human enterprise, and our search for transcendence.

But Judaism takes this idea of generational transmission one step further. It claims that authentic religious merit travels upward to the previous generation as well as downward to the next. Every day children cast a glow onto their parents, who created and nurtured them. For Jewish parents, deriving such "*nachas*" (Yiddish for "pride" and "pleasure") from children and grandchildren gives meaning to life, because parents receive their true reward when their children live productive lives. Excellence resonates, enhancing all the lives it touches.

The opposite is also valid: The departed carry into the next world the influences of those who were beloved by them. Whether we enhanced or burdened their lives, the individual who has now passed on became a different person because of our effect upon him or her. Are we not then, in a metaphorical sense, accompanying our departed to the new world?

What Is Death? A Spiritual Answer

What is death? Is it merely the cessation of the biological functions of living? Is it but the tragedy to end all other tragedies? Is it the disappearance of the soul, the end of consciousness, the evaporation of personality, the disintegration of the body into its elemental components? Is it an end beyond which there is only black void? Or is there significance, some deep and abiding meaning to death—one that transcends our puny ability to understand?

With all of our modern sophistication, our brilliant technological achievements, our impressive scientific progress, our discovery of new worlds of thought, we have not come any closer to grasping the meaning of death than did our ancient ancestors. Though philosophers and poets have probed the idea of immortality, death stubbornly remains, as always, the greatest paradox of life, a mystery yet to be solved.

What death means to mourners depends very much on what life means to them. If life is a stage and we, poor players who strut and fret our hour upon it and then are heard no more; if life is a tale told by an idiot, full of sound and fury, signifying nothing; if life is an inconsequential drama, a purposeless amusement—then death is only the heavy curtain that falls on the final act. It sounds its hollow thud, and we are no more. Death has no significance, because life itself has no lasting meaning.

If life is only the arithmetic of coincidence—human beings only chance composites of molecules; the world a haphazard conglomeration without design or purpose, where everything is temporal and nothing eternal, where values are dictated only by consensus—then death has no transcendent significance, since nothing in life has had transcendent significance. If such is our philosophy of life, then death is meaningless and the deceased need merely be disposed of unceremoniously and as efficiently as possible.

If life is only nature mindlessly and compulsively spinning its complicated web, and human beings are only high-level beasts, and the world is, as philosopher Arthur Schopenhauer noted, a great battlefield; if values are only those of the jungle aimed at the satisfaction of animal appetites, then death is simply a further reduction to the basic elements, an adventure into nothingness, and our existence on this earth is but a cosmic trap. In this scheme, life is surrounded by parentheses, a brief pause unnoticed by nature. Death simply brings to an end a cruel match that pits human against beast and one human against another. It is the final slaughter. In this scenario, we sink furtively, irrevocably, despairingly into the soil of a cold and impersonal nature, our life having been without purpose, our death without significance. Our graves need not be marked. As our days were a passing shadow, without substance and shape, so too should be our final repose.

If life is altogether absurd and we are bound to its course by impersonal fate or iron-clad circumstances that prevent our achieving real freedom and that expose us to only dread and anguish, then death is a welcome release from our chains of despair.

On the other hand, if life is the creation of a benevolent God, the infusion of the divine breath, and if we are not only higher than the animals but also "a little lower than the angels"; if we have a soul as well as a body, and if our relationship is not only the "I–it" of human beings and nature but also the "I–Thou" of creature with Creator, and if we temper our passions with the moral commands of an eternal and transcendent God—then death is a return to the Creator at the time set by the Creator. And then life after death must be the way of a just, merciful, and ethical God. If life has any significance, if it is not mere happenstance, then we know that some day our bodies will be replaced, even as our souls unite with Eternal God.

In the idea of immortality, we find the fulfillment of all our dreams. The Sages likened this world to an anteroom to a great palace that is the glorious realm of the future. We spend our lives in this anteroom, waiting to be admitted for our audience with the king. Thus, for the truly religious, death has profound meaning, because life is a tale told by a saint, not an idiot. Although it is full of sound and fury that sometimes signify nothing, more often life bears eloquent testimony to the divine power that creates and sustains us.

The Rabbis pointed out that *"hai alma k'bei hilula damya"* (this world can be compared to a wedding). At a wedding, two souls are united. Together, they bear the seed of the future. Although the partners will eventually die, the seed of life continues to grow, and death is thus ultimately conquered: The seed of the future carries within it the germ of the past. So it is with our world. We are briefly united with the natural cycle of life and then depart from it, leaving behind the seeds of new life to carry on after us, whether through our children or through our deeds.

Death has meaning if life has had meaning. If there was meaning in the life of the deceased, then be assured that this death has meaning, too—whether or not we are able to discern it.

PART IV

MAKING A
FUTURE,
NOT SETTLING
FOR ONE

Chapter 12

Searching for a Usable Future

Over the nowhere arches the everywhere.

—Rainer Maria Rilke

The experience of mourning is not the same for everyone. Some people go through the process and emerge strengthened and renewed. But in the majority of cases the normal outcome of mourning is not positive. In fact, most of us, when we mourn, do not consider outcomes at all, perhaps because instinctively we feel that death is simply a natural part of life and that our grief will spontaneously resolve itself. This is rarely the case, however.

After the first blow delivered by a death, many of us feel that we are futureless without our loved one. As our grief ages, we come to realize that indeed a future lies ahead for us, but we don't believe that we can influence how our great loss will affect it. We assume that in time our reaction to grief will take care of itself. As we wait for this to happen, it usually does not dawn on us that our future might be enhanced, that the promise held out to us by spirituality can make elevation possible.

As mourners, we face a choice: We can continue being depressed over our loved one's death, not giving up on our love, not wanting ever to forget, not wanting things to be different from the way they were. Or we can recover our old energies and our own self and move on. We don't have to be geniuses to acknowledge the truth in the Greek philosopher Heraclitus' phrase: "The road uphill and the road downhill are one and the same."

Just as we have gone down into the pit of sadness, so we can climb out of it. Yes, it took only an instant for us to become traumatized, whereas we climb upward only gradually—but as the Greek wise man said, the distance is the same. Each of us has the power to affect the outcome of our mourning; we need not be passive in the process, accepting whatever happens. And even if we do remain passive, the odds are still good that we will make a successful transition.

But we can do even better for ourselves: We can choose to transcend trauma and reach for a better outcome as we move through our grief. While this is difficult and takes much self-control and strong character, it can be done. And by doing so we might become so energized and changed that our mourning launches us into a new life.

During the process of shiva, it is generally outsiders—friends and distant family members—who worry about outcomes for the mourners. The mourners themselves are more concerned with the past. The intensity of their bereavement keeps them in its grip. To persuade them to grapple with possible outcomes is to shift their focus to the future, which they are not likely to be emotionally prepared to do. But in time, as the grief process proceeds and mourners become disentangled from their initial trauma, they are able to return to their search for a usable future.

The grieving process does not proceed in a linear fashion. Nor are its effects uniform or predictable. It affects us all in vastly different ways, and it intrudes into our lives in a strange multiplicity of ways—in dreams, at traffic lights, in the supermarket. It runs its course on different timetables for everyone. The only consistent rule is that its outcomes are as diverse as are human personalities. What primarily determines each outcome are the character of the deceased; the complexities affecting relationships among the mourner, comforters, and other mourners; pre-existing personality variables; the nature of the mourner's prior relationships; and the history of death experiences that each mourner brings into the present situation. During the grieving process, mourners exhibit a striking variety of clinical signs, changes in appearance, degrees of withdrawal, and physical complaints. And the duration of intense bereavement varies considerably from mourner to mourner, although some recovery from grief is usually evident within a year after a loss.

In this chapter and the next, I describe four possible outcomes of bereavement, exploring their intellectual and emotional underpinnings. To illustrate each I draw powerful lessons for modern times from our very human biblical heroes, whose weaknesses are portrayed in Scripture and Talmud just as surely as are their strengths.

The first outcome, *standstill*, is quite prevalent and unremarkable; it is negative and represents a pathological reaction to death. The second outcome, *transition*, is healthier and allows life to continue comfortably. The mourner's life proceeds in a horizontal movement, a transitional outcome, most often realized unconsciously. The next two outcomes are rarer, but they are as rewarding as they are exceptional. *Transcendence* represents a very positive and thoughtful outcome. But the highest outcome of all is *transformation*, exceptional but not unheard of. In this outcome, mourners transform themselves, with often creative and stunning results.

Standstill: "It Should Be Like It Always Was"

After the death of a loved one, life will indeed never be the same—that is the truth. But when we as mourners insist that life cannot continue because it will never be the same as it was; when we claim that the family will be haunted forever, that life will forever be a vale of tears and nothing else; and moreover, when we believe that it rightfully should be so—because anything less would dishonor the dead or because life without the deceased will not be worth living—these are pathological responses. Other pathological responses include a total absence of grief, a much-delayed grief, an excessively prolonged or intense grief, excessive anxiety when recalling memories of the deceased, forbidding all references to the death, and not tolerating general expressions of sympathy.

Inappropriate grief and stunted personal growth, especially in young mourners, are serious causes for concern. One symptom of inappropriate grief is a mourner's denial of the death, expressed in the belief that it never occurred, or that the deceased will magically return one day as if from a long trip. Those who deny death do not so much deny that a loss has occurred—everyone sees the actual burial or hears the news of it—but rather deny that there exists for them any usable future now that the loved one is no longer here. It is the same as saying that life can never work again without the person who has died. Such a state of mind is tantamount to the mourner's own death.

The Road Less Traveled

It is highly advisable that mourners who show such symptoms be accompanied in their travels through grief by a healing personality—a child or sibling, a doctor or member of the clergy. This is often more worthwhile than formal therapy, which of course must be sought if the symptoms become pathological.

I would say this to those who offer healing: In seeking to help mourners recover from severe grief we need to implement that healing with softness. We need to exert our humanity, conveying to the mourners that we care deeply, that the night of grief lies between two days, and that, by extension, their loss is our loss. We do not heal grievers with a momentary smile, by tranquilizing their reasoning powers with soporifics, by diverting them from their troubles by encouraging them to forget, or by temporarily derailing their anger with a trite joke.

Rather, the role of spiritual healers is to be *with* mourners, not to be there *for* them. Unlike that of grief counselors, our role is not to be transference figures, cognitive structurers, or behavioral trainers. The healer and the mourner are separate persons who ideally occupy the same space—mutually confirming each other's underlying common destiny and shared angst.

The best place to search for human sentiments needed in healing is in the Torah. Scripture has survived for much of recorded history, embodying a high truth, authentic and profound. Its words are the most widespread in any language. Its heroes are paradigms, which is why we study how they experience the end of days, even though we peer through the lens of sometimes more sophisticated eyes. The Torah is absolutely fascinating in the way in which it deals with grief. Learning from a patriarch's challenges can give us insight into our own selves. Though I have already related Jacob's story in passing, here we will examine it in depth.

The Jacob Case

The patriarch Jacob was a renowned dreamer, a great thinker, and a spiritual giant, but he could never resolve his grief. When his ten sons reported to him that his favorite young son, Joseph—the seventeen-year-old brilliant, handsome dreamer—had been killed by wild beasts, and they showed him Joseph's shredded and bloodied shirt as proof, Jacob could not, would not, believe that this was so, not because his sons' report was not credible—indeed, their trumped-up story had the ring of authenticity, since forests populated by wild animals surrounded every town in ancient times. Jacob could not digest the truth of what he heard because he had so much invested in Joseph's destiny as a leader, as God's messenger, as a saint, as a bit of his own immortality, and as a gift of God. But there was more: He adored Joseph right from his birth, and he was the first child of the wife that he adored.

Jacob's bereavement reached such profound agony that the family members arose together to bring him comfort, to assuage him in some way with words, assurances, and praise for the "dead" child—though, of course, his remaining sons knew the truth. Jacob reacted strangely: He rejected them, but not because he suspected their foul play. He rejected their offers of consolation, he rejected their visits, he rejected any palliatives because these would only confirm the profoundly unacceptable fact of Joseph's death.

Many Torah commentators, perhaps most, point out that Jacob rejected consolation because he had *"ru'ach ha-Kodesh"* (divine vision): He knew in the depths of his soul that Joseph did not really die. This interpretation is quite reasonable. We would assume that a biblical patriarch's blatant refusal to be comforted would have to rest on a firmer foundation than simply the idea that his son's death was unthinkable. (I have met a number of deniers who think, based on the Jacob story I am sure, that they, too, have a divine assurance that the dead person didn't die but is only lost and wandering and will one day be found.) Yet even if we set aside Jacob's divine gift, we can still appreciate his impulse to deny his beloved son's death. Such conflicted emotions are entirely understandable.

The greatest of the biblical personalities were great precisely because they were, at bottom, also human. They were not unworldly saints; therefore, their example can be emulated. Jacob rises in my estimation because he is so soft-souled that he could actually deny a hard fact when it was too horrendous to accept. What is positively brilliant and heroic about biblical personalities like Jacob are the dimensions of their sanctity. They are so close to God, yet so much the humans that God created; they are so little below the angels, while just higher than the animals; they have a spiritually powerful wingspan, yet they lie on earth's floor, their heads on a common rock, and they find the very gateway to the heavens. This is their heroism. This is Jacob's story, and in a more human dimension, this is the story of a mourner envisioning only a hole in the ground and yet reaching into God's heaven.

From my reading of the plain biblical text, there is every indication that Jacob simply was not able to contemplate so violent, purposeless, and horrendous a fate for such a divinely gifted son, and therefore rejected the notion out of hand. Later, during a deadly drought, when

Jacob's sons returned from Egypt with the news that the Egyptian over-lord—not yet revealed to them as their brother Joseph—was demand-ing Benjamin as a hostage, Jacob confessed to them that he could not endure a second such death.

Knotted Souls

A single word in the Torah—"*keshurah*" (knotted)—describes Jacob's deep and complex relationship to his youngest child. Benjamin, the only full brother of Joseph, the last child Rachel bore and for whom she died, is the only remnant of both Jacob's loves: his young wife and his teenage son. The Torah says of that relationship: *ve'nafsho keshurah be'nafsho* (his soul [Jacob's] was knotted with his soul [Benjamin's]). If Benjamin was knotted to Jacob because he was so close to his dear Jo-seph and his dear wife, what shall we say of Joseph and Rachel them-selves, his most intimate loves?

Let me describe it this way: When two ropes are twisted together they come loose and disconnect when each is pulled in opposite direc-tions. But when they are knotted together, no matter how loosely, the knot is tightened when the cords are pulled, and the tighter the pull, the firmer the knot.

Jacob was knotted to Joseph as tightly as a father could be, and of course he was knotted to Rachel, locked in permanent embrace (*kesher shel kayama*). Jacob could not resolve his grief for Rachel because the Joseph catastrophe happened right after her death and disrupted any possible resolution. Jacob could never resolve his grief for Joseph be-cause he was fresh from burying his beloved Rachel, and Joseph was to be her presumptive replacement. His two loves in this world—Rachel whom he loved more than Leah, Joseph whom he loved more than any other child—had vanished, without reason and without warning. The two sudden catastrophes tugged at his heart from all directions; the knots grew tighter with every sigh of grief. He had every reason to be-lieve the knot would last his lifetime, would never be loosened or un-tied. The double knot was the symbol of Jacob's mature life.

"Knotted souls" speaks of intertwined egos, of tight embrace, of unrelenting love. What happens when one of those souls expires, as Joseph had, as Rachel had? What happens with the remaining living soul, in this case, Jacob's? It drags the lifeless souls behind Jacob wherever he wanders, and the tight knot grows limp and gets heavier until it drags him into the grave. Jacob admits as much to the brothers, to Pharaoh, to Joseph when he finds him alive, to whomever will listen. In very close families, people often become knotted to memories, which they embrace forever.

We readers of the ancient biblical narrative whisper: "Unravel the knot, Jacob!" But this he cannot do. "Lay their souls to rest and live again, unknotted!" But he will not separate, and his entanglement wears him out. When Rachel dies, Jacob is critically wounded; when Joseph dies, Jacob dies.

He Cannot Get Over the Deaths

Jacob could not make the transition to a life without Joseph, just as he could not manage to make the transition to a life without his beloved wife Rachel—*"metah alai"* (she died on me). He could never achieve the closure from either calamity that would have enabled him to move on. Although he continued to live for many years after this event, all joy and hope had gone out of his life.

When his beloved wife Rachel suddenly died in childbirth, Jacob did not bury her in the ancestral grave in the cave of Machpelah, where his parents and grandparents were buried; he built her a tombstone on the side of the road. Jacob could not "put her away" forever, her remains to be hidden in an outlying field. The cave of Machpelah was isolated in the center of a large field, marginalized and inaccessible. Instead, he buried Rachel at the hub of his community's goings and comings, in the midst of its thriving culture and also its destiny, where she would always be reachable.

Indeed, centuries later, the prophet Jeremiah graphically described Rachel weeping for her children (the people of Israel) when they were exiled from the Holy Land and passed by her on that same road. The prophet comforted the people by assuring them that she was pleading for their return, as eventually it came to pass, when they would march by her grave once again on their way home from exile. To this day, the site of Rachel's grave receives more visits from people in trouble who ask for her intercession than the graves of all the other patriarchs in the cave of Machpelah.

But Jacob's sentimental gesture of Rachel's roadside burial blocked the possibility of closure. At her burial, he tore no clothes—a ritual he had introduced later after Joseph's body was supposedly torn by a wild beast; he did not formally eulogize her, and he did not bewail her, as the Torah explicitly notes Abraham did for Sarah.

In fact, he took immediate action in only one regard—he moved his personal residence away from his other wives: "[He] pitched his tent [ohaloh] beyond Migdal-eder." In regard to this verse the Torah does a strange thing: It uses the feminine form of the word "tent," but insists it be read in its masculine form. This, the commentators say, indicates that the tent was both "his" and "hers." Once Rachel had died, Jacob chose to move their shared tent away from his other wife and concubines. There and then he entered widowerhood, shut down, isolated from his family. As though to confirm this end to all Jacob's procreative desires, his eldest son Reuben then moved in with Jacob's former concubine. Here the sentence abruptly stops, pauses, and then as if in yet another confirmation of Jacob's new status as celibate widower, states very specifically that Jacob had "twelve" sons, as though to announce, "twelve and no more." With Rachel's death, Jacob the Patriarch retires from his familial role. All life-enhancing activity shuts down. All creativity shuts down. The joy of living has permanently been sucked from Jacob's life.

Both Rachel and Joseph died sudden deaths. Both were too young to die. Both were the pictures of success, stunningly beautiful, the people Jacob loved most in this world. He had never conceived of life without them, and unlike his father and grandfather, he could not move on.

When Rachel died on the roadside, Jacob had no time to mourn. There was no one to comfort him. But when Joseph died, long after the family had settled in the land, Jacob mourned him desperately, his grief an open wound. The tear in his heart was never sewn up or even basted, but remained festering for a lifetime. When Joseph died, Jacob suspended his grief over Rachel. He simply could not handle the successive tragedies—*vayema'en*; he refused the comfort offered. He was never consoled.

When Jacob was finally reunited with Joseph in Egypt, he cried that he had fully expected to go down to the grave without ever seeing his son again. Such are the words of one who knows in the subvaults of his being that his son was dead but who couldn't bring himself to think about it and certainly didn't want to be consoled for it.

When Joseph first appeared before Jacob, as though from out of the grave, Scripture describes their embrace: "he [Joseph] presented himself to him [Jacob] and, embracing him around the neck, he wept on his neck a good while" (Gen. 46:29). Jacob feels compelled to tell Pharaoh how old he is because he looks so aged, well beyond his years. He cannot restrain himself because his lifelong grief is bursting from within: "Few and hard have been the years of my life" (Gen. 47:9). This self-description is significantly at variance with Abraham's "sated with everything," and with Isaac, who died in wealth and rest. Clearly, the catastrophes that have befallen Jacob—the sudden death of his beloved wife and the image he has painted for himself of the ravaged body of his beloved son—have obsessed Jacob and dominated his life. These calamities have never been released or replaced in the bank of his memories. He never could conceive of living without them, and he never does.

Chronic Grief

When a ship founders, it runs aground on a shifting sandbank. When mourners are grounded during shiva, cemented to their lowered chairs, unable to navigate the shoals of life, they are foundering in the soft soil of a broken heart and dreamy memories. Stuck in the grieving process, mourners experience an inability to work through grief. Somehow this paralytic state seems preferable to the hopelessness they anticipate suffering if they ever relinquish their lost relationship. They find themselves fending off all threatening emotions too painful to bear.

Chronic grief is defined by psychologists as persistent grieving without diminution in intensity despite the passage of time. It is the most common type of pathological grief. Some of the symptoms of such inappropriate grief are not accepting death's irretrievability, denying or rejecting the fact that life can ever work again, and feeling too weak to spark the effort necessary to be dislodged from the reef.

Professional help is clearly indicated for those who exhibit the same level of distress one year after a death as they did during the first few weeks. Phrases such as, "I don't want to live anymore," "I have no interest in anything anymore," can be expected in the first days, but if they continue into the first year, there are serious problems with the bereavement process. When mourners say, "I want it to be like it was," they cannot expect to receive assurance; they already know that life will never be the same.

Does God Want Life to Go Dark?

God has so structured life—from subatomic matter to distant galaxies—that there needs to be death in order to make room for life. "One generation goes," Ecclesiastes says, and "another comes." At the most basic level of life, death clears the way for new lives, sometimes following a natural course, other times hastened by disease. When cancer cells live on, refusing to succumb to the natural process of cell death, they eventually destroy the healthy cells of their host organism. In healthy bodies, cells, the building blocks of life, are programmed to terminate to make way for another generation of cells.

Death, in this sense, is not always a crushing disaster. It must sometimes be framed as the instrument of God's mercy, which it often is. The frame of God's kindness enables mourners to think of death in this way.

Joshua Loth Liebman, in his book *Peace of Mind*, exquisitely framed the final moments of life in the following metaphor:

> For each one of us the moment comes when the great nurse, death, takes man, the child, by the hand and quietly says, "It is time to go home. Night is coming. It is our bedtime, child of earth. Come; you're tired. Lie down at last in the quiet nursery of nature and sleep. Sleep well. The day is gone. Stars shine in the canopy of eternity."

For a mourner to declare that his life is at an end because another's life has ended is to thwart God's plan for His universe. The midrash says:

> "The Rabbis taught: Three things entered God's mind that He must create, and if they did not, they should have—that a dead body should decompose, that the memory of the deceased shall evaporate from the mind, and that plants should rot." Because if the dead did not decompose, people would not bury their dead; and if there were no burial, they would never forget their relatives.

Of course, it is not forgetting a beloved relative but remembering that is of great value. When the Rabbis speak of forgetting, they mean that we should not let the deceased possess our minds, paralyze our thinking, and force us to live in the past instead of moving into the future. The phrase for this kind of forgetting is, as I have noted earlier, *"yishtakach min ha'lev"* (forgetting, or evaporating from the heart), what we today would call "closure."

The Rabbis of the Talmud deliberately established an edict (*gezerah*) that a person should not commemorate or remember the trauma of death for more than a given amount of time—twelve months for parents and thirty days for other relatives—so as not to strain the mourner's mind to retain an active memory of that death. We could not progress, even survive, if such memories hung around in our acute awareness. They would paralyze us, freeze all of life into one hour, and we could not then make the transition back to living—surely not transcend the death or become transformed and re-energized.

Through this ruling, the Sages are saying that, yes, time does and should diminish the intensity of grief. Such is the intrinsic quality of our human nature, without which we could not survive trauma after trauma; otherwise grief would weigh upon our persons, burden our hearts, and bring us to our knees. So powerful did the Rabbis consider this closure, given us by God through the medium of time, that the halakhah had to insure that the opposite did not happen. They instituted memory-sparking events, commemorations (*she'lo yishtakach min ha'lev*), so that we should not totally forget those who died.

Mourners ideally should learn to accept with a full heart the remedy of *nechamah* (comfort) that God sends us—"namely, that grief will slowly diminish and that we should not make bereavement hard on ourselves, as we are wont to do, but should realize that actually we are not permitted to grieve excessively."

The First Law of Jewish Life: Live

There is no religious edict that encourages mourners to drag whole families and communities into profound grief following a death, no matter the raw intensity of the tragedy or how shocked our senses may be. That is why the halakhah does not encourage excessive mourning, does not encourage extensive visiting to the cemetery, cuts short the full year for reciting *Kaddish* by a month, and develops firm practices for sewing up the torn mourning clothes.

The Psalmist sings: "You turned my lament into dancing, you undid my sackcloth and girded me with joy" (30:12). Ecclesiastes says: "[There is a] time for wailing and a time for dancing ... A time for ripping and a time for sewing" (3:4, 7). That is why it is appropriate, not gauche, for visitors at a house of mourning to express the wish that they meet in the future at celebrations. What the Law and the Psalms and even the cynical insights of Ecclesiastes are saying is that a life is not a life if it is only a dirge, sackcloth and tears, a gash in the collar.

In this modern age, we have learned firsthand another lesson, this one from Holocaust survivors. They experienced a hell unlike any other in history. Paraphrasing the Torah, the survivors wore their sackcloth inside, upon their souls. "What is there to rejoice about?" "How can we allow life to go on?" "How dare we not commit suicide?" Yet the survivors, many of whom continue to suffer varying degrees of "survivor guilt" simply for not having been being murdered while family and friends were being slaughtered by the thousands, have been able to invigorate Jewish communal life in the United States and Israel, to join in creating the State of Israel, to marry anew and raise large families, to enhance the Jewish community—and, above all, to teach us their lesson. The lesson of the first mandate of Jewish life is: Live!

The Mitzvah to Get Well

That people should take care of themselves requires no special emphasis. We have an obvious obligation to preserve our health, to use the best medical assistance we can find, and to adopt a healthy lifestyle. We may not voluntarily put our bodies or limbs in danger and we may not refuse medical treatment while we have a chance of being cured. Mourners need to hear such statements because there is a tendency among many to deny themselves good health in an effort to feel at one with the deceased, who has been "denied" life itself.

The very first meal mourners eat when they return from the burial, the condolence meal, is called *seudat havra'ah* (the meal of regaining health, or of renewing life), because, say Jewish thinkers, mourners feel at this point in their grief like offering up their own lives, ignoring their own basic needs, either in atonement for hurting the deceased or in general sympathy for the fate of the deceased.

Getting and staying well are not suggestions or gentle advice; they are religious mandates. The Torah requires that we achieve our optimum health and well-being: "Guard well your own souls" (Deut. 4:15).

Essentially, "souls" here means "persons." This mitzvah is even implied in a seemingly irrelevant biblical law that obligates a person who finds a lost object to return it to its rightful owners. By extension, when we are at risk for losing our good health, we have a duty to our own selves to return it to its "owner."

By excessive mourning, mourners achieve only a negative outcome. No perceptible religious good comes from self-induced wailing, turning a deaf ear to the words of comfort that others offer, refusing to be reintegrated into society in a natural fashion, resisting going back to work or school. Not only are such attitudes antithetical to the spirit of the traditional mourning laws, but they undoubtedly are not what the deceased would have wished. Mourning, crying, intense sadness, yes; but exaggerated grieving is altogether unwarranted.

Of course, mourners who remain paralyzed at the end of the full mourning period will not be content to follow this spiritual counsel. There may well be complex psychological reasons for their being unable to manage their grief. In such cases, they should certainly seek professional help. Grief unresolved can cause pain for a lifetime. Think of Jacob.

You Can't Preserve the Past by Freezing It

Science is already experimenting with freezing people at the moment of death in the expectation that they can be thawed out once a cure for their disease has been found. Although it may prove possible some day to restore the human body to material health, such future fantasies are irrelevant to the mourning process. The past cannot be preserved by cryogenics.

The overarching goal of restoring ourselves and others to health is to vitiate the idea that we should not try to cope, that we can never overcome tragedy. The goal is to prevent paralysis, to give mourners courage to move forward, to help them express their grief so that they can share it with others and receive their consolation. Mourners need to be helped by hearing that God so structured this world that we all suffer so that we can learn to incorporate our troubles and build on them to fulfill God's purpose. The process of getting well and making others well is a divine cycle. Everyone, grievers and consolers, must participate. Comforting the bereaved bolsters the salutary effect of Jewish mourning practices—such as mourning rituals, shiva, and *Kaddish*. All are designed to keep us from freezing our emotions and losing our will to live.

Transition: "I Want to Be Myself Again"

The most likely outcome of mourning is to become "normal" again, to "recover" from the trauma of a loved one's death, as though from a terrible illness. Such an outcome is likely to result without therapeutic intervention, even without conscious effort, just with the passage of time. God has so ordered this aspect of life that it resets itself, and life is resumed, albeit changed. The rational mind cannot achieve what time does.

But symptoms triggered by bereavement do not simply disappear; we are not automatically restored to exactly the same state as before. But we do adapt. Reactions to our loss recur most often around birthdays, religious holidays, family outings, and deaths of other relatives. Clinical observations of psychiatric patients show that such events can trigger serious pathology in vulnerable persons; but even such reactions are usually transitory.

A healthy grief process for one person may be different from that of another. For example, as I noted earlier, a man's typical reaction to a loss may include not talking, not weeping, and internalizing his grief. In contrast, a woman characteristically may worry about the future, weep for the past, and search for companionship to share her grief.

Healthy bereavement for both men and women includes recovery of lost functions; an investment in day-to-day life; feelings of hopefulness; the resumption of planning; and adapting to new roles and new status, different tasks, and social discontinuities. It involves recovering, returning, and renewing life in order to begin to blossom again.

Adapting to the New Configuration

Most mourning ends with an acceptance of the new world. The recovery may be either slow or speedy, but it essentially announces: "Life goes on. We must get back to where we left off when the tragedy occurred." Recovering signifies an adjustment to the new circumstances, squeezing life back into approximately the same niches. Yes, a widow without her husband, a widower without his wife, parents without their child, a child without his or her parent feels like a fifth wheel and will find it difficult to re-enter normal social circles. But mourners gradually adjust to the demands society makes upon them; life slowly rearranges itself.

At the end of the formal seven- or thirty-day period of mourning, or perhaps at the end of reciting *Kaddish* in the eleventh month, or at the unveiling, or on the yahrzeit at year's end, there will be a sense of closure—and with that will come a new beginning: New relationships will form; surprising new satisfactions will be felt. Mourners will return not "just" to where they were, but perhaps will emerge from their experience enriched by this fierce, mysterious, complex, and lonely passage of a human being from this world.

The mourning process gives rise to recognizable personal development—a bereaved child seems to mature, a surviving spouse not only accepts this new role but also begins to learn new skills previously managed by the deceased, becoming ever more self-sufficient in the art of living. Suddenly, the mourner discovers that a newfound courage emerges as if from nowhere, or a keen business sense that had been dormant comes to life, or seldom-used social talents suddenly reappear.

Overcoming the sting of tragedy, mourners recuperate from all the negatives associated with loss. They begin to adapt to normal life. Slowly hope returns, and they begin to invest energy in the future. Although their actions may seem to betray a somewhat shallow response to deep misfortune, revealing to others that they seem to have learned nothing from a profound experience, the important thing is that recovery has begun—slowly, cumbersomely, but eventually.

Does this mean that such adaptation has only brought us back to our starting point, save for the loss we have suffered?

Restoring Is Only a Partial Consolation

In the mysterious calculus of the human spirit, God sometimes delivers a replacement for the departed so that the equation of life seems to survive unchanged. Of course, no human being is replaceable. The mourning garment, once ripped in despair over a parent's death, can never be sewn up again; it can only be stitched and covered over to approximate its former wholeness; one can only try to get on with the business of living.

Of course, a child can never be replaced, but having another child may help the parents recover somewhat from their loss and divert them from their constant grief. Similarly, there is a restitution of sorts, when a wife remarries after her husband dies. Siblings may have other siblings, and spouses may find new mates. In the second half of the last century, we have seen this frequently as Holocaust survivors who saw their entire family perish before their eyes marry or remarry and begin new families. These families are quite often well-balanced, integrated into their social environment, free of internal conflict or abuse, and socially quite successful. Such life-affirming behavior is a modern replay of Job's consolation.

But did Job's new family truly compensate him for the loss of his first family? Not really. When an object is lost and then recovered, restoration seems to set things aright and serve justice. But neither a human being nor a human relationship is ever exactly replicable—and certainly not replaceable. Yet in the immense complexity that is human society and the nature of human loss, restoration does serve as a partial condolence, offering us opportunity and "permission" to move on and live life fully again. Since genuine replacement is not possible, restoration is significantly better than simple closure.

There is a truth embedded in the reverse of a biblical axiom; not only "God gives and God takes" (Job 1:21) but also God takes and God gives.

The Spiritual Community

In addition to assistance from Habitat Shiva—the rituals and spirituality of Judaism—there is something else that helps us make a normal transition to life without the deceased: the spiritual community.

The spiritual community is fundamental to Jewish law and tradition. This is evident in Judaism's rich historical experience and even more so in the ways it connects people: a *minyan* brings together ten people for a religious quorum; *zimmun* makes a single unit of three who eat and express gratitude together by reciting the Grace After Meals; and *hak'hel* gathers a national Jewish community in a united, massive celebration of Torah learning. During shiva, the community must fulfill its duty to bring the first meal to mourners upon their return from the cemetery, and community members are instructed by Judaism to visit even strangers who are mourners. This emphasis on community seeps into everyday Jewish thinking, reminding us constantly of a preachment that functions with the force of law: "All Israel is formally responsible for one another."

This feeling of unity creates a wellspring of support for the distressed as well as for those healthy individuals naturally in need of belonging. The sense of spiritual community is a mother lode of strength, even for those who have withdrawn from all its functions. For such people, the power of community emerges as an unintended consequence of their membership in the Jewish religion, one that they never expected but are likely to be gratified to discover at times of mourning.

The spiritual community, unlike an economic entity, thrives not on competition but on cooperation. When regular attendees are absent from the synagogue and when mourners fail to show up to say *Kaddish*,

the community seeks them out. Numerous accounts record the cama-
raderie that mourners, previously unattached to the Jewish community,
find during their days of grieving. The Jewish community shares their
grief, recites the amens to their *Kaddish*, brings its tears to support them,
and offers the strength of sheer numbers to them—as though the community were waiting to be used just at this moment to help this family
or that individual. How often one hears mourners say after shiva,
"Where did all these wonderful people come from? I didn't know they
cared. I didn't know that they even existed."

A story is told of a little girl who returned home late after visiting
her friend. When her mother asked the reason for her delay, the child
said, "I was helping Jane. Her doll broke." The mother asked, "Did you
help her fix it?" The child responded, "No. I helped her cry." A spiritual community helps mourners cry in their hearts, and it relieves their
loneliness, weakness, and their fear of abandonment. It is one of many
ways that, imperceptibly, without argument, without even utterance,
mourners are coaxed to return to society and to resume living.

The Classic Transition Outcome: The Abraham Case

The ritual of the Jewish funeral and burial service follows the pattern
enacted by Abraham when Sarah died; the rhythm and sequence of his
feelings are all incorporated in today's funeral service. Although I have
touched on this briefly in passing, here we examine it in greater depth:

> Sarah died in Kiriath-arba—now Hebron—in the land of
> Canaan; and Abraham proceeded to mourn for Sarah and to
> bewail her. Then Abraham rose from beside his dead, and spoke
> to the Hittites [asking to buy a burial place, the cave of
> Machpelah] (Gen. 23:2–3).

After Sarah died, Abraham went about systematically arranging her
burial, expressing his own emotion, but primarily, assuring *kevod ha'met*
(the honor of the deceased) for Sarah. The service he conducted was

formal—first, only speaking praises for his wife, the first matriarch; and, after that, weeping over her loss. Abraham could hardly hold back his weeping until after the eulogy. The word for "weep" is written strangely in the Torah, with a diminished letter *khaf*. The Sages comment that this demonstrates that although Abraham was genuinely suffering, he acknowledged that Sarah had reached a ripe old age and was expected to die. He cried, but in a controlled manner. Then Abraham bought cemetery plots for Sarah, for himself, and for their family, paying an outrageous price because he needed to bury her immediately, for her honor, a practice that has become Jewish law.

Rabbi Joseph Soloveitchik notes that the covenant and communication between God and Abraham continued only so long as Sarah lived. At her death that communication ended, as it did for all the patriarchs when their spouses died. Abraham's exalted spiritual creativity shut down with Sarah's death and with the beginning of his grief. This marked the end not only of Sarah's history but also of Abraham's. This towering human figure diminished in a moment.

With Sarah's death, Abraham returned to being the great, masterful "individual" that he was before he ever came into close connection with God, and became the founding patriarch of the Jews. Through his mourning process, Abraham made a smooth transition to normal living, continuing to be fully functional and tying up all loose ends in life.

The very first thing Abraham did after burying his wife was to guarantee the future of the patriarchate and the future of his son Isaac, who was destined to receive the family's earthly fortune. He embarked on the crucial task of finding a wife suitable for his heir, one who was spiritually, morally, and ethically appropriate to be a successor matriarch to Sarah. He took great pains to arrange every detail of just how this wife was to be found.

Finally, Abraham completed the transition by marrying a woman named Keturah. Clearly, she was not intended to be a replacement for the noble, spiritual, and beautiful Sarah. That chapter of Abraham's life was now closed. So who was this woman whom Abraham married in his old age? Most sources say that it was Hagar the Egyptian, his former concubine, with whom he had fathered Ishmael and whom he had to expel at Sarah's behest. Abraham now was able to redress an old grievance, an old injustice, by remarrying the woman he had once divorced, and with her to give birth to six more children and many grandchildren. But Keturah was the wife of Abraham the individual, not Abraham the awesome patriarch and progenitor.

(One ancient source offers the fascinating theory that Keturah was not Hagar, but a third wife, after Sarah and Hagar. She descended from Japhet, the third son of Noah, whose three sons were the progenitors of the ancient civilized world. According to this interpretation, Sarah was descended from Shem, Noah's first son and progenitor of the Semites, the Jews, Muslims, and Christians. Hagar was descended from Ham, Noah's second son and progenitor of the Egyptians and Africans. And now, to fulfill God's promise that Abraham would be *av hamon goyim* (the father of the multitude), Abraham marries a descendant of Japhet, becoming the "father" of Greece and Rome.)

A successful transition from mourning is marked by a smooth return and renewal of living after suffering grief. It encompasses not only a renewal of relationships but also the starting of new ones, reconnecting, remarrying, and rebirthing, while undergoing a personal renaissance. After Abraham dies, the Torah describes him as having lived to "a good ripe age, old and contented" (Gen. 25:8), and after Sarah died, it described him as blessed, *"ba'kol"* (blessed in all things) (Gen. 24:1).

This contented end of life is in stark contrast to Jacob, his grandson who almost died of grief, which made his life short, his years bitter. The outcome of Abraham's mourning and simple transition is the pattern of most people. It is moving on, continued normal living—but it is not reaching for the apex.

Chapter 13

Striving for an Exceptional Future

Pain provides an opportunity for heroism; the opportunity is seized with surprising frequency.

—C. S. Lewis

Consoling is a surprisingly complex operation. When we mourn we are living in a semiconscious miasma of forgetting, forgiving, and self-forgiving, trying to fill the sudden crater in our brain. We seek permission from within to separate from the deceased but are conscious of our own ambivalence—even as we aggressively strive to return to life with strength, we tenaciously hold on to the deceased who once was so vital to our existence, perhaps even a bone of our bones.

Transcendence: "I Have to Change My Outlook"

To succeed at consolation, comforters need to provide mourners with the framework for renewing their energy and their outlook. But it takes faith to turn this complicated framework into credible action, to strike a perfect balance within mourners so that they focus on the future while keeping the past alive, enabling them to face the world and to press forward.

A spiritual outlook motivates mourners to believe that it is possible for them to reach a higher goal even from this low point in their lives; that they can grow and not simply survive; that they can not only live through the present but can stride into the future, can lead a successful life, not just an acceptable one. The promise of Jewish spirituality carries us from grief to growth, inspires our desire to emerge creative from the morass of despair, to reach for new achievements and realize our full potential with renewed energy and a revitalized outlook on life.

After a death, many human forces are brought to bear on mourners to accept this death and to carry on with their lives. Most mourners do just that—and no more. But another force that is at work during the mourning process, a higher power, can spur mourners onward, beyond a simple resumption of the status quo, to reach exceptional goals. Jewish history and the social sciences know this dynamic well. When we are moved by this higher power, not only do we recover from our loss and go on living, but we also blossom with new creativity. A response to trauma can indeed result in a surge to triumph.

As mourners we may not believe that we have the ability to transcend so overpowering an emotion as grief, which has dragged us to the ground and lower. But a future does await us, and we have the right, the duty, to craft a vibrant one for ourselves. Accepting our loss is necessary to getting well, but we need to see such acceptance as a passive response—and only the first step. We need to regard the domain of shiva as only a threshold to what comes next. On day eight, after the visitors leave, the domain of the future opens before us.

Climbing Up

Rabbi Mendel of Kotzk used to tell his disciples that if they wished to know the world, they should soar above it. For only those rising above are able to see clearly what is happening below. So, too, if we place our problems in perspective, we have taken the first step toward transcending them.

To "transcend" means "to rise above." As a metaphor, it means to be lifted up, to gain a new perspective. Ashley Davis Prend, an expert on bereavement psychology, illustrates the phenomenon of transcendence through the example of this common experience: If you fly out of an airport on a rainy day, you first fly into the storm, but once above it, you find yourself in bright sunshine. You must transcend the darkness to find light. So it is with grief. Even as the sun shines overhead, the tempest still rages on the ground. Though grief is painful, it has transcendent meaning.

Transcending loss is about striving to make the experience an ultimately positive and redemptive one; it is about using our pain in a meaningful and inspirational way. It means making the best of a terrible situation, letting grief teach us important lessons about life.

There is something invigorating about transcending yourself, about lifting yourself out of the gray and rising to the radiant clouds above. Everything looks different. Everything seems less weighty. Such perspective is very consoling. Achieving perspective means shaking off your usual self-involved focus to gain a larger vision of life. Reaching this transcendent perspective changes the quality of life over time—there is a shift from focusing inward to focusing outward toward the larger world.

Transcending loss is a process of structuring a world of meaning, a holistic worldview that incorporates an instinctive response to loss, to fate, to the thousand and one "slings and arrows of outrageous fortune" that afflict us every day. It is a way of looking at the world. By rising above our own misfortune, we gain perspective; we view life from a distance, observing how every event forms a piece of an ordained puzzle. Transcending loss means rising above our grief rather than combating it. It means understanding it without fighting it, realizing that no amount of fighting can overcome a fatal misfortune.

A defeatist attitude defines you as a victim—and a victim only. But to see yourself only as a victim is to live a life choked by self-pity and martyrdom. When you define yourself as a survivor, you are stronger, wiser, and more compassionate as a result of your experience, and you can achieve transcendence and live life more fully than before.

When Biblical Heroes Lament: The Isaac Case

We can gain strength and hope by probing the internal strengths and weaknesses of great individuals in the Bible, who can be seen as useful role models for human behavior. Isaac, son of Abraham and Sarah and the father of Jacob and Esau, was the second Jewish patriarch, the only one of the three who is characterized primarily by stability and sturdiness. Isaac, however, was no Abraham. He was more devastated by grief than his father, yet he responded to it in a different way: To recover from loss, he did not simply return to his old world but instead rose to incredible spiritual heights, transcending his grief. Abraham suffered the loss of his wife in advanced old age, but Isaac suffered two major losses in quick succession and at a young age: his own near-death experience when he was brought to the top of Mount Moriah to be sacrificed; and then, perhaps worse, the devastating death of his mother upon his return from Moriah. Jewish tradition explains that Sarah died when she heard where her husband had taken her only child and what he planned to do. (Another legend offers an alternative scenario: Sarah's heart bursts with joy when she heard that God had spared her son, and she died content.) What Isaac suffered in nearly losing his own life at the hands of a loving father may have been overshadowed by his pain at losing his mother at a young age, especially if he blamed her death on his father, or, even more devastating, if he blamed her death on himself.

While Abraham's experience of death was more typical and his response more natural, so that he easily made the transition back to the world he knew so well, Isaac's situation was altogether different. Isaac was a purely other-worldly, spiritual man, mystical and contemplative. He was not by nature suited to handle this double grief. Fortunately, his father understood him well, and so, right after burying Sarah, he turned his attention to comforting his son. He realized the devastating effect that the black hole made by Sarah's death would have on his son, the emptiness of a home without a mother, and with it the loss of all the fruitfulness of their relationship, especially since Isaac was Sarah's only child, the son whom she had been molding to lead her people into the future.

Unlike Abraham who found his Sarah, and Jacob who found his Rachel, Isaac would not or could not seek his own wife. Instead, Rebecca came to him from afar, summoned by Abraham's servant. What she found when she arrived was not a lord of the manor nor a passionately engaged student, but a young man wandering and meditating in a field. Now this "field" was probably not an ordinary green meadow, but a metaphor for a "wild place." (When Isaac's son Esau is described as a "man of the field," we understand that "field" as a metaphor for "wilderness.") Perhaps Isaac, feeling cut off from his moorings by his grief, was wandering in the field because he was "lost." Normally a homebody, so unlike his arrow-shooting wild half-brother Ishmael, Isaac was now adrift in the wilderness. Stripped of the protective shield once provided by his mother, Isaac now felt her spirit vaporized and the house hollow. His home no longer possessed meaning for him; now it only reminded him of his mother's absence. And so he could not bear to be imprisoned by its walls.

Perhaps, as the Zohar states, Isaac, after his near-death experience, was numbed and blind to reality, as though he were dead inside. Henceforth he turned his eyes only toward the heavens. So what was he now doing out in the field? The Torah says, *"lasu'ach ba'sadeh"* (he was "talking" in the field). Midrash interprets this spiritually as "conversing with God," that is, this great, solitary man was praying the afternoon *Mincha* service. Is it not also possible—since *"lasu'ach"* means "talking," "conversing"—that he was talking to himself as he wandered aimlessly in the wilderness, that he was searching for himself? These are the symptoms of trying to manage grief: wandering, not being able to focus, being disoriented, one's intactness shattered, life's meaning evaporated.

Isaac's wanderings ended when Rebecca arrived, and he brought her into his mother's house. In telling the rest of Isaac's story, the Bible doesn't speak of the wilderness again; only of the tent: "Isaac then brought her into the tent of his mother Sarah, and he took Rebekah as his wife. Isaac loved her, and thus found comfort after his mother's death" (Gen. 24:67). His vacant heart was filled again.

What exactly happened to bring about Isaac's consolation? A midrash suggests that everything lost at Sarah's death was recovered with Isaac's marriage to Rebecca. When Sarah lived, a candle burned in her tent from Sabbath eve to Sabbath eve, the challah was blessed, and a divine cloud hung over the tent as a sacred shelter. When Sarah died, all that disappeared; but when Rebecca entered the tent as Isaac's wife, it all resumed. Rashi notes that Isaac saw Rebecca in Sarah's place.

But even though all physical signs of Sarah's presence could be restored, Rebecca remained Rebecca, not Sarah. The Bible does not yet suggest that after this event, Isaac's consolation was complete. For Isaac had not yet resolved his grief.

The medieval kabbalist Nachmanides points out that the midrashic interpretation noted above falls somewhat short because it does not take into account the term *"va'ye'ehaveha"* (and he loved her), specifically used in this verse (Gen. 24:67) to indicate Isaac's recovery. (This term is rarely used elsewhere in the Bible.) Nachmanides observes that an earlier verb in this verse, *"va'yevi'eha"* (and he brought her), describes the process of Isaac's physical restitution, which he achieves by putting Rebecca into a new role of replacing Sarah. But only when he expresses his love, *"va'ye'ehaveha,"* does his mind return to normalcy. In Freudian terms, he only began to resolve his grief when he invested his emotional capital in a future project: his wonderful new wife, who had qualities rivaling those of his beloved mother.

Only after declaring that Isaac loved Rebecca does the Bible immediately insert the words "and thus [he] found comfort." Isaac was comforted because he found a new and appropriate love for his future; a mother for his future progeny, the grandchildren of Abraham and Sarah, and a future matriarch for the Jewish people. His love for his mother then receded into the past, as it should, and all the physical manifestations of a life returned to normalcy fell into place: The illumination from Sabbath to Sabbath brightened his path through the wilderness of life, he finally found resolution for his grief, and the tent once again became the center of his life. Whereas earlier he had been immobilized, numbed, and thrown into confusion because of his bereavement, the future now opened up before him, and he was once again blessed.

Isaac was finally able to transcend the horrific double death he had experienced and to detect God's plan: the continuity of Jewish leadership, his father's blessing, and the restoration of blessedness to his mother's tent. This was transcendent consolation.

How a King Mourns

King David is the most dynamic, profoundly human, inherently powerful hero of the Jewish people, divinely bestowed with talents ranging from leadership and military expertise to the gifts of expressing soulful love and sublime poetry. David was known as the "Sweet Singer of Israel." We learn from him still, especially on matters of grief.

In its moving description of how David responded as his first child by Bathsheba lay dying, the Bible powerfully validates the concept of transcendent consolation:

> And the Lord afflicted the child that Uriah's wife had borne to David, and it became critically ill. David entreated God for the boy; David fasted, and he went in and spent the night lying on the ground. The senior servants of his household tried to induce him to get up from the ground; but he refused, nor would he partake of food with them. On the seventh day the child died. David's servants were afraid to tell David that the child was dead; for they said, "We spoke to him when the child was alive and he wouldn't listen to us; how can we tell him that the child is dead? He might do something terrible." When David saw his

servants talking in whispers, David understood that the child
was dead; David asked his servants, "Is the child dead?" "Yes,"
they replied.

Thereupon David rose from the ground; he bathed and
anointed himself, and he changed his clothes. He went into the
House of the Lord and prostrated himself. Then he went home
and asked for food, which they set before him, and he ate. His
courtiers asked him, "Why have you acted in this manner?
While the child was alive, you fasted and wept; but now that
the child is dead, you rise and take food!" He replied, "While
the child was still alive, I fasted and wept because I thought:
'Who knows? The Lord may have pity on me, and the child may
live.' But now that he is dead, why should I fast? Can I bring
him back again? I shall go to him, but he will never come back
to me" (2 Sam. 12:15–23).

Before the child died, David and Bathsheba made superhuman efforts to save him. But after he expired, David rose, transcended the tragedy, comforted his wife, and moved on with his life.

To begin to achieve such transcendence we need to climb a strange
spiritual ladder. Every step seems tiring and counterintuitive, but climb-
ing empowers us to transcend not only this loss but also every one that
may come after. Adopting this attitude of transcendence ultimately
implants in us a spiritual resilience, enabling us to distill meaning from
our loss and to believe, even at the vortex of acute sadness, that it is
possible to love and hope.

We can rise above a particular loss through our spiritual appreciation of what has happened through this particular death. We can come
to a sublime trust in God, learning from the example of Job. In the dawn
of religious history God consoled Job—not by reason but by challeng-
ing him to embrace such trust: "Where were you when I laid the earth's
foundations?" (Job 38:4). How can we refute such an appeal? If God has
been good enough to make peace in the heavens, as the *Kaddish* declares

in its climax, cannot God be trusted to make peace for us on this puny planet?

In my many pastoral encounters I have met numerous people who have developed for themselves a sublime spiritual philosophy of trust and wisdom that we would usually expect to find only in reclusive saints and elderly sages. These "ordinary" people have been able to rise to extraordinary spiritual heights through their wholehearted trust in God, through a faith that is palpable and that sustains them.

Such a philosophy does acknowledge that there are limits for each and every one of us, in terms of what we can and cannot achieve, of what we can and cannot do to alter the facts of our personal reality; but those who possess unwavering trust have empowered themselves to accept the inevitabilities of life as the will of God. Their trust raises them above earthly horrors that might otherwise devastate them. This is surely one of the delicious benefits of living an authentically spiritual life.

Psychologist Victor Frankl claimed that one of the ways we human beings can find meaning is by the stand we take toward suffering. He said:

> Through the right attitude, unchangeable suffering is transmuted into a heroic and victorious achievement. ... Even the helpless victim of a hopeless situation, facing a fate he cannot change, may rise above himself, may grow beyond himself, and by so doing change himself, and turn personal tragedy into triumph ... and turn his predicament into human achievement.

Reaching for a Higher Level of Acceptance

To react spiritually to so traumatic and life-altering an event as the death of someone we love requires that we realize that the event comes from God, that it cannot be altered, and that God's judgment must be accepted as right. It means that we rise to a higher level of acceptance—

first, by accepting the death itself through refusing to deny it, no matter how shocking it is; and second, by accepting the death in order to
transcend it.

This higher level of acceptance is known as *kabbalat din shamayim*
(accepting the judgment of heaven). It means that we acknowledge that
no matter how apparently unjust the death may seem, no matter how
random or excessive or undeserved it appears, that we regard it as the
decision of God, who is just and fair, although utterly inscrutable and
beyond the farthest reaches of human reason. Clearly, it is not easy for
rational human beings to accept something like this, which defies our
very rationality. But at some level we all must acknowledge that life and
death, the idea of God, and the concept of divine justice are simply
beyond the ken of human beings, despite all our sophisticated science
and tools of discovery.

By accepting that this death was God's decision, that there was no
way that any human being could have changed it, and that the only
choice we have now is to proceed with life, we become able to rise
above the immediate circumstances of the tragedy. We can appreciate
that this is the natural way of the world and of humanity. We affirm that
no one can avoid death, that we will ultimately lose the people we
love—some in predictable circumstances at the end of a fruitful life, and
others in circumstances that defy comprehension.

The Cost of Living

Accepting means understanding that death is the "cost of living," not
as an economic index, but as the price we pay for living and loving. This
is inescapably our destiny: These are the number of our years, our sufferings and enjoyments, our loves and fulfillments, our frustrations, and
the evils we must endure. "*Azoi vil Gott*," as we say in Yiddish: "This is
God's will." We pay on the way out.

King David's rebellious son, Absalom, was killed in the course of
battle, leaving David a broken man, beset by political dissent that threat-

ened the future of his united kingdom. The depiction of David's incon-solable grief for this unworthy son is one of the most touching scenes in the whole of the Bible: The king wanders from room to room, crying over and over, "My son Absalom! O my son, my son Absalom! If only I had died instead of you! O Absalom, my son, my son!" (2 Sam. 19:1b).

Yet, in his heart of hearts, King David knew that once the *Sturm und Drang* of Absalom's rebellion had ended with his son's death he would have to mourn his son and eventually get on with his life and his rule. Even though it seemed that nothing could calm David's anguish and his wish to die in Absalom's place, even though this son had wanted to defeat him, David did finally respond to his minister Yoav's prodding: "The King arose and sat down in the gateway." In time, David arose from his mourning and returned to his rightful place, the throne.

Beyond Acceptance to Heroism

As mourners we have an opportunity to reach beyond acceptance to heroism. We are called on to be heroes in handling our somber task. Ordinarily, people in this circumstance might be expected to weep and rage, to question the justice of God, even to deny it. To expect us to accept the judgment of God is to raise the bar of human capacity. And to accept it with serenity, without recrimination, is to be positively heroic. To respond to tragedy and yet not doubt God's justice is, in fact, to surrender to God—not because we are vanquished, but because we recognize God's superior will and judgment.

To keep the moral and religious dictates of Almighty God is to be genuinely religious; to accept loss and sadness without rebelling against God is to rise to the level of moral heroism.

Symbols of the Heroic

The Jewish mourning rituals put such heroic words onto the lips of mourners at the most crucial moments of the funeral service. Immediately after the casket is lowered into the grave and the covering takes place, when the deceased has disappeared from the face of this earth, we recite the *Tzidduk ha'Din* (The Justice of the Judgment). This prayer, consisting of fourteen short phrases, affirms in the clearest terms the rightness of divine judgment, repeating incessantly that God's judgment is perfect in every respect, that God does not always demand punishment for every transgression, and that although we cannot fathom God's ways, God's will should be accepted as a matter of faith.

Maimonides said as much in the strongest terms: "It is likewise one of the fundamental principles of the law of Moses our Master that it is not possible that He, may He be exalted, should be unjust."

In essence, what we are saying in this prayer is that this horrific event is not what God *wanted*; it is what God judged *must be done* for the sake of the world and humanity. *Kal d'avad Rachmana le'tav avad* (all that the merciful God does is for the good)—though it flies in the face of reason or even accepted morality, it is for the ultimate good. We find statements sprinkled all through Jewish literature about how God grieves for the very lives that God has taken! God joins Isaac in mourning Abraham; God mourns the death of the sons of Aaron, Nadav and Avihu, even more than does their stunned father; God grieves for Moses more than do his doting mother and worshipful student; God ends the lives of Moses, Aaron, and Miriam—and by implication, the patriarchs and all the righteous of the world—with a kiss! God mourns them, all the beloved heroes, the carriers of God's word to the people, and in the same "breath," as it were, determines their destiny: that they must die in this way and at this time. Human destiny is ineluctable—never desired, but absolutely necessary.

The word "destiny" shares the same origin as the word "destination"; God determines what our end will be. Medicine can delay death and gerontology can ease the aging process, but in the end we all will reach the same destiny, the same destination. God knows this destiny, and it arrives by the judgment of Almighty God.

But destiny is not fate, and Jews are not fatalists. Fatalism implies that we live our lives in a state of resignation, since, after all, God or randomness decides our fates, no matter what we do. No, Jews fervently believe that all beings have a divinely determined destiny, yet must strive to better their lives and their neighbors' lives, cure their illnesses, and stave off the advent of death rather than resign and languish passively until fate strikes. But once our destiny has been sealed and death has taken its toll, despite our best efforts, we need to fully accept the judgment of God.

Accepting God's judgment and God's design, and coming to terms with the fact that our own judgment is not God's empowers us to look at all of life as the destiny scripted for us by the Almighty. Such acceptance allows us to transcend the misfortunes of our life. Surrendering to God's judgment enables God to fill our inner beings and bring us consolation.

The Rabbis of the Talmud highlighted the need for transcendence in a favorite saying: "Just as one makes a blessing for the good, so should one make a blessing for evil." Over good we say, "Blessed are you, O Eternal, our God, who is good and does good." Over evil, we say, "Blessed are you, O Eternal, our God, who is the true Judge." We can obviously understand why we make a blessing for something good that happens, but why bless God over a death, which is an evil happening?

The answer is that a blessing is not a thank-you note, even though many blessings do convey gratitude. In the case of both good and evil, the blessing is an attribute: If I benefit, it is from God; if I suffer, its source is also God. The blessing over evil, *Dayan Ha-Emet* (the True Judge), is a sharp, eloquent statement by mourners that affirms that though death is life's most evil aspect, it is the work of God's judgment, and as such, it is "true," perfect, and unassailable. The phrase *"barukh Dayan Ha-Emet"* (blessed be the True Judge) is recited by traditional Jews whenever they hear of a death, any death, and it is also part of the formal funeral service.

The acceptance of God's judgment, which is accompanied by a prayer such as *Tzidduk ha'Din* and preceded by the blessing *Dayan Ha-*

Emet enables mourners to transcend the tragic occurrences in their lives and to reframe them positively in a religious fashion.

Homily on an Egg

As though to underscore this idea of spiritual acceptance and to allow mourners to transcend heroically the evil that has befallen them, Judaism slips into the mourning rituals the meal of condolence that family and community prepare for mourners to eat upon their return from the cemetery. The menu for the meal of condolence must include an egg. Why is that? *Machzor Vitry* answers, "Because it has no mouth." An onion, an orange, an apple all have stems, "mouths" where one begins to open them up. But an egg is elliptical, smooth, unbroken, with no stem. "It has no mouth," that is, it does not open its mouth to chastise God. So too mourners, like religious heroes of all eras, should accept with a whole heart the painful decisions of a just God.

The idea of raising one's voice to chastise God in the face of death finds even fuller expression in the following:

Rabbi Meir was at the house of study, giving his weekly Sabbath afternoon lecture, unaware that his two beloved sons had suddenly died at home. The boy's mother covered them with a sheet, and since it was the Sabbath, she forbade anyone from mourning on a day sacred for its peace and joy.

After the evening services, Rabbi Meir returned home and asked for his sons, who had not come to the synagogue. The rabbi's wife ignored his request, brought him the evening meal, and asked the rabbi to say the *Havdalah* prayer concluding the Sabbath.

Then the wife said to her husband, "I have a question for you. A friend once gave me two precious jewels to hold for him; now he wants them back. Shall I return them?"

"Without doubt," said Rabbi Meir.

The rabbi's wife took him by the hand, led him to the bedroom, and drew back the sheet. Tears burst forth in a bitter torrent from the saddened couple. "You see," said the wife, "these jewels were entrusted to us by God on loan. They belong to God and now He has taken them back."

––––––––

Job echoed those sentiments as well: "[T]he Lord has given, and the Lord has taken away; blessed be the name of the Lord" (1:21).

Spiritual Valor

My brother, Dr. Norman Lamm, once noted: "Given the nature of this world, death is necessary. Because death in itself need not be a punishment but a transition to a more spiritual existence, it is not truly painful for one properly prepared." This explains the custom practiced by certain saintly individuals to calmly wash their hands before dying, as one would in preparation for any other religious ritual.

A Kotzker Hasid on his deathbed requested some spirits in order to drink a l'chaim. He explained that whenever a Hasid prepares to perform God's will, he does so with joy at the opportunity to do a mitzvah. "If God has willed my death," he said, "I am now performing His will. And it is proper to do so in a joyous spirit!"

Rabbi Abraham Isaac Kook recounted a similar story about his ancestor Rabbi Isaac Katz. As he lay dying, Rabbi Katz reproached the disciples and relatives who surrounded his bed, their faces drawn and glum: "Is it not written, 'and she laughs at the time to come'" (Prov. 31:25)? He requested that candles be lit in the Sabbath candelabrum and that musicians play their instruments and sing to accompany his soul on its joyful journey.

––––––––

Such cheerful equanimity, of course, is beyond the spiritual or psychological reach of most people. But it is inspiring to know that such a reaction to death is possible, that heroism in the face of appalling tragedy is humanly attainable. Although such spiritual heights are rarely achieved, it is reassuring to see that the souls of humans can move beyond the grasp of fear.

Transformation: "I Became a New Person"

There are times, admittedly rare, when the outcome of grief reaches for its highest level, soaring beyond transcendence to a personal transformation that is as awesome as it is bewildering. In such cases, grief morphs into a springboard that propels mourners to heights they never dreamed of reaching—to creativity, to prosperity, sometimes even to extravagant success.

Soulful and Successful

Examples abound of artists and industrialists, the scholarly and the materially successful, who have enriched and broadened their lives—and have become more alive, joyful, and self-confident—precisely because they experienced grieving. Bereavement can mold pain and sorrow into opportunities for growth, spiritual advancement, connection with a sense of the sacred, and breakthrough creativity.

The landmark psychological study on achieving personal transformation after a death was done by psychiatrist G. H. Pollock, who called the concept the "Mourning-Liberation Process." He analyzed artists, scientists, and other professionals, some very well known, who had been impaired by grief. What he discovered was that creative personalities such as Nietzsche, Goethe, Oscar Wilde, Van Gogh, and Gustave Mahler all demonstrated that creativity can clearly be a direct outgrowth of bereavement. Pollock concluded from his studies that the successful completion of grieving might well result in generally increased creativity among even those less gifted than these geniuses and can also result in other very substantial growth-producing effects. Surprising new relationships and new achievements quite often follow a bereavement.

When Grief Drives Creativity

Remarkably, this creativity does not necessarily reflect a successful working through of grief. To the contrary, creativity may represent a valiant attempt to cope with intense grief via some ersatz restoration or reparation, without actually resolving the causes of loss and separation. In other words, it is possible for creative artists and great intellectuals to develop their talents even out of *unresolved* grief. Somehow, grief—whether resolved or unresolved—triggers a growth spurt. The psychologist Hannah Siegel wrote:

> "When the world within us is destroyed, when it is dead and loveless, when our loved ones are in fragments, and when we ourselves are in helpless despair, it is then that we must re-create our world anew, reassemble the pieces, infuse life into dead fragments, re-create life."

Transforming grief liberates us from the burden we have naturally assumed and empowers us to re-examine the world, and to bring creative resources to the task of rebuilding it. It happens as silently and imperceptibly as a person grows. The process is nonetheless stunning to witness.

Numerous psychoanalysts have noted the strong link between loss and creativity, for example, in Beethoven's sonata op. 81a. The sonata expresses one of the permanent features of the human condition: the experience of irretrievable loss. It is Beethoven's artistic reaction to the horrific death of his brother. The first movement depicts loss; the second, mourning; and the third, personal resurgence. The sonata has also been interpreted in terms of how it expresses the sentiments of grief—alternating between full acceptance and the denial of death—the left hand on the piano representing denial, the right hand, acceptance. Thus, personal creativity of the highest order can be a possible result of unresolved grief.

Ralph Keyes, who trains writers to transcend their fears, describes this dynamic:

"Fear flushes clogged pores of perception—Ears listening for the crunch of bears' paws, eyes scanning the horizon for enemy soldiers, and noses sniffing the air for the smell of fire, have heightened awareness ... Intense stress illuminates everything in sight when we feel frightened."

Isn't it true that scar tissue is the strongest part of the body? Herein lies a lesson for mourners: From the wound of death itself comes superhuman strength. Sir Walter Scott likened adversity to the rain: cold, comfortless, and unfriendly to humans and animals. Yet from the rainy season come the flowers and fruit that bring us beauty and nourishment.

An example of personal growth emerging from grief is the story of Michelle Z., a grief-stricken widow in my congregation. She was frozen in fear about how she would be able to navigate solo through a "man's world" at a late stage in her life. Michelle's husband's sudden demise left her abandoned and alone, thrusting upon her radically new responsibilities for which she was totally unprepared. Interestingly and unpredictably, Michelle decided that the only way out was through, and she discovered enormous internal energy to transform herself into a taker of risks, a seizer of new opportunities—handling the store, opening up another business next door, taking a new business partner, and redefining herself in important new ways. She developed new interests, acquired surprising new skills, and began to develop a very healthy respect for her self-worth.

Within time Michelle became a leader in the mail-order catalogue business and a board member of three charities. Where had she been all those years? Why had she become productive only after her husband's death? And why, after all this success, was her husband's death still causing her grief and sleepless nights?

Many mourners successfully manage their grief and transmute their losses into growth because circumstances compel them to redirect their native talents and find appropriate channels to express them. They appreciate that suffering is a part of their lives that must be accepted and that they must grow beyond it, and this propels them to connect with a larger meaning in life. Often they revisit and resolve earlier losses, but sometimes, like Michelle, they still silently grieve, crying into their handkerchiefs, pining for someone they truly love, in the very midst of their resounding success. They even learn how to play and to laugh—although it hurts—and to take care of their inner selves.

When Adversity Triggers Purposefulness

The nineteenth-century Jewish leader Rabbi Samson Raphael Hirsch made an insightful observation about uses of adversity through an ingenious reading of a familiar verse in Psalms: "My God, my God, why [*lamah*] have You abandoned me" (*Eli, Eli, lamah azavtani*; 22:2)? This cry by the Psalmist sounds like the persistent question of those who require constant explanation: "Why?" "Why me?" Rabbi Hirsch subtly redirects the speaker's meaning by noting that since Hebrew has no vowels, we might be reading one word of the phrase incorrectly. Instead of *"lamah"* (why), the text can be read: *"le'mah"* (for what). In other words, the speaker may be asking a question about himself, not about God: What is the purpose of my suffering? What can I do with it? What can I learn from it to make me a better person? "My God, my God, *for what* did you abandon me?" This is the question asked by those who constantly seek the spiritual: not why but to what end?

The question of "why?" so paralyzes people that all religions make some attempt to answer it, and all fall short of the mark because the question itself, in theological terms, is beside the point, as Job discovered. It is not the answer that fails, but the question. C. S. Lewis, the theologian, said: "I think many of the questions we ask God are like nonsense questions. Our saying 'Why?' is like saying 'Is orange square?' or 'Is yellow round?'" We often hold childlike concepts of God, especially when we think we can understand God just by calling God on the phone and asking for an answer. As adults, we need to appreciate that there are givens in life—and that these givens are often imponderables.

What Produces the Thrust to Transform Oneself?

Without digging deeply into psychological and anthropological studies, but rather by intuiting the serpentine reasoning so characteristic of grievers, we can divine the motivations that empower those in mourning in rare cases to transform themselves. In such cases, mourners achieve unanticipated creative success due to an injection of energy unleashed by their mourning experience that can be redirected to build a business, renew old relationships, reinvigorate study, change roles, recharge old batteries, and undertake new ventures. In a remarkably intuitive way, mourners sublimate the energy of grieving and channel it into creativity.

When we become mourners, we are energized this way for one of two reasons. First, we are motivated to fulfill the life of the deceased by being better ourselves, achieving goals the deceased sought for us, or by simply wanting to make the deceased proud of our accomplishments. We find this most often when children of any age are bereaved of their parents—"If Mom [or Dad] could see me now." Indeed, this may be the dominant motivation behind personal transformation. Actor Matthew McConaughey once said: "I became a man the day my father died. Nothing in my life gave me more clarity and a stronger sense of responsibility. I've become a better lover, a closer friend and a kinder stranger."

Out of love may come sorrow, but out of sorrow can come light, the brightest light we have ever seen.

Or we may act out of another motivation that is just the reverse: for example, if the deceased was perceived as a ceiling over our heads, discouraging our risk-taking or stealing our self-confidence. Sometimes, adult orphans in grief need to recover from their parent's *life*, not from their *death*. For example, the day after his father's death, H. L. Mencken, the great essayist, rushed his essays to the post office and was published in short order for the very first time. He suddenly became liberated; the shadow over him had been lifted. He could not grow in his father's shadow, since the man seemed to him a superman. Mencken was convinced he could not be better than his father. But when the father died, his son's creativity soared.

In fact, a 1978 study found a link between the early death of a parent and a child's future career success. The study, focused on 699 eminent persons, found a significantly higher than average incidence of early parent loss among these successful people. The author of the study theorized: "If feelings of insecurity, inadequacy, emptiness, and especially guilt can inhibit functioning" after an early parent loss, "then the mastery of these feelings may be a springboard" for success. For some, then, sustaining a loss finally allows for fulfilling the promise that has been hiding within.

Transcendence, transformation. Such high-sounding words convey a sense of the unreachable. But when we break them down into living ideas, as I have tried to do, they make good sense. I close this chapter with an anecdote about a great human being who transcended a sudden, frightening situation and transformed it into an awe-inspiring, breath-taking, unforgettable moment. And it happened in front of thousands of gasping people.

Transcending and Transforming: Itzhak Perlman

On November 18, 1995, the renowned violinist Itzhak Perlman came on stage to give a concert at Lincoln Center in New York City. Those who have been to one of his concerts know that getting on stage is no small achievement for Perlman. Stricken with polio as a child and wearing braces on both legs, he walks with the aid of two crutches.

He walks across the stage one step at a time, painfully and slowly. Yet he walks majestically, until he reaches his chair. He sits down slowly, puts his crutches on the floor, undoes the clasps on his leg braces, tucks one foot back, and extends the other foot forward. Then he bends down and picks up his violin, puts it under his chin, nods to the conductor, and proceeds to play.

Audiences who have seen Perlman perform are used to this ritual. They sit quietly while he makes his way across the stage to his chair. They remain reverently silent while he undoes the brace clasps. They wait until he is ready to play.

But this time something went wrong. Just as he finished the first few bars, one of the strings on his violin broke. Everyone could hear it snap—it went off like gunfire across the room. There was no mistaking what that sound meant. And there was no mistaking what he had to do. People who were there that night thought that he would have to put on his braces again, pick up his crutches, stand up, and make his way offstage to find another violin. Or he would have to wait for someone to bring him one.

But neither of these things happened. Instead, he closed his eyes and waited a moment before signaling the conductor to start up again. The orchestra began, and he played from where he had left off. And he played with more passion, more power, and more purity than ever before.

Of course, all of us know that it is impossible to play a symphonic work with just three strings on the violin. I know that; you know that; but that night Itzhak Perlman refused to know that. The audience could see him modulating, changing, and recomposing the piece in his head. At one point, it sounded as if he were retuning the strings to get new sounds from them, sounds that they had never made before.

When he finished playing, there was an awesome silence in the concert hall. Then people rose and cheered. An extraordinary outburst of applause exploded from every corner of the auditorium. Everyone was on his feet, screaming and cheering, doing everything he could to show how much he appreciated what Perlman had done. The great violinist smiled, wiped the sweat from his brow, and raised his bow to quiet down the audience. And then he said—not boastfully but in a quiet, pensive, reverent tone—"You know, sometimes it is the artist's task to find out how much music you can still make with what you have left."

What a powerful statement that is! Perhaps it can even be regarded as a way of life, not just for an artist but for all of us. That night, a man who had prepared all his life to make music on a violin with four strings found himself all of a sudden, in the middle of a concert, playing with only three strings. And the music he made with those three strings was even more beautiful, more sacred, more memorable than any he had ever made before, when he was able to use all four strings.

So, perhaps our task in this bewildering world is to make magnificent music with all that we have. And, when that is no longer possible, we must *transcend* our private, personal tragedies, retune the strings of our life, and *transform* the divine instrument we each embody to make still more beautiful music with what we have left.

Chapter 14

"You Have Transformed My Mourning into Dancing"

A long life is not good enough; but a good life is long enough.

—Rabbi Meshulem Jungreis

In unexpected ways, Judaism impels mourners to rise above pain and to re-create themselves, to go beyond survival to self-elevation, to move from passive transition to transcendence to awesome transformation. The prophet Isaiah (61:3) phrased it elegantly:

To provide for the mourners in Zion—
To give them a garland instead of ashes [pe'er instead of efer],
The festive ointment instead of mourning,
A garment of splendor instead of a drooping spirit.

Surprisingly, Judaism brings about this spiritual transformation by guiding mourners through the process of personal repentance. Death is linked with the religious emotion of *teshuvah* (repentance, return, regeneration), which is so powerful a feeling when it is sincerely under-taken that it can be life-changing, virtually creating a new individual out of the repentant mourner.

We can experience this repentance in two ways: First, we might harbor regrets about our relationship with the deceased—slights, angers, and lapses of decent conversation as well as our not having paid enough attention, not having given him or her well-deserved satisfaction, and not having been considerate—lapses that we commit unthinkingly in the busyness of everyday life. As we now take our moral inventory, we not only grieve the loss of an individual, we also lament any of our own misdeeds that may have caused anyone unnecessary sadness. We repent for not having appreciated all that our loved one had to offer.

A talmudic story illuminates this process.

When the eminent scholar Rav died, his disciples accompanied his body to the burial site, and on their way home, stopped to eat at the Danak River. They came upon a legal problem and couldn't resolve it. One of them, Rabbi Ada bar Ahava, rose and made a second tear on his clothing, which he had already torn as an act of grieving. For this moment he realized how dependent he had been on his teacher and felt his loss even more grievously, recognizing that he had not seized the opportunity to learn more from him when he was still alive. Thus, the rabbis all mourned once for his death and a second time for having for-ever lost their chance to learn more from him in his life.

———

A second kind of repentance is spiritual. We repent for our failings in our religious commitment and in our ethical living. Both sinners and mourners suffer from losing closeness to God. Rabbi Joseph Soloveitchik, referring to the moral shortcomings of the entire Jewish people, cites Jeremiah (31:3) tellingly: "The Lord revealed Himself to me of old. Eternal love I conceived for you then." Once God was close, but because we have fallen short in our ethical and religious goals, have been insensitive to God's presence, ignored God, or taken God for granted, we have grown remote from God's love.

So, too, mourners experience profound grief when they perceive their deceased relative or friend now only from afar, when they understand that their loved ones are slipping out of reach forever. The emotions of sinner and mourner are remarkably alike. That is why sitting shiva is equivalent to doing *teshuvah* (repentance). Both involve traumas of loss—one, human; the other, divine.

Becoming a New Human Being

Maimonides, when he wrote about repentance, said that when a person truly regrets a deed and decides never to repeat it, that person is transformed and becomes a new person. Spiritual regeneration sparks personality regeneration.

In a poignant book on the personality transformation undergone by one who does *teshuvah*, Roy S. Neuberger, son of the noted financier and founder of the Neuberger-Berman investment company, described his remarkable trek from Central Park to Sinai. Despite having been raised in legendary wealth on New York's Fifth Avenue and having attended Oxford University, Neuberger still searched for a meaning to his life. "Why when I have everything, do I feel as if I have nothing?" This son of a very privileged family tried the door to every philosophy and every major religion—East and West. He failed them and they failed him. Finally, nothing was left—not his marriage, not his education, not his society. Of course, he absolutely *knew* there was no God. He wrote such things as: "Nobody normal believed in God." "The problem was that I felt I *also didn't exist*. ... Suddenly, I began to turn the whole question around. Like Hagar in the desert, my eyes opened and I saw something I had never seen before. There was one unopened door ... the door to God."

And then both he and his wife simultaneously discovered the God of the Jews and the Torah—and turned their lives around 180 degrees.

Although they had grown up attending Sunday school at the Upper East Side's Society for Ethical Culture, they profoundly transformed their goals and lifestyle, becoming devout members of a community of deeply committed and observant Jews on Long Island.

Through the transformative process of Jewish ritual and spiritual regeneration, mourners who repent during bereavement are moved to change their inner direction and grow at a furious pace, as if they were now reborn to another destiny. Their sense of life is enriched—life is good.

The Egg Again

In religious symbolism the egg conveys a cornucopia of subtle meanings. As I said above, it is eaten at the meal of condolence because it has no mouth, symbolizing to mourners that they should make peace with God without opening their mouths in protest against death.

To me another profound symbol expressed by the egg is that it holds within itself the seed of the future. An egg represents the possibility of new life. A chick breaks its shell and either becomes a hen, capable of laying hundreds of eggs every year of its life, or a rooster, able to fertilize new eggs. As we make our way through our grief in the shattered world below, we anxiously journey toward our new destiny—from calamity to renaissance, collapse to resurrection. All this, embodied in a simple egg.

The High Jewish Art: Wringing Blessing from Tragedy

At the heart of Jewish existence is a special survival mechanism, hidden in the folds of Torah, a propelling force in the continued existence of the Jewish people. It is knitted into the fabric of original creation, into the whole cloth of "Israel," and clothes the earliest childhood experiences of the growing nation of Israel.

It is the sublime talent and energy to transcend tragedy and to transform it into triumph. It is the very same strength that I encourage people who are grieving to find within themselves.

This genius of the Jews empowered us to rescue ourselves from near death to mass resuscitation and then on to a religious renaissance. This is not just reversing a religiously backsliding, idolatrous population, but a full-blown phoenixlike resurgence. We have been able to repeatedly rise and decline and then rise again, often more powerfully than ever. Although it borders on the incredible, these reversals of history occur consistently—in different ages, in critical circumstances, and with extraordinary intensity. How does such a thing happen?

In the story of humanity, it is the story that drives humanity. Ancient narratives told over and over again become the spiritual energy that moves passions, goals, and ideals. It is not the teaching, but the telling. The heroic narratives of the human race are absorbed as bedtime stories; in kindergartens, yeshivas, and in Sunday school classes; in textbooks on the Homeric legends, in the myths of Greece and Rome, in Aesop's fables, in the stories of the Founding Fathers, in the heroes of the Old West. These stories follow the same pattern as the narratives that mourners love to tell and rework. They slip unnoticed into the storehouse of people's memories and then at the appropriate moment are sucked into the reservoir of our assumptive lives. For example, the story of Jacob is a formative tale rooted in a person's memory, dormant until it is summoned. Then at once old Jacob comes alive and the story is re-enacted, on the international stage as in private life.

The rabbis say: *"Ma'ase avot siman le'banim"* (The deeds of parents are guideposts for children). The word *"ma'ase"* evokes two meanings: "facts" and "story"—*ma'asim tovim* (good deeds), and also *ma'ase b'Rebbe Eliezer* (a story of Rabbi Eliezer).

The narratives that follow are seminal stories in the Jewish tradition of patriarchs, prophets, priests, rabbis, and scholars, and have imperceptibly become the guideposts for the children of Israel. These tales, told and retold through successive generations, have shaped the intuitive Jewish response to poverty, sickness, war, suffering, and death.

Here, we look at just a few of the Jews' peak experiences, and in each *ma'ase* we will find the salient quality of self-transformation, which reveals an astonishing instinctual drive to rise from despair and grieving to spiritual renewal and then even higher—to a reinvigorated leadership.

The peaks on which we will alight are instances of this magical rebirth after horrific expulsions, when individuals, families, and whole communities were driven from their homes. We visit expulsion from the Garden of Eden to humanity's first diaspora; the fleeing of Jacob and his family down into the killing fields of Esau; the escape from Egypt into a desert infested with hostile nations; the forced exile from Jerusalem and the Temple down to pagan Rome and the irons of slaves; the wanton expulsions from one bleak shtetl to another, ravaged by successive pogroms; and, finally, the expulsion from the human race through unspeakable horrors of the Nazis. They span from the Garden of Eden to the Holocaust, the birth of humanity to the death of human decency.

Taking Back the Future

The Garden of Eden was not a paradise for man, not for woman, not even for the animals; it was a proving ground. The first human beings failed the test: They could not achieve perfection equal to the perfection of nature that we might have expected of them; they did not achieve the necessary spiritual greatness in that perfect Garden; and they, the Divine's creations, were not in the least creative. Moreover, they did not even pass the basic citizenship requirement for the right to live in such a garden by obeying local ordinance. Indeed, so much of a disappointment was the entire experiment that fiery swords forever stand guard, signaling permanent lockout. No going back, not ever.

Traditionally, Jews therefore picture their true paradise not as a beginning but as an end—a place to be yearned for and finally earned. Henceforth Adam and Eve are not in a paradise, out of this world. They are very much in the world, steeped in a new geography, East of Eden, humanity's first diaspora. In this real world, there is suffering and pain, catastrophe and death. At the outset God squares with them, preparing them for what they are to face. "You should know who you really are, 'You are dust;' and you should know where you are going, 'you will return to the dust.' The very earth will rebel against your eating of the perfect fruit you tore from its beautiful branch." God expelled Adam. No more serenity; now struggle. Adam and Eve are morally crippled forever by the shrapnel of their explosive arrogance. Cursed.

Herein lies the first lesson of the Jewish people, and of all mankind. Adam and Eve are cursed, but they are alive and strong and thinking. They decide forthwith to reverse the direction of civilization; they will yet transform the curse of God into the blessing of God. Ultimately, they will find a place in *olam ha'ba*, the pleasures of the world to come, because they will deserve it.

The very first verse after the catastrophe sets the tone: "Now the man Adam knew his wife Eve, and she conceived" (Gen. 4:1). In this world, the human creature creates, once and again and again. People suffer the pains of childbirth and the worse pains of childrearing. Their grandchildren build whole cities, tools, musical instruments, and languages—new cultures, a microcosm civilization. Their families commit grievous offenses and they suffer a flood of grievous consequences, but the world is renewed on a new moral base that they have fabricated out of scraps of toil and anguish.

For many centuries thereafter, praying Jews have passionately reached for a seemingly unreachable goal, *Chadesh yamenu k'kedem* (Renew our days as of old). These words beg for deeper understanding. *Kedem* is not only a time word, but also a place word. *Kedem* means "old" but it also means "east." When God expelled Adam and Eve, it was *mi'kedem l'gan Eden* (East of Eden). It is East of Eden where the genius of Judaism began to take hold and to flourish and where our oldest ancestors began to create human society. And it is this geography, the first of many easts to which the world "orients" itself in prayer, in which the Jews triggered the recurring surges of national genius for transforming near-death curses into the creation of blessings, miraculously rescuing their faith both from inner decay and external force. "Renew our days as in the East."

The Killing Fields of Esau

This narrative, especially as it is elaborated in Talmud and Midrash, describes Jacob wrestling in the night with a mysterious creature who is a fusion of the Divine and the human, the spiritual agent of Esau, the primordial incarnation of evil. The wrestling represents the life and death struggle Jacob anticipates in meeting his terrible and terrifying brother, who had sworn to kill him for having appropriated his father's blessing. Gentle Jacob is petrified, but he wrestles in the night with courage and subdues his enemy. This in itself is a grand and unexpected victory, a classic end to the story. But Jacob does not consider his survival a huge accomplishment; the climax is yet to come.

The Bible adds three short verses:

"Let me go, for dawn is breaking," [said the stranger]. But [Jacob] answered, "I will not let you go, unless you bless me." Said the other, "What is your name?" He replied, "Jacob." Said he, "Your name shall no longer be Jacob, but Israel, for you have striven [*sar*] with beings divine [*el*] and human, and have prevailed" (Gen. 32:27–29).

This visionary, who has dreamed of a staircase to heaven, needs to win physically, of course. But he is Jacob; he needs to achieve a historic change, a spiritual goal, rather than only physical endurance on earth. He had anticipated the obliteration of half of his family and with it the possible termination of the whole Abrahamic heritage; he needs to be blessed with a conclusive spiritual triumph. He was willing to risk everything on earth; he wants a touch of heaven.

The blessing is his heroic transformation and is symbolized by his name change, from Ya'akov (Jacob)—who was born grasping onto *ekev*, a man's heel; that of Esau, his twin brother—to Yisrael (Israel), a hero who has struggled with a human being and with an anger and is now grasping onto God's word. He descends into the killing fields of Esau, and is not content to walk away with a simple physical sign. He insists on a spiritual blessing, the ancient power symbol of triumph and transformation, from Esau, who plotted to kill him for taking from him the original blessing of their father. Jacob transforms himself into the ancestor of Jews, who in his image wrestle in every generation against the evils of contemporary Esaus, who limp away from the killing fields, but who are "Israels." Forever will they transform themselves from victim to victor.

Like humanity itself, the birth of the spiritual entity known as "Israel" is the drama of rebirth from the night of near death to the dawn, when they will emerge as the chosen of a merciful God.

From Pit to Peak: A Nation Is Born

Jacob goes into Egypt to save his family from famine, but in the end his children are spiritually starved in a night of anguish. This seems to be the last act of the brief Jewish drama: The Jews are enslaved by Egypt, the mightiest power on earth, and their sons are mercilessly drowned. They are losing the physical stamina to keep their heads up, losing their heritage, quickly losing moral energy needed for the good life, losing their legendary ability to endure, losing their will to remain in their own integrity, and finally beginning to lose even their identity. Israel, the almost-nation, is reverting to Jacob's birth-status, individuals digging their heels into the clay of peons, slowly sinking to the lowest rung of spiritual impurity (tum'ah), almost touching moral bottom. The Haggadah spins the narrative over and over, expanding it through the centuries of exile: they "cried," they "groaned," they "screamed," they "moaned." The descriptions flood their mouths, they don't know what to call it: "our affliction," "our burden," "our oppression." You could sense the Romans in their decline: *Delenda es Carthago.* (It's gone.)

Abruptly, after centuries of slavery, history takes a radical turn. The brick-laying Jewish helots split apart the ankle chains of their Egyptian masters and miraculously drive to the shores of a raging sea. God lays a straight path across waters and they part politely, welcoming the wild-eyed slaves. Moses sings, and Miriam dances, and the people cannot contain their glee. The rabbis of the Passover Haggadah still cannot contain their glee two thousand years later, and the greatest minds are given to conjecture: How many were the hidden miracles—and how many plagues thrashed our slave masters? It can't be only ten; some say fifty, others two hundred, still others two hundred and fifty! No matter, it was *pele pela'im* (miracle of miracles).

Hundreds of thousands of former slaves dashing from Egypt to Sinai, they race across the harsh desert—thirsty here, hungry there, complaining, whining—yet in three months they arrive at the foot of the mountain, prepared to receive the Ten Commandments and the Torah from the hand of God. Yesterday a dying breed, today preparing for the holiest moment in history, God's Revelation, which will forever change the face of the civilized world! They were perched precariously in the center of immensities, in the conflux of eternities. The Jews were in a spiritually compacted moment between two colossal episodes.

How do you get from one to the other without going mad? You fly.

There is a single verse in the Bible that is a bridge between the near-death experience of the Exodus story and the inconceivable rise to the highest level of sanctity at Mount Sinai; between servitude to criminal overlords and service of song to Almighty God.

This is what God tells Moses to tell the people before he gives them the Tablets: "You saw what I did to the Egyptians, and how I bore you on eagles' wings, and how I brought you to myself" (Deut. 19: 4). The verse has two pillars: "What I did to the Egyptians"—to extract you from their iron grip; and "how I brought you to myself"—took you to my heart, as I promised your fathers, and embraced them with my covenant that you will be mine forever. But how did you get to this place? The Torah inserts an unforgettable metaphor as the nucleus of the story that links exodus to revelation: "I bore you on the wings of eagles."

First, understand: The eagle is the picture of swiftness. God cannot wait for your embrace while you slog, start, and stop in the hot sands. Fly to me, "I brought you to myself."

Now understand further: Why are you being carried by eagles? Because an eagle is the highest flying bird with a huge wingspan. She carries her fledglings on top of her wings to protect them from the low-flying carnivorous predators. "I want you to be safe," you can hear God say, as it were, to be safe, to be whole, and "I will not allow you to be devoured by the villains."

Most important: The eagle lives at the top. She instinctively soars to the highest perch—on the summit of the mountain, on the tallest tree, on the highest branch. There she is most secure, most contented, most vigorous, breathing the cleanest and sharpest air. She transcends the bottom feeders and the middling sprinters. Perched at the top of the world she has a commanding view of the panorama of life. Above the eagle there is only heaven. "Over the nowhere there arches the everywhere." "I bore you on the wings of eagles."

Herein lies the wisdom that speaks to the Jewish condition and also to those who are bereft of someone they loved. The eagle can gather its young and its food with its talons and transcend the screech of predators, the suffering and the pain, and rise precipitously from the pits, soaring to the peak. This is the historical task of the Jew from the giving of the Torah to tomorrow: to go from the tar pits of the Egyptian pyramids to the blessed foot of Mount Sinai, to fly over tragedy and find the olive branch of blessing.

We thank God not for rescuing the Israelites from under the heavy hand of the Egyptian overlords, but for granting them a new powerful moral vocation. Now the Jews are free to declare independence, to seek a Promised Land, to become the conduit of religion and morality for a broken world. This event determines the future course of Jewish history, the journey from bondage to moral grandeur that required the transformation of their national character and culture.

No Cursing

The Balaam narrative breaks the pattern of expulsion and resurgence. It is cast not in the mode of exhortation or moral teaching, but of a declaration of love. In it, the Israelites are not active as a party to the conflict and they are not at immediate risk. They are not even aware of the thunderous debate—between God and Balaam, and Balaam and Balak—hovering over them, and the fate that is in the balance. As usual, they are the objects of scorn, the feared enemy of a paranoid king, the kind that Jews know well from their short history.

Like Egypt, Moab is an ancient superpower and its King Balak, afraid of an Israelite incursion to pick Moabite fruit or drink from their wells, seeks to crush the Jews in a single stroke—not by armed might but by enlisting the renowned gentile prophet Balaam to curse the enemy. Balak summons Balaam to do the demolition job and after Balaam's feeble attempts at avoiding confrontation with the Israelites, he is persuaded to climb to the pagan altar on the heights of Bamot Ba'al, where he is able to see the entire Jewish encampment and issue the vile curse that will trigger dissension, idolatry, internal strife, wild immorality, and finally inner decay.

But to no avail. Despite Balaam's intention to curse the Israelites, he returns to Balak discouraged—he feels compelled to bless them. Again and again, Balak moves Balaam to one then another vantage point, searching for a weak spot that will call forth the prophet's curse. Like a magnifying glass that concentrates the sun's rays to burn a small hole through wood, now Balak hopes to focus the curse on a small section of Jews that would not appear to be religiously formidable.

But the wily king and the heathen soothsayer simply cannot make it happen. God twists Balaam's tongue, and the words that pour from his bellyful of curses reformulate themselves into glorious blessings on three occasions. At one point, he breaks out in the most precious blessing ever bestowed on the Jewish people: "How comely are your tents, O Jacob, your dwellings, O Israel" (Num. 24:5).

What is fascinating is what the Jews did with that blessing in subsequent generations. One would expect the tradition to ignore this unintended praise and to let it sit in its context in the Torah. Instead, they feature it as the opening statement of the prayer book, one of Judaism's greatest gifts to world religion, and make it the very first words a Jew recites on entering a synagogue, before any other prayer. Thereby it became an invitation to all the blessings in the prayer book, courtesy of a hysterical king and a frenzied prophet, who were going to use it as a sledgehammer to bludgeon them.

In this narrative, the Jewish nation, though it is a sizable mass moving through the desert between established nations, is nonetheless not a real threatening force; it has no trained army, no supply lines to sustain it; it is not competently organized; and it formally declares that it seeks no military confrontation, only minimal hospitality in the arid desert (which is never forthcoming).

What appears to constitute a more substantial threat for the desert kingdoms is their perception that the Jews are in fact God's chosen people, whom He will protect and for whom He will fight: *Ha'shem ish milchamah*, God is a God of war. But if that is truly what they fear, why is there never an attempt to appease God or to pacify His people?

It is not for us to decide these matters but simply to note that whether it is divinely initiated, or caused by the backsliding of the Jews, or by the fear of their enemies, the curse-blessing connection is a fixed characteristic of Jewish existence.

What is frighteningly similar is the old dynamic at play again—which is now negotiated by God Himself: the need to convert near death to blessing. While the story's apparent purpose is to demonstrate the protective custody of the Jews by their Creator, the subtext is that the Jews, the "peculiar" people of God, are vulnerable simply because they are who they are.

Note the abridged version of this story in Deuteronomy (23: 5–6): "*Vayahafokh ha'shem elohekha lekha et ha'kelalah li'verakhah, ki ahevkha hashem elohekha*" (But the Lord your God turned the curse into a blessing, for you, because the Lord your God loves you).

The Balaam narrative is a textbook illustration of *vayahafokh*—the word that Torah uses for turning things on their head, the same word that *Megillat Esther* uses to portray the reversal of the fortunes of Mordecai and Haman, and the word we as individuals use when confronting disaster. The story is so powerful because the action is sparse, the language crystal clear, the events accomplished miraculously by God Himself, and the motive of the reversal is plainly declared: Because the Lord your God loves you.

A Turning Point in Jewish History

Another critical turning point in Jewish history, the radical breach in the historical tradition, is the destruction of the Second Temple by the Romans under Titus in the year 70 C.E. Had it not been for conscious rabbinic intervention at the time of the Temple's destruction, Jewish history would have almost certainly come to an end; as it was, the Jewish people at this moment were teetering on the edge, a moment away from their own death and the death of their faith in God.

The mourning that followed this catastrophic destruction was not only grief for the Temple itself but for the core of Jewish faith represented by the structure. The Roman conquest was not only a defeat for the people; it was also a disaster for the Torah, the constitution of the Jews. This could easily have triggered the end of Jerusalem, of the Promised Land, of a whole people's future.

But the Jewish people survived and transcended this calamity. The Sages introduced practices that transformed a nation's near death into a life-protecting armor that has shielded the Diaspora for 2,000 years. They universalized the central Temple originally in Jerusalem. Now every synagogue and study hall in the world is a *mikdash me'at* (miniature Temple); the ritual sacrificial service of the Temple is recited faithfully every day in synagogues as if each one were the sacred Temple itself; the holiest of prayers are recited by Jews facing east toward the site of the Temple in Jerusalem, even though it lies in ruins, survived only by a wall that has wailed every year of the Jewish exile.

Jerusalem still occupies the central space in every Jewish heart, even as the Temple lives again in every synagogue. Yet the Rabbis instituted an annual fast, Tisha be-Av, not to forget the catastrophe. What this incredible spiritual inventiveness accomplished was to make the Temple and the people permanently impervious to every plotting Titus. Though enemies might destroy one temple or ten, they cannot crush the Temple in every town, the Jerusalem in every soul. Because of this ingenious management of public Jewish mourning, the Rabbis guaranteed that the Jewish people will not only be universal but eternal. Even the crushing body blow of the Nazis could not vanquish them.

The Temple was spiritually retrieved. In the miniature temples of the exile they re-enact the temple service, yet also pray for the rebuilding of Jerusalem Temple every day. The Rabbis never settled for another mountain on which to build another temple, another city they could call Jerusalem, an edict that would allow them to supercede the old Temple so that they could survive. The third Temple someday will be rebuilt on the same holy site, Mt. Moriah, but the fate of the Jewish people will never again hang on the goodwill and designs of their human enemies.

With the Temple's spiritual rebirth, total destruction was averted. The Jewish people once again squeezed a blessing out of the catastrophe and went to thrive creatively throughout history in foreign lands, as the Rabbis had designed. The drama of death and rebirth perseveres; the curtain will never fall on it.

A Past That Was Futureless

The eighteenth-century Hasidim living in Eastern Europe suffered the most abject poverty conceivable. Not only did they subsist on minimum living standards; their labor was unproductive and famine was widespread. They were often hungry, homeless, and—worst of all—utterly futureless. How could they live through the day, not knowing whether there was a tomorrow? They could not develop a trade or build their homes because they might be expelled at any moment, unceremoniously, like Tevye from Kasrilevka in *Fiddler on the Roof*. They were constantly subject to being drafted into the army or succumbing to illness.

Yet astonishingly, the culture of Hasidism is built upon joy. This incongruence is acknowledged on the walls of Jewish homes everywhere: pictures of Hasidim dancing, singing, studying, and laughing.

How was such a thing possible? The Hasidic rabbis could not combat the social and economic evils endemic to medieval cultures. Their only recourse was to forbid sadness! Defiantly, in the midst of suffering, they actually banned sorrow, or *atzvut*, thereby creating an opening for hope to slip unnoticed into their lives. To modern ears, this borders on the absurd: Can one mandate a mind-set? But that is exactly what they did.

The Hasidic rabbis acted not as intellectual despots outlawing a natural behavior, but as loving, caring healers, prescribing a cure for their patients' chronic suffering. They functioned not by fiat, but with devices that were positive and uplifting: singing full-throated songs, dancing with the Torah, shouting their gratitude to God for giving them life (such a life yet!). Then there was the crown jewel of their joy, a celebration unlike any other: They transformed the observance of the weekly Sabbath from a halakhically defined bastion to a weekly wedding hall, celebrating the marriage of the Jewish laborer with the Sabbath Queen herself, as she arrived ceremoniously in the mud-spattered streets of the old shtetl.

In his Polish shtetl, one of my scholarly ancestors was called "Der Hoicher" (the Tall One). Actually he was quite short and appeared even shorter as he seemed always to be bent over his worktable. But when the sun began to set on Friday evening people said that he suddenly grew a foot taller! Like all Jews, when he prepared for the coming of the Sabbath banquet he suddenly straightened up, donned his Prince Albert caftan, and went to greet Her Highness, the Sabbath Queen. He became transformed into a courtier, as stalwart and proud as any in the king's court. Jewish serfs thought of themselves as superior in learning and devotion to their feudal lords, and on the Sabbath they showed it.

The process of wringing beauty from ugliness, joy from despair, dance from dirge, and blessing out of sheer hell was the special gift that the Hasidim gave to the Jewish world. Rising from the ranks of the economically and academically downtrodden, the Hasidim became messengers of hope, reinvigorating Judaism and serving as the engine of resurgence in every country of the Diaspora.

The Hasidim struggled and in the end survived; but they went far beyond merely enduring. They went on to win ...

Fate said to them: "Mourn your misfortune"; Destiny said: "Dance."

"You turned my lament into dancing, you undid my sackcloth and girded me with joy, that [my] whole being might sing hymns to You endlessly; O Lord my God, I will praise You forever" (Ps. 30:12–13).

The Holocaust and the Holy Land

When we mourn the Holocaust, we grieve for six million murdered individuals. And we also grieve for what could have been the annihilation of the whole Jewish people, the disastrous near termination of Jewish history as we envisioned it. Fifty years later we still cannot catch our breath when discussing it; we still see a possible holocaust in every anti-Semitic act. But the Jews found hope amid the bones and blood on the Nazi killing fields. The immigrants who were turned away from country after country, the prisoners of war who were abandoned, the scraps of people who could never find relatives they desperately searched for, were given a permanent refuge. The perennially stateless suddenly were handed a land—the State of Israel, where they would forever be free from the brutality of pitiless pursuers.

We dare not claim that the Jews had to go through a holocaust in order to achieve an Israel. God forbid. God does not ask of people such horrendous sacrifice. No dream is worth that nightmare. We dare not seek for cause and effect; we can not know God's purpose and cannot possibly comprehend the scales of God's justice. We can only have a bird's-eye view of history, never a God's-eye view. But with Jewish independence following so swiftly on the heels of the Holocaust, we marvel at this mysterious regeneration of our refuge, the Holy Land. Once again, the Jewish people have walked the mourners' path from collapse to renewal.

What occurred in Germany and Europe in 1933 could never have been anticipated either. The Nazis began their goose step across the continent, and in short order a mountain of corpses erupted. Jews suddenly were flung into an inferno, thrown down from the top of society into the sewers of the Wehrmacht. Their hopes and plans had not only been dashed, they had been buried for all time.

But in 1948, God breathed life into the dried bones in the valley of death that Ezekiel described many centuries ago. In a historical instant, the Jews are pulled out of that vale of tears and their dream for twenty centuries—a veritable mountain of opportunities, of futures, of hopes, and the possibility of smiling once again—became real. Three months after burying their dead, they were making plans for their new lives.

Is such a thing plausible, even imaginable? Can we take such a thing in stride? Is it at all possible that there is no linkage between two such colossal events—concentration camp and Jerusalem of Gold? Is there a whiff of a chance that this is sheer coincidence? The conjunction of the two events—the closeness, the suddenness, the steep downward and steep upward in a blink of an eye—can we ignore such a dramatic happening? In point of fact, is there not one God? Are we not His one people? Who understands the forces at work here? Can this possibly be the random history of Henry Ford's description—one damn thing after another?

Indeed, the two events may not be related as cause and effect, but we cannot deny they are indeed related spiritually and existentially. On a spiritual scale, the grief of the Holocaust years acted like a springboard to propel a suffering people forward beyond the creation of the State of Israel: to self-realization and spiritual regeneration, to physical might with which to defend ourselves, to national creativity, to a prosperity that just months before would have been an outrageous prediction.

Here is compelling proof that Israel has been a blessing wrested from the catastrophe of the gas chambers: Fifty years afterward you need only witness the enormous achievements of Holocaust survivors and ask yourself: "Could these be the same people who hopelessly grieved for their entire families and will always feel bereft of a whole world that has vanished?" They vanish, but with a trace! The Jewish people have risen once again.

A Nation's Genius; a Person's Gift

This astonishing drama of resilience, which is the silent heritage of all Jews, is a source of profound comfort in days of personal grief. Its effect on the entire Jewish people has filtered down to enrich each Jew's grieving for a single soul. Our ancestors have demonstrated so much inner conviction in their drive from grief to growth that it has become the pattern for their descendants. We now know that if we have the inner resources, we can transcend tragic events and reinvigorate our lives.

The talent of the whole Jewish people has always resided in this intuitive response of individual Jews—drawing out whatever good could be found in evil, refusing to bend to blind fate, and sublimating the energy used to fend off a great evil and funneling it into an engine for personal achievement. Our wounds become our strengths: The pogroms made us more alert, the old Jew-hatred brought us closer to one another, and the Holocaust eventually alerted even our somnambulant neighbors to the madness of our enemies. We exulted in the realization that we could survive the worst of all tragedies and then move on to accomplish so much for our people and ourselves.

It does not satisfy us to be called "survivors." For although we delight in our "Jewish continuity" and in our unlikely survival, which are of course achievements of enormous proportions, by itself this is not a rich source of pride. What this people wants is that its *banim* (children) become its *bonim* (builders). The nation has braved death and grief not merely to live to see another day, but to make of our people a "Holy People," to bring peace to all people, to grow closer to God and live exemplary moral lives.

Such can also be the case when we mourn personal losses. When we grieve the loss of a beautiful child, a beautiful parent, a beautiful spouse, a beautiful relative, or a beautiful friend, we can transform our intense sadness into blessing. As we rebuild our lives in reaction to our grief, as we grow from loss to fulfillment, as we bring joy back into our own lives and into the lives of those we touch, we bring others and ourselves close to God. This dynamic of transformative outcome—the mourner's ability to move from sadness to greatness and not settle for survival and continuity—is the heart and soul of Jewish history.

Characteristically, the Jews have lost the battles but won the wars. Characteristically, the Jewish hero has been utterly unlike anyone in the enemy's pantheon of classical heroes. To wit, we were crushed dramatically by an arrogant, jubilant, young Titus at the head of an invincible conquering army. Not so the Jewish hero who, in a mode immortalized by Jacob, emerges triumphant—if only to snatch a blessing—a change of name, a new mission, a safe harbor for all his family, an entitlement to worship his God in the way he was commanded, and then goes limping off into the dawn of a new life. This recurring metamorphosis is hidden from plain view, but it is vital.

Lessons from Nature's Book

Nature is a textbook that is often a resource for understanding human events and even for clues to what God asks of us. One summer, as I traveled cross-country, I took the road west out of Kansas, my senses lulled by the placid and the predictable scenery in a dreaminess of endless sameness. The road slipped quietly into Colorado, and the earth burst in front of me, and my mind was abruptly awakened by a radically different landscape. At Colorado Junction, on the left side of the road, the mountains leap from nowhere, enormous peaks following closely upon one another like a massive herd of elephants bullying its way through the brush. Precipitously, the peaks fall into a bottomless gorge and just as abruptly climb sharply, mounting up, up, and out of view.

As I neared the edge of the colossus, an eerie pounding from the right side of the road became increasingly louder, then suddenly the roaring waters of the handsome and fierce Colorado River burst in front of me. The heaving waters hurtled headlong, recklessly, boisterously, foaming, rushing to some hidden destination. The river was screaming at me: Stop; look up; listen up; loosen your uptight attitudes; stare in awe. Do you know where you are?

I pulled off the road. My jaw dropped and I froze in dismay. No one prepared me for this; something is happening here. Does anyone understand? Mammoth elephants were mocking my five-and-a-half-foot frame and the river's earsplitting shriek calling for me to just think. I was stunned out of my torpor; I was surrounded by enormities! I was in the presence of greatness. My senses were crashing inside my brain. If you can't wonder, you can't be religious.

Ask Like a King

After having studied the four outcomes of grief and the numerous gradations between them—standstill to transition to transcendence to transformation, and even beyond, to repentance and reconciliation with the Almighty—how should the griever proceed? Dr. Norman Lamm, to whom this book is dedicated, provides us with helpful insight. He quotes the Psalmist:

> "One thing I ask of the Lord, only that do I seek: to live in the house of the Lord" (Ps. 27:4).

The talmudic Sage Rabbi Abba bar Kahanah claims that what David was asking for here was *malkhut* (royalty)—to become the king of Israel. Clearly, the rabbi did not mean to turn what seems like a straightforward spiritual request—"to live in the house of the Lord"— into a political campaign. What he meant was much more profound and more spiritual.

Enemies—such as the warrior Goliath, King Saul, and David's rebellious son Absalom—besieged David, scheming to destroy him at many points of his life. He was forced to flee and act insane, hounded and hunted like a wild animal the field. If he could ask for any single thing, it should have been a surcease of hatred, a fortress to protect him, a few years of peace. But David didn't pray like a beggar, groveling for crumbs. Rather, *malkhut sha'al*, he asked *like* a king. He did not ask *to be* a king; he already was one. No, he asked to dwell in the house of the Lord, an even grander palace than that which he presided over heretofore. He was not reaching for a handout; he was asking as a sovereign.

Grievers are beset by pain and suffering, overwhelmed by a pervasive spirit of decline, a wasting away. In such a situation, Jewish tradition points them to the example of David: ask like a king, reach for the sky, hope the ecstatic hope.

But some words of caution: Perhaps such reaching, such hope is too much for you to ask of yourself at this crushing moment. Perhaps you are not ready to transcend or transform your grief; perhaps it is too early for you even to fully accept the death that has occurred, especially a sudden one, or a young death, or an accidental tragedy. Please know this: if this is the case, you should not force yourself to do that which is too difficult, maybe even hurtful. Growing from grief takes place only in the context of healing, when the mind is ready to become whole again. Even then, you need to acknowledge that everyone heals at different rates and to realize that Jewish law and tradition never ask of mourners that they do more than they feel they can.

You may also feel that this demand to transcend grief, to be transformed by it, seems arrogant. Does any person have a right to ask to be strengthened as a result of grief? The answer, I believe, is that people do not know their inner strength until they seek it. It is difficult, but it is a goal worthy of everyone.

Most assuredly, we have the moral right to demand of God that He empower us to find a creative, productive, fruitful life. Merely asking this of God takes us halfway there. It is everyone's right to hope for healing, to reach for the heavens, to demand compassion from God.

Ask like a king; you may have a royal surprise.

Words for a Loss, When at a Loss for Words

The consolers must feel the mourner's pain, as with ancient Job; and they should speak with him words of consolation. Divrei tanchumim, words of consolation must be given and also taken.

—Kitzur Shulchan Aruch, 34, 7

He [God] performs a miracle for every mourner who accepts the medicine of consolation given him by others, and in that way he heals them from the anguish of grief.

—Rabbi Eliyahu Dessler

Palliatives: Words That Soothe

To resume living a quality life, mourners are told by Jewish tradition to be "*mekabel tanchumim*" (a receiver of comfort)—that is, to receive and not resist the comforting words of visitors, the suggestions of well-meaning people who come bearing compassion and understanding and who fervently commiserate with the grieving. Jewish ethicists call these comforting ministrations "medicine" (*refu'ah*) for the soul.

GIVE AND TAKE

Comforting others must be placed in a proper framework: God implanted in us the ability to be consoled and then commanded others to deliver the consolation. Mourners should swallow the prescription, even when the ideas and phrases that are offered are lightweight or trite. They should not dismiss them too quickly, for some common-sounding phrases are deceptively profound. The French writer Charles Baudelaire once said: "The immense profundity of thought [is] contained in commonplace turns of phrase—holes burrowed by generations of ants." Generations of Jews, reciting the same phrase, have burrowed deep into their hearts; mourners are well advised to consider what is being said. The words may have a healing resonance.

Resisting the words of comfort is not unknown to Judaism. The most prominent example of such rejection was Jacob the patriarch, whose entire family sought to comfort him in bereavement when he thought his son Joseph had been killed by a wild animal. Jacob rejected their attempts. There was nothing they could say that would be of any value to him, and he rebuffed them, never allowing words of comfort to reach into his soul. Earlier, when Rachel, the wife he deeply loved, died and he buried her in a solitary grave on the roadside, Jacob was in no position to receive comforters. It is likely that the patriarch never overcame his beloved's demise, never learned to process the news of her death, and ultimately he dragged the image of her coffin behind him all his life. Undoubtedly, his long years of grieving for Rachel and for Joseph (who he thought was dead) were the major triggers for his telling Pharaoh that, although he was not very old, he had lived a life of excruciatingly painful days.

Recently, I was astonished to find myself in an analogous situation. Six years after teetering on the edge of paralysis and enduring a suffering I had never known before, I was told that I was a particularly difficult patient to comfort. And my wife, who agonized with me through every crisis, was equally difficult to assuage. I was astonished, I contemplated, I understood, and I learned a vital lesson. I am the founder of the Jewish Hospice movement in the United States and my wife is its executive director. We had already heard every phrase, thought, and word of comfort, and therefore encouraged no one to speak words of consolation to us in our misery. We not only did not accept consolation, but like Jacob, we dismissed it. In consequence, those who came to help left frustrated at their every attempt and we were not helped; nothing entered our ears that could possibly soften our hearts.

All aspects of consolation can be triggered or thwarted by a comforter's choice of words, whether he presents them properly and tenderly, whether he makes them acceptable to the mourner's ears. Nathaniel Hawthorne said about using words: "... so innocent and powerless as they are, as standing in a dictionary, how potent for good and evil they become, in the hands of one who knows how to combine them!" The comforting of the bereaved is severely compromised by well-intentioned visitors who misspeak or who speak too forcefully, too dogmatically, or who instruct and seek to persuade by pleading, cajoling, or being overbearing.

A mourner must learn to be *mekabel tanchumim* (a receiver of comfort), and the *menachem* (comforter) must learn to deliver the condolence artfully. It is when mourners swallow the words that their resolve and hopes are strengthened. Unpronounced sentiments are like pills prescribed but not taken. Perhaps particular sentiments will be ineffective, but the cumulative effect of many well-intended wishes and thoughts may prevail.

Traditional Farewells

Jewish tradition understands the quandary of those who want to comfort mourners but cannot articulate words of comfort, so it provides a formulaic religious response to what is essentially an inexpressible emotion. Thus, consolers are able to express their sentiments in a soothing and spiritual way without fear that they might become tongue-tied in the face of irretrievable tragedy.

THE CROWN JEWEL OF JEWISH CONSOLATION

> May God console you among the other mourners of Zion and Jerusalem (*Ha'makom yenachem etkhem betokh she'ar avelei Tziyon vi'Yerushalayim*).

This traditional farewell of mourners instituted by Judaism is carefully constructed and profound. It conveys positive feeling with layers of ever-deepening meaning, even for those who don't understand the literal Hebrew or who can hardly remember the words or even pronounce them correctly. This formula also relies on God to take primary responsibility for consoling the mourners—to comfort is human, to console divine. Mourners might find it hard to fully accept a human being's personal words, but they may feel more readily consoled by an invocation of God's participation in mourning. The ideas embedded in this phrase are a summary of the religious and spiritual devices the tradition uses to bring the mourner some consolation.

Ha'makom

In this blessing, God is referred to by a specific and little-known name, "*Ha'makom*," which translates simply as "The Place." God is referred to as "place" because space affirms stability, solid ground, rootedness—the opposite of ethereal. A "space" term is used instead of a "time" term such as the Tetragrammaton, the four-letter word for God's name, which signifies eternity, because mourners need to inhabit the here and now.

Space is the framework for grievers—the *place* of shiva, changing one's usual *place* at services. Time, in contrast, is infinite, mercurial, and unmanageable.

Further, the use of the word *"makom"* averts a possible negative response from mourners. Calling God by this consoling name avoids thrusting God's more familiar, awesome name into the face of mourners who have been shaken to their roots by God's irreversible decree. That is, in fact, also the reason for not greeting mourners with the usual "shalom," since shalom is another name for Almighty God, a name hard to embrace at this disquieting time.

Yenachem

The second word of the classic farewell blessing is the Hebrew word for "console," but it is not one always used for this purpose in the Bible. When the Israelites betray God's trust, God is depicted as *va'yenachem*—"regretting" the creation of human beings or "regretting" taking Israel out of slavery. This seems to have everything to do with God's undergoing a change of mind, as it were, and nothing to do with God's consoling.

But we need to understand a link that is not immediately visible. Intrinsic to all consolation is a sense of deep regret. Regret gives rise to a need for change and triggers an acceptance of loss, which leads inevitably to profound consolation. It compels people to review, reassess, and readapt to a world that has permanently changed after a friend or relative has died. It points to a change in direction—adjusting to a new status and new relationships among all members of the family or business or inner circle, and submitting to self-transformation, if that is possible.

Betokh She'ar Avelei Tziyon vi'Yerushalayim

The formula is incomplete, however, without its second half: "Among the other mourners of Zion and Jerusalem." This phrase emphatically moves the consoler away from the natural tendency to focus solely on those presently grieving. It connects both the specific griever and grief in general in two salient and subtle ways.

First, the phrase broadens God's consolation to include "other mourners"—of Zion and Jerusalem—thereby expressing a critical imperative in the process of grief work: the universal need for mourners to share their grief, the natural interconnectivity of all mourners. Grievers are not alone, and they must know this so that they do not feel singled out unfairly by God, specially targeted for suffering. The phrase also brings the mourners to the realization that death, in all its guises, is suffered by everyone, "other mourners," and that it is an inherent quality of life. Subliminally, yet another level of meaning is implied: Others are genuinely able to share their pain.

More subtly tucked into the folds of the phrase "the other mourners of Zion and Jerusalem" is the teaching that the mourners' past grievous losses are connected with their present loss. Indeed, within our lifetime, we suffer and grieve for many losses: a loved one, a dear friend, a business relationship, a livelihood, or our prestige. Or we may mourn a ravaged community, perhaps a sacred city like Jerusalem, or a devoutly held idea like Zion. Many never resolve old grief; horrific incidents of the past may cast their long shadow over a new trauma. Even night has its shadows. Grieving should be seen as an ongoing process of acknowledging cumulative misfortune rather than only a recent disaster. An entire collection of past losses thus insinuates itself surreptitiously into the fresh grief, though most mourners regard the new loss as a single monolithic burden.

In English, "grief" has no singular, no plural, only a comprehensive sense. Similarly, the Hebrew word for grief, "*avel*," is a comprehensive term. So, too, is "*hefsed*" (loss)—we speak of *hefsed merubah* (great loss) and *hefsed mu'at* (minor loss), but not in the singular or plural as such. On the other hand, "*nechamah*" (consolation) has a ready plural—"*tanchumim*" (many consolations). Thus, centuries of Jewish usage, expressed in the common forms of daily language, shine a light on the significant contrast between accumulated grief and separate consolations. This linguistic insight into Judaism teaches two counterintuitive truths: First, all mourners, no matter how diverse their losses, share a common sadness, forming a communal net of sorrow, although each is unique. And yet a single mourner's particular experiences of grief form a personal net of troubles, shared by no one else.

Jewish tradition, in its Ashkenazic and Sephardic formulas, requires that this special Hebrew phrase be spoken because it incorporates a fundamental tenet of Judaism: We are the concerns of God, not only as unique individuals but also as one among many others who are suffering and who must always be included. In fact, an oft-repeated teaching of Judaism is that God heals us only if we first ask God to help others. This is particularly true when we turn to God not to seek comfort for a personal loss, but for the survival of Zion and Jerusalem. That is why, when extending God's blessing to sick people, we mention *"she'ar cholei Yisra'el"* (those others in Israel who are sick). We affirm that God is concerned not only with individuals but also with the whole community of Israel. God is at once the public God of the People Israel and also the God of persons, of Abraham and of Isaac and of Jacob, as we recite in every religious service. The French Catholic philosopher Blaise Pascal, one of the keenest minds of the seventeenth century, had this phrase sewn into his coat lining—"I believe in the God of Abram, Isaac, and Jacob, not of the philosophers nor of the wise"—because it reflected his closest personal belief in a personal God and because he wanted to guarantee that it went wherever he went.

"REST IN PEACE" AND "MAY HIS MEMORY BE A BLESSING"

The literature of the Jews generally uses two phrases interchangeably after mentioning the name of a deceased: *"Alav ha'shalom"* (May he rest in peace) and *"Zikhrono li'vrakhah* (May his memory be for a blessing). Yet there is a fine distinction, not traditionally emphasized, between the two. *Alav ha'shalom* focuses exclusively on the deceased: "May this one *rest in peace." Zikhrono li'vrakhah*, on the other hand, means "May this one's *memory be for a blessing*," focusing on the effect that the deceased had on all who remember him.

Yes, we surely want our departed loved ones to rest in peace. But since the overwhelming majority of those who die are good people, their families feel assured that they will achieve this eternal test. Indeed, the Rabbis, using the mystical computations of the Midrash, hold that all who die will ultimately find that rest after the first year of posthumous judgment. But we who survive them, we who struggle with earthly temptations and desires and who may not be the souls of perfection, are not convinced that we will find such peace in our own lives. That is why we ask for the blessing of those who have gone to their eternal rest.

When I think of my own father and mother, I realize what a source of blessing they have been for me and my children. Their memory evokes thoughts of kindness, honesty, and faith. I do not have the slightest doubt that they have found rest and peace.

We are encouraged by the memory of the departed—blessed, not weakened or disabled by it. We ask ourselves: Does the memory of the deceased have this effect on me? Does it make me a better man or woman than I would otherwise have been? Does the image of his approving smile stimulate my courage to do right? Does the pressure of her invisible hands guide me in a better way? If the answers are positive, the loved one's memory will remain among us for a blessing. *Zikhronam li'vrakhah*.

GOD GAVE AND GOD TOOK BACK

The verse "God gave and God took back" (Job 1:21) is the central prayer that mourners recite after the burial. It affirms God's justice and assures us that this death was not merely a random catastrophe, not just happenstance, but an intentional, specific decision of the Almighty, who blessed us by having given life to the deceased.

It implies that if we protest God's decision to take our loved one, we must also remember to thank God for having given us the opportunity to share with the person we have lost.

MAY WE MEET AT JOYOUS OCCASIONS

It is customary to say to one another at funerals: "May we meet next at a joyous occasion," colloquially referred to as *simchas* (Yiddish for "joyous times"). This wish expresses the insight that we should remember not only the tragedies for which we gather from afar but also the celebrations that have brought us together in joy. It underscores the value of togetherness—in all of life's highs and lows—the moments that relieve us of our essential loneliness.

MAY SHE BE A GOOD INTERCESSOR

Many people pray that the deceased, now spiritually closer to God, will serve as a righteous intercessor on behalf of the surviving family. Yet we must make a crucial distinction here between what is a fond hope and what amounts to utter blasphemy. To pray directly *to* the deceased— that she or he heal the sick or guide the wayward—borders on necromancy, which is strictly outlawed by the Bible (along with the sorcerers, soothsayers, and enchanters who practice it). The Jew prays directly to God alone. Inquiring directly of the dead is considered an abomination, as it was in ancient times.

Why, then, do some Jews speak of the deceased as being an intercessor? To understand how Judaism sanctions this belief, we need to differentiate between a hope and an invocation—between invoking the help of the deceased directly and articulating an urgent hope that the deceased, who knows our inner heart's desire, will petition God on our behalf.

It is said that the Apter Rabbi, before he died, told his followers that the great Rabbi of Berdichev—both of them affectionately called "lovers of Israel"—had announced that he, the Berdichever, once he arrived in heaven, would protest to God about the troubles constantly plaguing the Jews. But when he arrived there, he was so struck by the wonders and grandeur of the world to come (*olam ha-ba*) that he completely forgot his mission. But the Apter vowed that he would not let the glories of the next world deter him from his mission, insisting that God lessen the sufferings of his people.

The hope that we express in asking departed loved ones to intervene on our behalf is very natural and truly harmless. It certainly reflects no corrupt theology or the influence of any ball-gazing charlatans. Indeed, we Jews do believe that we can maintain an abiding spiritual relationship with the deceased. As long as we understand this connection spiritually, then "consulting" or "informing" the deceased about a wedding or other celebration in the family or about an impending crisis may prove to be a formidable psychological comfort for mourners. Having a heart-to-heart talk with the departed may be the kind of conversation that mourners cannot engage in among the living. Of course, such communication should be resorted to only rarely; it should not be a regular routine.

THE MOST CONSOLING WORDS

Probably the most consoling words I have ever heard are these: "Tell me what your loved one was really like." The dialogue between mourners and consolers during shiva is not designed to distract the bereaved but to encourage the mourner to speak of the deceased—of his or her qualities, hopes, even foibles—and, of course, not to criticize the dead who cannot respond. Far from recalling the anguish of the loss, it gives those who are bereaved the opportunity to recall memories and to express their grief aloud. Psychologists assure us that mourners specifically want to speak of their loss. Eric Lindemann, in his classic paper "The Symptomatology and Management of Acute Grief," writes, "There is no retardation of action and speech; quite to the contrary, there is a push of speech, especially when talking of the deceased." Both the mourners' words and their tears should not be avoided or suppressed. For mourn-ers and for comforters, words truly make a difference. "Tell me what your loved one was really like" is a good beginning.

Problematic Farewells

When comforting a mourner, we often draw upon familiar expressions that we ourselves have heard others say in such situations. But unexplained, such expressions often convey messages that leave the mourner puzzled or upset. Be careful when using them.

WHAT THE MIND CANNOT DO, TIME WILL DO

When we have difficulty accepting a serious blow, we tend to cast our problem into the future and to take no action in the present. We rationalize this avoidance with gems of old wisdom: "What the mind cannot do, time will do"; "All in good time"; "Time will heal"; "Just give it time"; "Time heals all wounds." The trouble is that it doesn't. Time tends to cover up problems, not deal with them; to bury them, not make them disappear; to soothe over them, not solve them.

No doubt it is true that with the passage of time the piercing pain of grief will be blunted. But the future is little consolation to mourners. What the effects of time will be is only conjecture at present. Grief must be handled today. A promise that eventually everything will be all right is a therapeutic evasion practiced regularly when there is no immediate answer. But it is an empty promise.

Twentieth-century ethicist Rabbi Eliyahu Dessler said that grief will not just float away and consolation will not arrive spontaneously, given enough time. The days by themselves will not magically bring healing; only God can truly heal. *Ha'makom yenachem.*

GOD TOOK HIM BEFORE HE COULD SIN

The idea that a child taken by God is without sin is an ancient truth in the Jewish religion, since a person is considered sinless until he or she has attained the age of maturity (thirteen for a boy and twelve for a girl). Although such a teaching does not make the death of a child any easier to accept, it may somewhat lighten the mourner's suffering. Contrarily, it might be taken as a puny excuse for a child's death, or worse, as a justification that since the child did not sin, his or her death is not so bad. A visitor to the house of mourning must be sensitive to this and choose his or her words carefully.

Precisely such a concern is illustrated by a moving story of a talmudic sage:

When the son of the great Rabbi Yochanan ben Zakkai died, his disciples came to comfort him. Rabbi Eleazer said, "Adam, the first man, had a son who died, and he was consoled. You should also accept consolation." Rabbi Yochanan reprimanded him: "Not only do I have my personal suffering, but now you also wish to remind me of the first man's suffering."

Rabbi Yehoshua said, "Job had sons and daughters, and they all died. Yet he was consoled." "Not only do I have my personal suffering, but now you also wish to remind me of Job's suffering," said Rabbi Yochanan.

Rabbi Yossi entered and said, "Aaron had two great sons and they both died on the same day, and he was consoled. You also should accept consolation." Rabbi Yochanan said, "Not only do I have my personal suffering, but now you also wish to remind me of Aaron's suffering."

Rabbi Shimon entered and said, "David, the king, had a son who died and he was consoled, you also should accept consolation." And Rabbi Yochanan once again said, "Not only do I have my personal suffering, but now you wish to remind me of David's suffering."

Finally, Rabbi Eleazar ben Arach said: "I will give you an analogy to your situation. The king entrusted a precious object to one of his subjects. The subject became nerve-wracked and in a constant state of worry. 'When will I be able to return the object undamaged and unsoiled to the king?' My teacher, Rabbi Yochanan, you are in a similar situation. You had a son who was a Torah scholar and left this world without sin. Be consoled that you have returned in a perfect state that which the king has entrusted to you."

Rabbi Yochanan sighed: "Eleazar, my son, you have indeed properly consoled me."

Of course Rabbi Yochanan was a spiritual giant, and he undoubt-edly processed this spiritual consolation in the depths of his soul, and it was framed by his relationship with God. In fact, the Sage was con-soled by Rabbi Eleazar's words more than by any others. But we are not likely to meet such spiritual heroes in our communities, and the ques-tion that a comment such as "God took him before he could sin" might trigger is that if indeed the child is without sin, why did God see fit to take him or her at all? Even the thought of this question might cause the mourner more grief than consolation.

Some years ago, as I briefly mentioned earlier in passing, the four-year-old child of friends of ours in Palm Springs, in an unguarded mo-ment, walked into the family pool and drowned. My old friend Herman Wouk, the celebrated author, who delivered one of the eulogies, expe-rienced a similar tragedy with his own child at his home in the Virgin Islands many years before. In his eulogy he made this the essence of his remarks: "You are returning your child to God in a state of innocence." It proved comforting for the distraught parents, as indeed it must have proven so to the Wouks. Midrash refers to God's taking special care of children's souls, and in contemporary times, the renowned rabbi Ezekiel Bennet willed that he be buried only among the infant dead.

There is an additional spiritual benefit that derives from this idea of returning to God in innocence. Faithful Jews lay great emphasis on purity, especially at the end of life. The body of the deceased is very carefully ritually cleansed with water in a ceremony called *Taharah*, which means purification. The shrouds in which he or she is dressed are simple and white. The *Vidui* confessional prayer that should be recited before the onset of death is designed to purify the person's soul so that he or she appears before God guiltless. Returning to God after death in innocence, therefore, holds a very high place in the spiritual life of the believing Jew.

This emphasis on purity offers the mourner a comforting image—a state of whiteness. What a contrast to the tangled intubations, infec-tious fluids, and the body odors of the infirm, or to the horrific sight of a person killed in a car accident. The image of cleanliness and tidiness befits our image of children in their nurseries and leaves the mourner with a feeling of orderliness and fragrance in place of the griminess of dying.

MAY YOU KNOW OF NO MORE TROUBLE

Offering mourners the encouraging hope that they should know no more trouble is not a particularly helpful pronouncement. Would that it were true! Mourners as well as consolers know that such promises can not be realistically fulfilled. There will always be some form of pain; no one will be completely free of trouble in the future. There is absolutely no use denying it, even as an ecstatic hope; it is an impossible wish. Suffering is the universal balance of joy, as the night is of the day. Expressing such a hope tends to make all condolences sound like throwaway poppycock, and not serious, carefully considered wishes.

We find a similar-sounding plea for the impossible in the fervent prayer, traditionally recited at burial: "May God banish death forever." Do we believe that death will one day vanish from the world? Will death ever be conquered? The spiritual response to the prayer is: "Yes, by God, in some distant future." And if God can conquer death, can God also not obliterate trouble?

Unfortunately, this line of reasoning is a bit specious. This prayer, calling on God to vanquish death, is not meant to be a goody-goody, implausible supplication by frantic tell-me-anything mourners. It expresses a real hope that we can increase the human life span so dramatically that the thought of imminent death will seldom intrude upon our minds. Yet despite today's extraordinary medical advances, it remains completely unthinkable that we could wipe out something as endemic as trouble. Indeed, suffering is indigenous to the human condition, no matter how short or long a human life may be.

There is, nevertheless, a way to make the phrase "May you know no more trouble" usable. When extending this condolence, we can say instead: "May you know no more troubles of this kind" or "this severe" or "for many years" or "before you celebrate many more *simchas*."

Parables: Spiritual Wisdom from Everyday Life Episodes

In the very fabric of the Jewish tradition, we can find consolation, in the assumptions and expressions implied in legends, parables, and customs. At the seams connecting all our experiences, parables seep into our lives from every source—Sages of Talmud, Hasidic masters, literary giants, rabbis, mystics, and poets—to focus light on the predicament of the soul's pain in mourning.

WHEN SHIP LEAVES PORT

The saintly twentieth-century Rabbi Aryeh Levin applied this thinking to being born and dying. When a child is born, everyone is rapturous with joy, but the child itself cries. When someone dies and the spirit leaves the world, everyone grieves, but the spirit itself rejoices, because it has gone from a world of darkness to a world of light. The voyage of our deceased is completed and the soul's ship returns to a safe harbor. A parable:

Two ships cross in the harbor. One is just leaving port; the other is returning. All rejoice to send off the ship that is departing; the returning ship doesn't stir any rejoicing. A wise man thinks: It should be just the opposite. There should be no rejoicing over the ship that departs the port, for no one yet knows how it will fare. How many rough seas will it encounter? How many accidents may occur? But everyone should rejoice over the one that is returning to harbor, because we see that it has returned in peace from the perilous voyage.

LORD OF THE CASTLE

Rabbi Menachem Mendel of Kotzk once shared with his followers a parable he found in Midrash:

A man passed by a castle and, seeing it ablaze with no one putting out the fire, he thought that this must be a castle without an owner. That is, until the lord of the castle looked down at him and said, "I am the lord of the castle." When Rabbi Mendel said the words, "I am the lord of the castle," all those gathered around him were struck with awe. Mysteriously, the listeners deduced that the "castle earth" is burning, for the earth is the Lord's handiwork.

———

To mourners, it may seem as if the earth were on fire and that it had no ruler or that God were hidden and not putting out the flames. But mourners must know that even tragedy is overseen by God, the eternal Master.

A BROKEN HEART

These thoughts, derived from the words of the Rabbi of Kotzk, deserve to be pondered:

1. Nothing is so straight as a crooked ladder.
2. Nothing is so crooked as "straight" advice.
3. Nothing is so whole as a broken heart.
4. Nothing screams like silence.

Think about the following interpretations of the Kotzker's enigmas and reflect on how they pertain to your life and death:

1. All ladders that enable us to climb higher can be used only if they are slanted. Life is not always upright; it curves and twists unexpectedly, often it appears random. But God has built this system into life: The ladder is tilted and we can continue to climb. *Nothing is so straight as a crooked ladder.*
2. The important events in our lives are complex; the problems we face are complicated. We cannot solve the important dilemmas of life by simplistic, straightforward notions; such clichés deceive us and in the end may make matters worse. A death of someone we love is a rupture, an uneven tear, that often trig-

gers deep melancholy. Grief is not a sickness that a linear solution will cure; it is a tragedy that most often will gradually disentangle and find a natural resolution. *Nothing is so crooked as straight advice.*

3. When beset by tragic experiences, we conclude that we will forever be wounded, that our wholeness has been shattered and will never again be recoverable. This is the philosophy of those who cynically assure us that from the day we were born, we are only one day closer to death. But the "whole" of life, like the whole of every day, is made up of light as well as of darkness. Those who can sense the tragic will sense the true scope of living. *Nothing is so whole as a broken heart.*

4. We identify quiet with peace and equanimity; loudness with action, pain, and quarrel. We assume that people who are in pain shout with anger and that those who are silent have solved their problems and accept their situations—that they need not care or simply do not care enough to suffer. But silence is a cloak under which we seek warmth and protection; inside the folds of that cloak may hide immense sorrow and profound hurt that strains to be discovered. *Nothing screams like silence.*

WORKING ONLY UNTIL NOON

The Jerusalem Talmud recounts how Rabbi Bun was eulogized by Rabbi Zeira in a parable:

The king employed day workers for his vineyard. One very good worker took sick at midday and had to stop working. At the end of the day, the king paid all the workers equally. But the majority of the grape pickers complained: Why should the worker who took ill receive a full day's pay, since he worked only part of the day? The king explained, This person did as much in half a day as you did in a full day.

In the vineyard of the King of Kings, Rabbi Bun explained, some workers are tragically cut off while the day is young. But they receive a full reward, since the work they have done, their interest, sincerity, or sweetness, has enabled them to gather all the grapes of life in a fraction of the time it takes the rest of us. Yes, we wish they could have stayed all day; we cannot change that decision. But the King of Kings can be trusted to compensate them as though they had produced a full bounty of good accomplishments.

WHAT HIT ME?

I was once told this story about the eighteenth-century *tzaddik* Rabbi Hayyim of Sanz. He returned from the funeral of his seven-year-old son early in the morning, even before the first morning services began. After the prayers, he stood at his lectern and said to the congregation:

A man was walking peacefully down the street when suddenly he was struck by a hard smack on his shoulders. He whirled around angrily to see who had hit him and was astonished and relieved to find that it was his close friend, who had slapped him in friendship at meeting him after a very long absence.

Rabbi Hayyim explained: This morning, a powerful blow shocked me and shook my whole being. I was enraged. Then I realized who it was who had struck me. It was my beloved and almighty God who hit me. The blow hurt and my soul trembled with anguish. But now I accept this blow with love—my friend, God, did it in love.

———

In every generation, some Jews have been spiritual heroes, in that they regard their pain as "*yissurim shel ahavah*" (agonies of love). In other words, they consider their pain as deriving from the tough love by which the Almighty teaches the world. Even though they cannot divine the lesson, they attribute it to a loving God.

PEBBLES

When Victer Hugo, the great author of *Les Misérables*, was persecuted by the France he loved, he lived heartbroken in forced exile on the island of Guernsey in 1851. He climbed a cliff overlooking the harbor at sunset, chose a pebble, and stood, lost in deep meditation, before throwing it into the water. He seemed to derive great satisfaction in performing this strange ritual each and every evening. Some children watched him throwing the pebbles into the water. One of them grew bold enough to ask why he was doing this. Hugo smiled wryly, was silent a moment, and then, legend has it, he said, "Not stones, my child; I am throwing self-pity into the sea." Throwing the pebble helped him separate the facts of his situation from his own self-pity.

———

Traditional Jews have a custom called *tashlikh* (sending), when they throw pieces of bread onto bodies of water. Symbolically, they are throwing their sins into the sea. The sin of self-pity is among the most destructive pathologies of bereavement. Even modern behaviorists often recommend such symbolic gestures for helping us overcome hardships and negative thoughts.

A HAND CLASP

Mark Twain once told this parable:

Two children were overheard talking about the death of their grandmother. The five-year-old girl asked her seven-year-old brother how grandmother went up to God. "Well," said the boy, "it happened this way: First grandmother reached up and up and up as far as she could; then God reached down and down and down. When their hands touched, God took her."

———

TRUSTING FATHER

In reference to mourning, the Bible cautions the distraught griever: "You are children of the Lord your God. You shall not gash yourselves or shave the front of your heads because of the dead" (Deut. 14:1). The medieval Spanish commentator Ibn Ezra elaborated:

> Once you realize you are children of the Almighty and that God loves you even more than a mortal father loves his children, you will not grieve excessively over whatever He does to you. Whatever He does ultimately is for your good. At times you might not understand His ways, just as a young child does not always understand why his father does certain things. Nevertheless, a child trusts his father. You are also a child of God; you should trust the Almighty.

Coming Toward Me
I sought Your nearness,
With all my heart have I called You,
And, going out to meet You
I found You coming toward me.
                                        —Yehuda Halevi

ONE DOOR CLOSES, ANOTHER OPENS

The founder of Hasidism, Rabbi Israel Baal Shem, was supposed to have said that he had no particular fear of death because when one door closes, another opens. A new world appears, higher, more spiritual, and more satisfying. The inventor Alexander Graham Bell said: It is true that when one door closes another opens. But we are so obsessed by the closing door that we don't even notice the door that is standing open.

COMING HOME FROM BUSINESS

It is said that Rabbi Hayim Ben Attar, whose Bible commentary influenced early Hasidic thought, believed that a dying person does not simply disappear into oblivion. I was once told the following parable, which refers to this belief:

A father sent his son on a business venture to another city. After allowing his son a certain amount of time to make some profit, the father sent a message for his son to return home. When the son returned to his father, his life continued in that place. The son's existence did not end because he left the city. He merely moved from one location to another. Moreover, when he returned to his father, he was back home, and that was the best place for him to be.

BEING A WITNESS

Just as there must be witnesses at the signing of a legal will, so should there be witnesses that testify to a spiritual legacy. Elie Wiesel, the writer, has often urged anyone who lived through the Holocaust to feel duty-bound to bear witness to it. So, too, individuals need testimony to their personal experiences—the travails, the heroism, the great loss, the iron will—that mark him or her as a person of value. People need a relative or acquaintance capable of testifying at some time in the future after they are gone that they and their unique qualities are missed. It is more important than an investment; it is a legacy.

A SEED

A legend tells us one way to find joy even when we are mourning:

A sorrowing woman approached a great sage with the plea that he bring back to life her only son, who had just died. The sage told her that he could indeed comply with her request on one condition: She must bring him a mustard seed taken from a home that was entirely free of sadness.

The woman set out to accomplish what appeared to be a relatively simple task. But years elapsed and she didn't return. One day the sage accidentally ran into the woman but hardly recognized her, she looked so radiant. He asked her why she had never returned to him.

"Oh," she said, in a voice indicating that she had completely forgotten about his charge to her, "this is what happened: I went in search of the seed, as you asked. But I went into homes so burdened with trouble and sorrow that I could not just walk out. Who better than I could understand how heavy was the burden these people were bearing? Who better than I could offer them the support they needed? So I stayed in each home as long as I could be of service. Please don't be angry with me. But the simple truth is that I never again thought about returning."

––––––––––

There is no home that has escaped grief, no person who has avoided pain, no society that has evaded suffering. We are all connected by threads of sadness. Fortunately, we may find joy in sharing our burdens.

THE QUIET ONES

Psalm 19 describes the stillness of heaven: "There is no utterance, there are no words" (*Ein omer, ve'ein devarim, beli nishma kolam;* v. 4). In a sky filled with Big Bangs, crashing comets, and bursting stars, the Psalmist sees the sun and moon, our sources of day and night, as silent luminaries. So, too, there are refined people living in raucous surroundings who are islands of reserved, discreet, and nonverbal existence. Not by their decibels shall you judge them, but by their decency.

The Psalmist then completes the metaphor of the quiet ones: "Their voice carries throughout the earth, and their [unspoken] words to the end of the world" (v. 5). The quiet ones communicate not with shouts but with bright rays that shine upon others.

Rabbi Issac Luria, the great kabbalist, holds that at birth people are allotted not a number of years, but a number of words, emphasizing the quality, not quantity, that is paramount in their lives. This notion accounts for the many who have had great impact on others, even though their lives were short. Their rays of kindness silently illuminated many generations, their rays spread to the invisible ends of the world.

PRISONERS OF HOPE

The prophet Zechariah said: "Return to Bizzaron, you prisoners of hope. In return [I] announce this day: I will repay you double" (9:12). Targum, the Aramaic translation, renders "prisoners of hope" as "ye captives who have all hoped for deliverances."

One cannot compare the suffering of different people; each is unique. Picture the waiting room in two dental offices. In one, there are two patients experiencing pain; in the other, only one is in pain. Can you say the first room contains more pain? Just so, you cannot compare the effect of a death in one family with that of another. We should not compare one tragedy with another; each suffering is unique, indescribable, and exceptional. We also cannot console mourners by spinning competing war stories of death or grief, or by reminding them that some other person had it worse. Since nobody's suffering qualitatively is the same as anybody else's, comparing personal tragedies at such a time is futile and also insulting. Likewise, the quality and shape of each sufferer's ultimate hope. What is common is the desire to become whole and strong again, because all captives of suffering are like prisoners waiting for the return to their stronghold, Bizzaron.

Portraits: A Gallery of Unforgettable Paintings

The Jewish classics include many texts of profound consolation. These do not appear in the form of specific lessons directed at consoling mourners. Rather, they are stories, teachings, attitudes, and insights that are conveyed subliminally—almost as undertones or postscripts of a specific incident or a phrase describing one of the heroes of Torah.

Not only do we learn from the thoughts that are inside the folds of written texts; we learn also from the text of life itself—how it is lived and how it is ended. Judaism is a vibrant, rich tradition that has spawned a host of scholars and saints and leading thinkers in every generation. How did these exceptional people console each other? In this library of libraries, the shared text of life, we find a broad assortment of insights and perceptions, homilies, parables and anecdotes, and bold scriptural interpretations. Some may not apply to the specific circumstances of an individual's mourning but others will. I, therefore, paint a broad picture, with a variety of landscapes.

MEASURING A PALM TREE

"The righteous bloom like a date-palm" (*Tzaddik ka'tamar yifrach*; Ps. 92:13). The Psalmist uses a palm tree as a simile for an upright, firm, and morally erect person. Characteristically, a palm tree has no lower branches and grows tall, erect, and proud. It soon towers above every nearby plant. But its growth is only at the top. How do you measure that palm tree accurately? The Sages said: after it is cut down.

Like the palm, there are people who have high standards and who reach exalted goals in personhood, family, business, profession, and ethics, becoming exceptional, even saintly, in the process. In Judaism, you don't have to be an angel to be a saint. Our lives are measured accurately but, too often, after we have been cut down.

Carl Sandburg titled the last chapter of his biography of Abraham Lincoln "Measuring the Tree When It Is Down." This phrase has been widely repeated in articles, sermons, and obituaries for a hundred years because it touched a sensitive but very human weakness: our tendency to cherish people only after they are cut down. During the rush of life, when people are near us and standing tall, we rarely realize their stature. They become singularly important after they fall; and when they are gone, we are startled. "Why did I never realize how impressive she or he was?"

Whether we size people up during their lives or not, we instinctively do so when they die. This is why it is proper for comforters to speak of the deceased when they console a mourner. People deserve to be honored by becoming a subject of analysis by their own family and friends. Most often, we better appreciate a person at this final moment. We learn from a person's strengths and even from his or her foibles. Then, though the tree is fallen, the memory is of a majestic presence. A saint grows like a palm tree.

CANDLE ON A GRAVESTONE

There is beautiful legend told about one of the greatest medieval mystics and scholars, Nachmanides, known in tradition as Ramban. He decided to make his way to the Holy Land when he was exiled from Spain, where he had been one of the most illustrious men of his generation. As he was leaving, he told his many worried disciples that when a lamp appeared on his mother's tombstone, it would be a sign that he had died. One implication of this legend, as I see it, is that our deceased parents and relatives still care for us beyond their deaths. The mystical vision—Mother always knows!

A GOOD-BYE KISS

The Book of Genesis (2:7) records that God "formed man from the dust of the earth. He blew into his nostrils the breath of life, and the man became a living being." At the death of Moses, Miriam, Aaron, and others throughout the ages, God is said to have drawn out their last breath with a kiss. At our birth, God exhales breath into our nostrils; at our death, God inhales our last breath with a kiss.

The Rabbis spoke profoundly about the surprising lack of pain we feel when death finally comes, because the reward of dying may be a divine kiss:

Rava, while seated at the bedside of Rabbi Nachman, saw him sinking into the eternal slumber of death. Rabbi Nachman said to Rava: "Sir, tell [the angel of death] not to torment me."

Said Rava: "Sir, are you not also an esteemed man?"

Said Rabbi Nachman to him, "Who is esteemed, who is highly regarded, who is distinguished [before the Angel of Death]?"

Said Rava to him: "Sir, do appear to me in a dream."

Later, Rabbi Nachman showed himself to Rava in a dream. Rava asked him: "Did you suffer pain, Sir?"

He replied: "As [little as] the taking of a hair from a cup of milk; and were the Holy One, the Blessed, to say to me: 'Go back to that world as you were,' I would not wish it, for the fear of death is great."

A PAINTING AT DUSK

It is said that John Ruskin, a nineteenth-century author and art critic, observed that you can tell the genius of a painting only at the end of the day. It is when the little details are blurred in the dusk that you can see the grand design of the painter. This is a metaphor for being human; the grand design of a human personality is best visible at life's end. The details of life fade in the dusk; what remains is the impression of a whole person.

THE RAVEN AND THE SPARROW

The noted naturalist Loren Eiseley once described an episode most of us are never likely to see. He was in a little forest at the edge of a grass glade. He sat down with his back against a tree stump, gazing into the long sunlit glade, and fell asleep. Suddenly, he was startled by a commotion of screaming birds circling a tree.

On a protruding branch of a tall tree in the meadow sat an enormous raven, ominous and autocratic in its blackness, and in its beak was a tiny red nestling, squirming to be free. The horrified flock fluttered frantically in circles around the large bird. The raven gulped, perched, immovable and indifferent. Suddenly, from the whole field, there flocked hundreds of small birds of a dozen varieties, drawn by the cries of the helpless parents. They wailed in common despair. But the murderer, the black bird, sat satiated and unperturbed.

Then the naturalist saw the wondrous judgment of life against death. In the thick of this frantic grief, the crying abruptly faded into the sky. He listened, and a thin sweet sound touched his ears. He could hear the crystal note of a lone sparrow singing in the hush. Another bird picked up the song, as though on cue. Then another and another, until all the birds began to sing the sparrow's song—still in the brooding shadow of the raven. Because life is sweet, and sunlight is beautiful.

"In simple truth, they had forgotten the raven, for they were the singers of life, and not of death." The raven took life; the sparrow lifted life above death.

A NARROW BRIDGE

The thirteenth-century Provençal poet, physician, and philosopher Yedayah ha-Bedersi, in his *Bechinat Olam* (The Examination of the World), wrote an unforgettable parable:

The world is a tempestuous sea of immense depth and breadth, and time is a frail bridge built over it. The beginning of the bridge is fastened with the cords of chaos that preceded existence; the end is rooted in eternal bliss and illuminated with the light of the King's countenance. The width of the bridge is but one cubit and it lacks guardrails. And thou, son of man, against thy will thou art living, and continually traveling over it, since the day thou hast become a man.

———

The great Hasidic rebbe Rabbi Nachman of Bratzlav, responded to that vulnerability—to the fact that, when confronted by powerful forces, we become afraid to live, always seeing ourselves falling into chaos. Rabbi Nachman sang of it and encouraged his people: *Kol ha'olam kulo—gesher tzar me'od—ve'ha'ikar—lo le'fached klal* (The whole world is a narrow bridge. But most important: Don't be afraid). He speaks not of specific fear, but of the imagination of disaster; the fear that, because we are vulnerable before God, terrible things will happen to us. That is also the sense of the phrase said at the end of all our daily prayer services: Do not walk in fear that something terrifying will strike you suddenly—*pitom*—from nowhere.

In our meandering through life, we, the small creatures with the massive brains who can grasp both heaven and earth, who stand in the center of enormities—we must cross bravely on that narrow, rickety bridge without rails. Not by coincidence is the word for pain "*tzarah*"—literally, "narrows." Tragedy does happen, but life goes on. Do not be afraid and you will go from the narrow to the broad spaces; from a fear of death to a full life.

THE SHADOW

What could be more transitory?

> Man comes from dust and ends in dust. ... He is like the potsherd that breaks, the grass that withers, the flower that fades, the shadow that passes, the cloud that vanishes, the breeze that blows, the dust that floats, the dream that flies away.

> For we are sojourners with You, mere transients like our fathers;

our days on earth are like a shadow, with nothing in prospect
(1 Chron. 29:15).

We are not like the shadow of a wall or tree. We are like the
shadow of a bird in flight.

If sometimes we feel invisible or illusory, like a passing shadow, we
should be more like the shadow of a wall or a tree, not that of a bird.
A stationary shadow is not quite so ephemeral—although it is only a
blip on the historical stage. Passing shadows give shade and protection
if only for an infinitesimal moment, a fraction of nothing. Fleeting shadows are illusory, without substance and without remembrance.

We learn about life's transitory nature from the name of Bezalel, the
biblical architect of the desert tabernacle. His name is a contraction of
two words—"be'tzel" (in the shadow) and "El" (God). Bezalel performed
art in the shadow of God. Some people we mourn may have lived like
birds in flight. In human terms, on this earth, in our lifetimes, their
fleeting shadows may have achieved permanence, serving as a cool,
refreshing interlude in the heat of our quotidian struggles. Even in mi-
nuscule ways, they may well have changed the way we live and, through
us, changed the lives of our children, too. In that sense, they were not
shadows of birds in flight, nor that of walls that may collapse, nor of
trees that might be struck by lightning. Their shadow dwells yet in
places unimaginable.

Influence
This learned I from the shadow of a tree,
Which, to and fro, did sway against a wall
Our shadow-selves, our influence, may fall
Where we can never be.

—E. Hamilton

THE DANCE

Rabbi Nachman of Bratzlav was a master of sorrows. No man was more aware of suffering in his generation than he. Suffering, he said, was of three kinds: physical suffering, psychic suffering, and, above all, spiritual suffering. Everyone, he noted, is full of torment, but the law of life is that people must strive with all their power always to be full of joy. This is no mean task, as we can see in this parable:

Hasidim are dancing in a circle, high-spirited, energetic, fervent—they smile as they dance. They notice a man who is standing outside the circle, glum and sorrowful. Against his will, they draw him into the circle of dancers. Soon he gets caught up in the dance and he, too, begins to smile. They have forced him, against his will, to rejoice with them.

———

When we succeed in coaxing a person drowned in sorrow into our circle of happiness, the recalcitrant person is moved to rejoice despite his suffering—he is caught up in a *dance of joy*. This parable says that it is not enough to command a mourner to smile, because a smile does not always translate into joy. Rather, we need to draw the bereaved into the dance of life so that he can sublimate his suffering by accepting the irretrievable and searching for a transcendent meaning and grow from it.

We can distill from this parable yet another lesson, says Rabbi Nachman: Rejoicing, when it leaves melancholy at the periphery, raises the mournful person, but to only a low spiritual level. The mourner attains a higher level when he draws melancholy itself into the dance and allows sorrow to turn itself to joy.

THE FOX AND THE VINEYARD

Another familiar parable teaches us about the vanity of life:

A fox searches for a way to get into a tempting vineyard, where luscious grapes are waiting to be plucked, but a hole in the fence is much too small for it to squeeze through. The fox decides to lose weight in order to get to the other side of the fence. It fasts for days until it is able to squeeze through the hole. When finally it succeeds, it eats the grapes ravenously without stopping, ecstatic with its good fortune, and grows plump. Then the fox waddles back to the fence and recalls the grand and glorious world outside. Struck by wanderlust, it hunts for a way to return to that world. Yes, it's back to the old hole once more—but, of course, the fox can't squeeze through. So it fasts once again and succeeds once again. By becoming skin and bones like its old self, the fox finally forces its way out.

So, too, like the fox, we enter the world with hands clutching nothing, and we extricate ourselves from this vale of tears with palms open, taking nothing with us. In the vineyard of our lives, we romp and feast—but in the end, we learn that shrouds have no pockets. What golden goods can we take with us down into the grave?

Yet in the bountiful garden of our lives, we may also grow to become decent, good people, sometimes even achieving exalted goals. The beauty, the love, the faith, and the kindness we generate in this life are exactly what we will carry away with us when we depart this world for the world to come. How we spend our years in the midst of the tempting garden of life depends on the middle letters of the word "life"—"if." *If* we can grow in decency and kindness in the midst of this world, we are worthier and wiser than that wily old fox.

THE HALO OF INK

Midrash teaches that Moses' head was framed by a halo, but he didn't realize it. Where did this halo come from? Rabbi Yeshu'a, son of Nachman, said: "As Moses was writing the Torah, God realized that a drop of ink would remain after the manuscript was completed. So God took the leftover ink and circled it around Moses' head and created for him a halo. As it says: 'And Moses did not know that rays of light shone on his face.' "

A great nineteenth-century Hungarian rabbi and scholar, Moses Sofer (called "Chatam Sofer"), derived a scintillating insight from this story: All good people are given enough ink to script their entire lives. Special people are granted a bit more ink than they need. With that gift, God creates a halo for them. And they are not even aware of it!

Pearls: Meditations from the Deep

It is of no value to transmit thoughts and words if there is no one at the other end to receive them. The following meditations are pearls only if they are accepted and digested. Mourners should accept, or at least listen to, the consoling words that others provide.

SWEETNESS FROM STRENGTH

After Samson left home, walking on a dangerous road to Philistia, a lion suddenly pounced on him. He fought courageously and killed it with the superhuman strength of his bare hands. On his return, he found the dead lion—but he was struck by what he saw: In the lion's carcass was a hive of bees making honey, "*Adat devorim bi'geviyat ha'aryeh u'devash.*" It stuck in his mind, and later he posed it as a riddle to the Philistines: "Out of the strong came something sweet" (*u'me'az yatza matok*; Judg. 14:14).

The insight he drew from that scene—sweet honey being produced by busy bees inside the carcass of the dead lion—is penetrating. The English scholar Walter Pater began his great book on the Renaissance with these words, translated into Latin from the Hebrew scripture: "*ex forti dulcedo*" (from strength comes sweetness). Pater was saying that from the enormously powerful thinkers of the age came the sweetness of the Renaissance. I have these words embroidered in silver on the *atarah* (collar adornment) of my tallit as the bywords of my life's goal: From strength comes forth sweetness.

When people who have exceptional strength of character die, we tend to think that a whole era has ended. But their legendary strength may have enabled them to produce rare sweetness, their remains bringing forth honey. Kindness, love, and caring very often do not come from softness but from strength, not from spongy adaptation but from steely determination.

I remember as a young man when my grandfather, a renowned

scholar and family patriarch, died; the family thought that without him everything would fall apart: his values would evaporate, his emphasis on Torah would be lost, and the family might even drift apart. But we underestimated the wisdom contained in Samson's remarkable riddle. Although the lion had died, the honey still flowed on.

HOLD ON AND LET GO

Judaism charges us with a strange task: We are to hold on strenuously to certain things in life and let go of others with equal determination. Danish philosopher and theologian Sören Kierkegaard once made the point that by letting go you lose your foothold temporarily, but by not letting go at all you can lose your foothold forever.

We learn to hold on to our children and give them unquestioned love. Family ties need strong glue to stay together. But there does come a time when, for the children's sake, we must let go, else mother love turns to smother love. The biblical tale of Abraham as father is paradigmatic. Abraham and Sarah raised Isaac with incredible care. The Sages said of Abraham: He did nothing but for his son Isaac (*Klum asah ela bishvil Yitzchak beno*). Father and son had a deep bond. Then God instructed Abraham to take Isaac to Mount Moriah and there sacrifice him. Abraham, the paragon of faith, opened his arms and full-heartedly prepared to let go.

In our own life dramas, we hold on tenaciously to the precious gifts of life, faith, and health. But we know there are many aspects of life that we must learn to let go of with free will and without remorse, such as the sharpness of our senses and resilience and energy as we age. There are those who cannot grow old gracefully because they cling too tightly to youth, cannot let go of their self-centeredness, cannot separate their minds from their egos, and are narcissistic until the day they die. We cannot live fully if we cannot learn to relinquish. This is the nature of things. Many of our qualities are given on a time-limited basis. Only if we learn to accept this situation can we achieve tranquility.

The most imposing and demanding "let go" in life is life itself. The most trying "hold on" in life is of a life that is listing and beginning to sink. More mysterious, if we are to survive the human losses that we all must suffer, these conflicting forces of holding on and letting go must be exercised at one and the same time. This is both imperative and virtually impossible. On the one hand, we must make our peace with inevitability, and on the other, we must hold on to all we hold most dear.

The Rabbis, despite their love of life, said, "He who would die, let him hold on to life." But they also noted, "One cannot hold on to life unless he is ready to die."

The stunning, paradoxical truth of human existence is that we must not hold life too precious. We need to be ready to sacrifice it! This strange law is written into the scheme of things: We must hold our existence dear and cheap at the very same time.

Of course, the tug of war between these two impulses triggers a terrible tension. How can we be expected to do both at the same time? The only valid answer we can give is—God! God is a third force that resolves the terrible contradiction—God gives life and God takes life. That is why at a family member's death, Jews recite the blessing, *barukh Dayan Ha-Emet* (Blessed is the True Judge). And then we say: "The Eternal has given and the Eternal has taken back." The two—hold on and let go—are logically irreconcilable. They are resolved only in the spiritual realm.

Rabbi Samson Raphael Hirsch noted that the Sages instructed us not to chain ourselves to anything we have, however noble, so long as it is transient. If we do, when someone passes on we decline with that person and thereby cast ourselves into the grave with the one who has passed away. It is wiser to be ready at every moment to return a loved one to the source. Life is dear, hold it tight; but also hold it loosely. Embrace life with open arms!

LIFE IS A BOOK

The Scripture-intoxicated Rabbis compared major qualities of our lives to one or another of the books of Jewish literature. The Torah sculpted the

Jewish soul, and the folk embraced the Torah, kissed it, and used it to characterize and depict an individual's lifestyle and *Weltanschauung*. Rabbi Tzadok Ha'cohen wrote this profound insight: The whole world is a book written by God, and the Torah is the commentary which He wrote on that book. The Rabbis used the titles of many books—of Torah and Talmud and their vast traditions—as chapter headings for their own lives. Life, like a text, holds mysteries that require commentary and commentary upon commentary, as surely as does Torah itself. For example:

The Book of Lamentations (*Eikhah*) is a metaphor for people's suffering—in illness, in raising children, in frustration when the goals of life evaporate before our eyes, in the loss of losing a loved one.

The Song of Songs (*Shir Ha'Shirim*) symbolizes the extraordinary courage and fortitude that people display when, despite a load of burdens, they manage to find hope and give love, to squeeze harmony from the maelstrom of chaos, to transform dirges into song, and to turn curses into a cornucopia of blessings.

The Book of Righteousness (*Sefer Ha'Yashar*) is a metaphor of our struggle for excellence, for being honest in the best religious tradition, and for standing erect in a profusion of schemers.

Which book best characterizes the dominant qualities of our departed relative? The title of the book becomes the inscription on the slate of your memory.

THE MERIT OF THE CHILDREN

We think of a parent as not only endowing a child with life itself but also with teaching the child the values of honor, decency, and a love of life. Rabbi Akiva added to these endowments looks, longevity, wealth, health, and a lineage of ancestors. If children receive well, they give their parents pleasure in return. They can bestow honor, merit, and credit on their mother and father. The Talmud refers to this as *bera mezakeh abba* (a child casts merit onto a parent).

This is one reason for a child's reciting *Kaddish* for a deceased parent. When reciting the *Kaddish* prayer, the child stops at the end of every sentence and the congregation responds by saying, "Amen." By reciting a prayer which elicits a communal religious response, the child becomes a catalyst for elevating others—whose "amens" are a spiritual affirmation of God. The child's deeds are witness to the majesty of God, who could create a society in which such a parent and such a child could exist and experience reciprocal tenderness and love.

THE WALLS HAVE FALLEN

At the death of a parent or grandparent or other leading family members, it feels as if the walls have collapsed and the house is teetering precariously at the edge of collapse. In a reference to someone having a nightmare of such a death, the Talmud makes a radical exception: Although on the Sabbath a Jew must be joyous, eat well, and certainly not fast, a person who dreams that the walls of his or her house have crumbled (*ha'ro'eh ba'chalomo korot beto she'naflu*) should fast, even though it is the Sabbath, as a fervent prayer to forefend against the disaster from actually happening. Horrific dreams are sometimes perceived as omens, and this Sabbath law acknowledges that human beings are only human after all.

If merely a dream is enough to provoke fear, what shall we say of reality? "Falling walls" can be interpreted as a metaphor for family catastrophe. Such a nightmare can be understood as referring to someone powerful and protective suddenly collapsing. Like a wall, that person had been strong and stable, enclosing and guarding us. When such a person passes away, it seems impossible to pick up the pieces. During such times, we implore a merciful God to sustain the household, to keep the family together, and to bring the tranquility of the Sabbath back into our home.

WATCHMAN, WHAT OF THE NIGHT?

"*Shomer, mah mi'lailah*" (Watchman, what of the night?). Answered the watchman, "*Atah boker, ve'gam lailah*" (Morning will come, as also the night came; Isa. 21:11–12). Isaiah asked: "Watchman, guardian, protector, how long will this night last?" The Watchman answered: "The morning must ultimately come, and it will chase away the shadows of the night, just as night sent morning away."

———

In the dark of night we tend to think dark thoughts. When we awaken during the night we see no sun in the sky—no fun, no future; only fear, fleeing, failing. The prophet assures us that the morning indeed will come. A rising sun will bring a new horizon, a different outlook, and mercifully renewed energy. We cannot truly assess this world by looking only at shadows. We need to discover the rays of brightness as well.

But Isaiah is enigmatic. He says not only that morning will come, but that night is equally inevitable. What he means is that comfort and consolation do not suddenly materialize by wishing that "may we meet only at happy occasions" or that "may we never know trouble." We will know trouble, unfortunately; there is simply no day without night. We define night by the absence of day, as we do day by the absence of night.

But this we learn: We can cope with night if we are confident that dawn will follow. And we will be prepared for the next night too (*ve' gam lailah*). Life is light and darkness (*boker ve' lailah*), love and lamentation, calm and confusion (*simchah* and *tza' ar*). It may not instantaneously transform sorrow into dancing, as the Psalmist implores God in Psalm 31. But it does empower us to hope for strength and sanity and to hope in anticipation of their arrival.

When I entered the military, as a chaplain after my ordination, my entire military class—twenty-six rabbis, priests, and ministers—sat silently in a lecture hall, hands folded at attention on the very first day of instruction. A colonel entered and turned to a large, blank white sheet on the wall. Without a word, he drew a black dot in the middle of it. "Look at this image for the next ten minutes until I return." Commanding this to graduate clergymen seemed to border on the absurd. But I never forgot his simple, graphic lesson. The officer came back and asked for a show of hands to describe what we saw. Every single one of us agreed that we saw a black dot. He said we were all wrong, and to look once more. Then he told us: We see not a black dot, but a black dot surrounded by a large white space.

For me, this was a valuable lesson. It becomes second nature to focus narrowly only on the black dots of life, ignoring the whole picture. In the nighttime of life, in the bottomless hours of our bereavement, we bemoan the tragedy; this event simply cannot be romanticized and turned into light. We look at the life that we mourn, and we see illness or missed opportunities or frustration or unrealized goals, and we are mystified at the utter futility of it all.

In our spiritual imaginings, we sense that God looks at the whole person. Only God can see both sides of the mountain at once—the road up and the road down. In God's divine perspective, the dark spots in a person's life may be infinitesimal; perhaps in God's-eye view the tiny dark may be a tunnel of light.

Generally, most people do not have a worldview that is wide enough. We need to be cautious when identifying life's experiences as either all good or all bad. Thus, from our human perspective, what happened to biblical Joseph—being sold into slavery, thrown into a pit, and sent to jail—might seem all bad. Jealousy and hatred are to be condemned. It is a vicious fate to be separated from an aged father and sold as a slave. But in the end, all of these events worked for the good, contrary to all expectations. As Joseph said to his brothers, "[al]though you intended me harm, God intended it for good" (Gen. 50:20). So, too, death is a night with all of its darkness, yet it is followed by a dawn.

If we stop the Joseph story at midpoint we see only defeat. But if we stretch all the way to the end, we sense a progressive fulfillment of God's purpose—no longer personal suffering but the saving of the entire family of Israel. It is analogous to looking at a mountain as only an obstacle to be climbed. But by experience, we know that we also get to go down on the other side, the hidden side we only picture but cannot see.

I knew a man of forty-five who never married; he was disheveled, never worked, lived on a meager inheritance. He was alone, like a cork on the sea, thrown hither and yon, without any apparent direction. I could imagine what endless sadness there must be in him. But he always smiled; and I always thought: "He's covering up." One day I noted that behind the smile he looked content. I persisted: If I were in his place I would be horribly depressed. He died young. At his funeral it occurred to me that I always saw a black dot behind his luminous smile. But he was the most contented underachiever I had ever met; he always saw the dominant white expanse of a good life. He, not I, saw the big picture. Who is to say there is no value in mere contentment?

In our conceit, we think we know people; we are certain of our appraisals. But can we ever fully enter another soul? Who knows what God sees when God looks into what we call darkness? And who knows what a person can see beyond that ubiquitous black dot?

A RUMOR OF ANGELS

There is a fascinating insight that maintains that we could prove the existence of God—not by scientific theories, nor by Scripture, nor by miracles—but by the existence of people who act selflessly, without being commanded to do so, without compensation, without fuss and fanfare. They become unremarkable, unassuming paragons of virtue. Jewish tradition calls this *kiddush ha'Shem*, the sanctification of God's name. People commonly call such individuals "angels." Spiritual-minded people call a story of such a simple yet incredible individual a "rumor of angels."

This fact by itself could testify to the existence of an all-wise God who created the world with a foundation of decency, *olam chessed yibaneh*. You don't have to be a saint to be an angel, but you do have to be a selfless, self-sacrificing person. If you are, you are testimony to the existence of a benevolent creator. Watch a mother caring for her sick child, kissing and hugging her, hovering over her bed all night, wishing she could be sick in place of her little girl. That is a rumor of angels. If a person can become an "angel," then a God of goodness must exist.

My Place Is with You

My place is with you, the world's humble,
the mute of soul, who spin their lives in secret,
modest in thoughts and in deeds,
the unknown dreamers, wanting in speech and gaining in splendor.
Your pleasing spirit is stored away within you like a pearl at the
    bottom of the sea,
and your distinction ripens, like berries in the woods, in a haven of
    shadow.
Your hearts—a holy sanctuary, your lips—its sealed gates,
you were not told that you are princes,
you do not know that you are the soul's swells.
Artists of the beautiful silences, ministers of the dumbness of God,
no stranger's eye will ever capture the rejoicing within you, or the
    mourning.
A single light is always in your eyes, a bright quiet glow,
a single smile is always on your lips, full of wisdom and
    forgiveness,
with which to reckon, but not to judge, all that befalls you:
the large things and the trifles, the just and the unjust together.
Gently, gently, as if on tiptoe, you move through life,
with a wakeful heart, and a heedful ear, and a ranging eye,
and a spirit that trembles with every rustle of beauty and every stir
    of magnificence,
you pass and, without exertion or intention, you scatter faith and
    purity around,
they drip from your being as azure trickles from the sky and shade
    from the flourishing forest.

Truly you are schooled in stillness, who stifle voices and words,
nothing grand will come from your mouths and nothing high from
    your hands,
your desires will expire in your hearts and your longings in your
    bosoms will cease,

you have no stake among the visionaries and no portion of the
    glamorous estates,
your steps will die without heirs, leaving no echo or trace.
But your lives—they are your finest visions,
and your glory—it is that you existed,
o diligent keepers of God's image in the world!
Day by day, drop by drop, by the light in your eyes and the lines in
    your faces,
the loveliness of your lives will pour into the universe, as a hidden
    spring
spills into a river to refresh it, without the river knowing.
Not a flutter of your lashes will be lost, I swear,
nor will the smallest tremor in your souls fall to the ground!
Like the singing of the stars they will rise and vibrate forever in the
    vault of heaven,
they will live still and be alive in the last generation,
when not a scrap of the songs of Heman and Jeduthun remains
and not a memory of the wisdom of Chalcol and Darda,
and they will be revealed once again in the eyes of a man and in
    the image of his face.

                  —Hayyim Nahman Bialik

THE MOTHER ROOT

The Talmud is in awe of the Jewish woman for the unparalleled devotion of her mothering—how it has molded society, kept Torah and Jewish life alive, and ensured Judaism's dynamic survival. If half the world are women, the other half know them as mothers. The Sages expressed the wonderment of women by citing biblical verses from the last chapter of the Book of Proverbs (31), which speaks of *eshet chayil* (the woman of valor).

A lost key to unlocking the Jewish concept of motherhood can be found in the Hebrew word "*em*" (mother; or in Aramaic, "*imma*"). "*Em*" is a basic foundation term that undergirds some of the most important concepts in the Hebrew lexicon:

It is a root of *"em-unah,"* translated as "faith" but embracing meanings from "stability" in the Bible to "faith" in the Middle Ages. "Em" is the mother root of what today is the broad spectrum from faith to trust to spiritual life.

"Em" is a root of *"em-et,"* which is a cluster term signifying "truth," "integrity," "decency," and "nobility."

Indeed it may be a root under the concept *"am-en,"* which is an untranslatable answer, an "indeed," to a blessing; the sacred response of people to the gifts of life, abundance of nature, and blessings bestowed upon us by God.

When a mother, an *em*, an *imma*, passes from this life, she leaves a special void. Who can replace her, the woman who brought us into the world, who sacrificed and loved and pampered us? She was likely the root of our faith, self-worth, stability, and decency—and the ready response to every blessing. She triggered a rumor of angels and now she has ascended to the place of angels.

FROM VICTIM TO VICTOR

At moments of deep sorrow, any one of us may turn on God in anger. Such a response is understandable. But we can turn to God, even at such low points, with hearts overflowing with gratefulness, not for what we have lost, but for what we had originally. We can choose our response to God—out of horror, or out of honor.

Over the last sixty years, knowledge of the Nazi Holocaust has generated much sympathy in the world for Jews. It also has spurred many Jews to adhere more assiduously to the laws of Torah. Although the underlying motivations were complex, one reason for both has been the realization that the Jews were at risk of being totally annihilated. But horror transmuted to honor: the re-creation, after two thousand years, of the State of Israel. Drawn to the Zionist prospect out of pride, we stood taller, fought harder, and became part of a winning team. We were victors.

Victors or victims, the deeds of ancestors translate into the lives of their descendants. Once again, *ma'aseh avot siman la'banim* (the deeds of the fathers are precursors for the sons).

The Torah records that Rachel, Jacob's wife, lay dying in the prime of life after giving birth to Benjamin, her youngest child. A strange dialogue, in Rabbinic literature, describes the scene. Understandably, she is angry, bitter, deeply disappointed. Cradling her baby, she is pictured sobbing:

Why must I die now? Who will care for you in the middle of the night? Strange arms will hold and comfort you. Another heart will delight in your antics. You will never know your mother, who dreamed for you, who died for you, who loved you. I will name you Ben-Oni, son of my affliction. You will remember my sadness in your name. You will remember me, if not in happiness, then in horror. *I will pray for you:* When your children's children stop at my grave on the road as they return to the Holy Land, I will plead for them and cry over them.

Jeremiah (31:15) records this epitaph: *Rachel mevakah al baneha* (Rachel weeping for her children).

But Jacob summarily rejects her entire demeanor, the name she has chosen for her child, and her understandable, but abject surrender to despair:

No, Rachel dear, the boy is not a son of your affliction! The child should not trudge through life remembering his mother at every mention of her name because of her suffering, Ben-Oni! Rachel, your son must not become a picture of horror, but a mark of honor. His name will be Ben-Yamin, son of the right hand—a symbol of strength, health, success, glory, and gratitude to God. Ben-Yamin must want to live, because life smiles.

Confronted by the choice of name—either Ben-Oni or Ben-Yamin, the Torah chooses Ben-Yamin. Both names are Jewish, both reflect a truth, each is proffered by the greatest of our ancestors. But Ben-Yamin is the high road, the way of nobility, whereas Ben-Oni is the preservation of catastrophe.

We should remember those who died, as Torah mandates, not primarily because their dreams were dashed, but because they could dream new dreams; not from fear of death, but out of love of life. We should not memorialize only pain, injustice, suffering, loss, tragedy, and tears, but also creative actions, the soul, and human values. The epitaph that enshrines the deceased should proclaim: Ben-Yamin. The undying hope is that our descendants will be not victims but victors. Tradition has decided: Rachel deserves our love, but Jacob was right.

PEOPLE ARE NOT DUST

"For dust you are, and to dust you shall return" (Gen. 3:19). Traditionally at the Yom Kippur service the elders and pious congregants tend to weep when reciting the phrase "*adam yesodo me'afar, ve'sofo le'afar* (man's origin is dust and his end is dust). After thinking about it, it really is a frightening thought: For all our vaunted posturing over a whole lifetime, dust is all we are. It is enough to shrink our self-image to its roots, puncture our prestige, diminish all our imaginings—in fact, reduce us to dust.

It is said that the nineteenth-century Seer of Lublin asked a simple question about all the weeping over this phrase; he asked, "Why do people cry? What have they lost?" If we came from gold and now we were being reduced to dust, that would constitute a cataclysmic loss, and crying would be an appropriate response. But if we emerged from dust and in the end are simply returning to that very dust, what exactly have we lost in the process of living? And if this is true, why such grief?

He answered the simple question with a simple, but profound insight. True, we come from and return to the dust. But between emerging from the dust and being buried in the dust, human beings, unlike dust, are able to grow, even soar, and become dreamers. Only if we do not grow in our lifetimes do we have something to cry about. We may have failed as human beings with God-given missions because we did not shake off the dust. But if we did grow—so that we were not only higher than the animals but also a little lower than the angels—then when our bodies are ultimately interred in the earth our souls ascend to heaven.

We, the descendants of primordial Adam, may "come from" and "go to" dust, but we ourselves are not dust. Our minds and our memories comprise a universe of love and meaning; our soul is a galactic expanse suffused with honest striving, the refining of character, and the pursuit of worthy goals even in the most desperate times. Our parents struggled to raise up a new generation—are they but dust? Relatives and friends, who are decent, kind, spiritually elevated, have sacrificed for family and ideals—are they but dust?

In sublime modesty, Abraham, the patriarch, said: "I am dust [*afar*] and ash [*efer*]" (Gen. 18:27). These words have always been thought of as synonyms, but they are not. Dust is and always has been; it has no past, no present and no future. But ash is qualitatively different. Ash has a history; before ash became the residue of the flame, it may have flourished as a leafy forest producing silken blossoms, fruit, shade, and lumber—even a temple of God. When we paraphrase Abraham saying, "I am as nothing now (*afar*, dust)," he quickly adds: "But I am also *efer* (ash). Once I was an orchard."

The human genome has a metaphoric significance, reflective of its profound scientific importance, which we have only recently begun to plumb. The genome not only contains the building blocks of humanity, it is also stuffed with other matter, which appears to manifest no discernible order. On the one hand, it is infused with life-creating talent and power; on the other, it seems to carry useless baggage. So, too, the person taken from our midst will return to the shapeless, inert dust. But his remains may become nurturing ash, for what he has accomplished or sought to accomplish is a rich past that not even his mourners may now realize.

There is much dust in the earth—what seems to be the useless baggage of our lives. But there is also ash—the stuff of the greatness we leave behind. The wicked may return to nothing but dust, but most of us resemble Abraham. Though we come as dust and return to dust, we leave behind an ash that bears witness to the greatness of the Creator.

Platitudes: When Sympathy Turns to Banality

We feel compelled to offer our consolations because of our human need to relieve the heavy burden of sadness that envelops mourners. By bringing comfort, we hope to help balance the moments of grief, although we know that one expression of sympathy, one conversation, or one visit cannot turn mourners' heads and hearts around. Still, we do it—out of love, compassion, and sympathy.

Generally, we find it extraordinarily difficult to convey this condolence appropriately—to be sufficiently sensitive to the nuances of mourners' feelings, to strike their mood squarely, and to devise thoughts and words that both soothe and edify. We need not flagellate ourselves if we fall short. How can we say what we truly feel? How can we convey it with sincerity and candor?

I myself experienced the power of reticence and careful speech while sitting shiva for my father in Israel. During this time, my family was visited not only by friends and relatives but also by distinguished scholars and rabbis, including the two chief rabbis of Israel. We were truly pleased and honored that they all came, not because of their words, but because their presence alone provided comfort. Their eyes mirrored compassion, empathy, and concern, and their frequent silences were eloquent. We derived much solace from their sensitive discretion.

Visitors to a house of mourning feel justifiably uncomfortable trying to compress noble sentiments into a few words, the size of a good-bye. In the face of death, we become tongue-tied. We feel compelled to seek some way to answer the ultimate question: Why has this tragedy happened? But we don't find it. Our fallback position is usually a cliché—a platitude that contains a grain of truth but is generally meaningless, often banal, and sometimes even hurtful. Death always has the final word.

Rabbi Israel Salanter, the nineteenth-century moralist, taught that writing is easy but that erasing is one of the hardest things for a person to do. It is the same with comforting: Speaking is easy; but having spoken, it is impossible to erase any nonsense we might have uttered.

Although mourners at this time desperately need to be understood, they often find themselves in the difficult position of having to understand their comforters. Mourners need to appreciate that words that sometimes seem insensitive are intended to be words of caring. They may need to comfort the comforters by being very understanding.

When we are mourners ourselves, we need to discount in advance the platitudes our comforters will offer us, not to dwell on how simplistic their answers are to life's most complex questions. We need to focus on our comforters' motivation, the authentic purpose for which they came. We need to accept their gift of solace in the true spirit in which it is offered.

And when we are the consolers, we may not know what best to say to those in the clutch of their suffering, but this should not keep us from visiting mourners. For when one person is genuinely touched by another's tragedy God instantly gives him or her the credentials to become an effective grief supporter.

BLUNDERS OF THE BENEVOLENT

Mourners and comforters alike should be prepared to hear a torrent of the most common platitudes and peccadilloes, offered, of course, as I have said, with the best intentions. Some contain nuggets of deep truth; others are simply inane. In most cases, it is impossible for the mourner to respond to expressions of sympathy such as:

> Some people have it worse.
>
> I feel your pain.
>
> How is everything?
>
> Be strong for your children.
>
> Your loved one lived; now it's your turn.

Count your blessings.

Better it happened to you; you can take it.

If there is anything I can do, just call.

The funeral was nice.

She's better off now.

You're young, you'll have another baby.

MORE BANALITIES

There are religious-sounding truisms that have the timbre of spirituality, but that are misdirected and utterly inappropriate, and also require no comment:

It's a sin to be angry.

Don't think too much; give it to God.

This happened because....

You must forgive.

This too shall pass.

Yet some of these comments, despite their being platitudinous, may elicit profound insights and bring comfort to the mourner.

LIFE GOES ON

An insightful Hasidic anecdote underscores the wisdom of the phrase "Life goes on." Rabbi Abi was an ardent admirer of the great Rabbi Naphtali of Ropshitz. Once during the joyous dance festival of the Jewish calendar, Simchat Torah, when the Hasidim in the city of Ropshitz were dancing feverishly, Rabbi Naphtali was informed that Rabbi Abi had died. The rabbi immediately signaled that the dancing should stop. But he quickly recanted, explaining: "If soldiers go out to war and the captain falls, should the soldiers flee? No. The battle must go on." He then gave a sign, and his followers continued to dance and rejoice, transcending their immediate sorrow.

For mourners, it seems as if the heart and the clock have stopped; life will never again be the same, even though it does go on without the deceased. In response to the comforters' assurance that "life goes on," mourners should remind themselves: "It is true that those who offer me this comforting advice won't notice my loss because for them life will go on. It is not the same for me: I will miss my loved one terribly. For me, life will not just go on." Even so, we will one day have to continue to sing and dance on life's stage.

SOME PEOPLE HAVE IT WORSE

Conveying to the mourner the idea that others have endured worse times is not only pernicious, it is also offensive, not worthy of a response. To the mourner, how much worse could it get? Comforters should avoid expressing this notion, for it actually makes light of a person's mourning. Furthermore, consolers need to realize that personal tragedies are not combat stories full of bravado and courage. We cannot compare one person's grief to another's. All grief is essentially incomparable.

I FEEL YOUR PAIN

But of course we don't. We comforters aren't privy to the depth, nuances, and complexity of the mourner's relationship to the deceased— even though his or her experience may appear similar to our own. What we need to convey as consolers, and what mourners should hear from us, is the sentiment: "I can't know exactly how you feel, but I'm sure you're hurting. And I hurt with you."

HOW IS EVERYTHING?

How could things possibly be for someone who has just suffered the loss of a loved one? How should a person who just suffered such a devastating loss feel? How can he or she be expected to describe it to others? Comforters probably ask such an awkward question because they want to start a conversation with the mourner and don't know where to begin. Yet as innocent as our intention is, it is very much like asking a sick person who is attached to a respirator, "How are you?" How much better it would be if we were to add just one word to our question—"How are things *today?*"—thereby changing the entire meaning of the question. It now encourages a much simpler answer: Today is better or worse—than yesterday, than at the moment of death, than at the funeral, than at the end of shiva. Even if this word isn't added by the comforter, mourners can best respond to "How is everything?" by assuming that "today" is what is implied.

BE STRONG FOR YOUR CHILDREN

It is very common for comforters to encourage mourners to be strong for others—their children, their spouse, or their aged parents. Without realizing it, they are implying that mourners can simply change their own feelings by an act of will in order to help their families. But no one can turn on a spigot that gushes internal strength. In fact, acting strong for our children or others when we are falling apart is not a good idea most of the time. It is also good for our loved ones to see us genuinely expressing our grief. What comforters should say is, "I'm sure you will be strong enough to handle this terrible situation—maybe even as an example for your children [or spouse or parents]."

YOUR LOVED ONE LIVED A LIFE; NOW IT'S YOUR TIME

When a mother or father dies at age ninety-five, it is clearly less wrenching than if she or he were just fifty-five. But a parent's dying at any age leaves us abandoned. Adults, not just children, become orphans. I often wonder why it is that as soon as we hear of a death we instinctively ask, "How old was he or she?" Is it our own demise we are thinking about and now measuring how close we are to it? In any case, this pronouncement intimates that mourners should stop thinking of their loved one, should stop mourning, should stop making a fuss. Hardly. Comforters should regard this phrase as a dead end; mourners should dismiss it as misguided.

COUNT YOUR BLESSINGS

All of us, including mourners, should count our blessings, should be grateful for each of them, some more, some less. But the days of grieving are meant precisely for focusing on a mourner's loss, not on any dividends life may give us; this is not the time for mourners to decide whether their lives add up to more pluses than minuses. All the blessings in the world cannot replace a single grievous loss. Much later, when our grief has lost its urgency and power, we may indeed conclude that on the whole we have enjoyed more blessings in life than tragedies.

Coming from comforters, such advice is a banner that shouts: "Feel guilty!" And: "Be satisfied with what you have; how many people have your good fortune?" We should never make mourners feel guilty, no matter how good our intentions, and no matter how true this statement may be. Better that we console the mourner with: "I hope all the blessings you're surrounded with will give you strength to mourn this terrible loss." Mourners should think of this when well-meaning comforters misspeak.

BETTER THAT IT HAPPENED TO YOU; YOU CAN TAKE IT

Once I heard a young, intelligent woman say, "Better that this happened to you because you can take it," when consoling a mother whose adult son had died and whose daughter-in-law had been declared psychologically incompetent to keep custody of her own child. The consoler actually meant to compliment this mother, telling her how good it was that she had a wealth of internal strength to cope with her loss and that if such a catastrophe had happened to a weaker person, the result would have been disastrous. But at this painful moment, this woman did not need compliments, but solace. What her comforter should have said was: "You're strong and that's fortunate for your grandchild; but this is such a painful experience." Mourners should try to accept such pronouncements as praise for their inner strength. Comforters should word such compliments more sensitively.

GOD NEEDS HIM MORE THAN WE DO

Consolers try to frame the loss of a loved one in noble terms; and yes, this affirms the special value of the deceased. But the idea that God needed your loved one can be invoked at a later time, after the initial phase of mourning has ended, when this notion can be digested and accepted. During shiva, when the mourner is still staggering under the blow, such a thought only triggers additional questions: "Why did God take back from me such a precious gift?" "If God needs him, why did He give him to me at all?" Refraining from expressing these ideas during the initial phase of mourning actually reflects halakhah. As Jewish law says, *Halakha, ve'ein morin ken* (It is law, but we don't teach it so). Later—weeks, months, perhaps years later—mourners may come to the realization, probably through their own devices, that no matter how unjust a loss seems at first, the God we believe in is indeed just, and God's actions and motives are beyond our knowing. Only then can we accept that our departed beloved is needed more urgently elsewhere.

Peccadilloes: Wrong Advice, Generously Offered

Peccadilloes are outright wrongs that tend to mislead. Because mourners often feel that they are inexperienced, that they need answers to many thorny questions, they tend to accept as revealed truth and indisputable dogma much that is said by more experienced, or smarter, or older comforters. It is good for both comforters and mourners to be wary of these comments and avoid some of the more common peccadilloes.

MOURNING LASTS ONLY A FEW WEEKS

The idea that mourning is over in a short time is simply not true. After the Vietnam War, a journalist asked the general public: "How long is it normal to mourn the loss of a loved one?" Many of those who responded thought that individuals should complete mourning between forty-eight hours and two weeks after a death! In my own experience, I have found that even physicians and nurses, who work with mourners on a regular basis often assume that mourning ought to be relatively speedy in these modern times.

But the reality of the human heart is quite otherwise. As Arthur Quiller-Couch, a British writer, once sadly commented, "All the old statues of Victory have wings: but Grief has no wings. She is the unwelcome lodger that squats on the hearthstone between us and the fire and will not move or be dislodged."

Jewish tradition has long understood that grief proceeds more slowly and in an extended cycle. Each year the sacred calendar re-enacts personal mourning on a public scale. We mourn for the destruction of the ancient Temple in Jerusalem that was sacked and burned by the Romans in 70 C.E. This mourning period extends the three weeks before Tisha be-Av, the ninth of Av, the day that commemorates the traditional date of the burning of the Second Temple. The period of public mourning is divided into two parts: an initial period commemorating the severe loss of Judaism's heart, the ancient Temple; and a longer period of consolation following the Fast Day of Tisha be-Av, when Judaism reassures the Jews that God remembers them and will redeem them. Curiously, the period of commemoration anticipating that terrible day of destruction lasts only three weeks; it is called "The Three [weeks] of Punishment," but the consolation period following the ninth of Av lasts for seven weeks; it is called "The Seven [weeks] of Consolation." In rabbinic tradition, the number seven always indicates "real time," as opposed to eight, such as in the eight days before circumcision, which the Rabbis referred to as "beyond [normal] time," outside our common timekeeping frame. In other words, consolation is not "beyond" our needs or capacities; it is reached in "seven," which represents the fullness of time, real time in our everyday lives.

This traditional division into three and seven weeks further illustrates that it takes less time for bereavement to set in than it does to reach a resolution of grief. If this is true for public grieving for an ancient Temple, how much more true it is when the grief is personal and life-altering.

Seamus Dean, Irish poet and novelist, wrote: "The doctor came and gave her pills and medicines. She'd take them and become calmer, but her grief just collected under the drugs like a thrombosis." The poet here aptly observes that grief sometimes flees momentarily in fear of palliative medicine, but rarely does it disappear so easily. More often it crawls underneath the surface of consciousness and pains us still.

Careful research into bereavement has made it clear that the effects of mourning linger far longer for most of us than we assume they will. Mourners should not expect to recover too quickly. And comforters should avoid setting general rules for time limits for mourners on their idiosyncratic process of grieving.

WOMEN TAKE MOURNING WORSE

There is a surprisingly widespread misconception that men are not affected as much by loss as are women. Why? Since men do not publicly demonstrate their grief as much, it is assumed that they recover faster than women, that they do not need the support of others to overcome their grief, or that they are not as disoriented by major loss as are women. However, research shows that each of these assumptions is false. We have learned that men and women demonstrate widely divergent styles of mourning, but they both experience grief in roughly equal measure.

As James J. Lynch, a professor at Wesleyan University who writes extensively about the criminal mind, has put it, "Loneliness and grief often overwhelm bereaved individuals, and the toll taken on the heart can be clearly seen. As the mortality statistics indicate, this is no myth or fairy tale. All available evidence suggests that people do indeed die of broken hearts, men as much as women." The misperception that men are not as affected by grief as are women, or that women are not as emotionally strong as men, seems to derive from societal expectations that men need to hide their grief and be stoic in order to demonstrate their masculinity. In the end, mourners and consolers should both be aware that male mourners may actually be at more at risk for serious psychological and medical consequences (such as congestive heart failure, myocardial infarction, and hypertension) than are women because they may deny themselves the catharsis of grieving.

GRIEVING IS A PRIVATE MATTER

Another misunderstanding about mourning is that people ought to grieve privately. Some mourners assume that the public mourning period should be kept short, even though the aggrieved continue to feel disoriented by their sorrow. Some mourners think it best to keep busy and return to public life, even though they find they do not have the stamina to do so. Such assumptions may lead mourners to believe that their continuing feelings of grief are abnormal. As a result, they may decide to keep their mourning a private matter rather than be exposed as people incapable of handling their mourning.

Almost all psychological studies reveal that most mourners worry about whether they should hide their grief. They seem convinced that the principle "out of sight, out of mind" can be applied to social relationships. Some are so successful in masking the disorientation stemming from their grief and their sinking sense of loss that they deceive even close relatives. Thus, when asked how a mourner is handling his or her loss, relatives often answer, "really well," simply because they do not see the mourner complain or cry.

Some professionals identify this attempt to hide mourning as constituting a "religion of privatism." The irony is that mourners who choose to keep their grief so private cut themselves off from sharing their grief with others, from the very friends and relatives they need to connect with so that they can avoid becoming disoriented. Privatism fails to provide the basic reorientation we need for healthy living when major changes occur. Mourners and comforters should strive to overcome this rather unhealthy idea.

WHEN YOU KEEP BUSY, YOU DON'T GRIEVE

A common misunderstanding is that the best way to handle grief is to suppress all thoughts of the deceased. "Keep busy! Don't think!" is heard commonly in houses of mourning. Many mourners do indeed try to handle the disequilibrium and the disorientation of their grief by becoming very busy. They change homes, communities, jobs—even spouses. Others feel it is important to take long trips or to buy long-wanted items.

Undoubtedly, mourners will find comfort in keeping occupied. But as I have said before, it is almost always an error of judgment to change one's lifestyle radically while still grieving. Self-generated change only adds stress to a system already overloaded by the psychological and emotional instability caused by the death of a loved one. Mourners often suffer emotional or physical problems when they step up rather than slow down the pace of their lives and when they complicate rather than simplify their responsibilities. Accelerating change increases both vulnerability and disorientation and decreases the ability to solve problems.

MEMORIES ARE PAINFUL AND SHOULD BE AVOIDED

Comforters sometimes advise mourners to forget their loved ones, to set their losses behind them in order to reinvest their energies in the future and to get on with living. Yet many mourners report that their greatest fear is that they will do exactly that—they will forget the deceased. When mourners cannot readily recall the details immediately preceding their loss, some conclude that they must be losing their minds or suffering the onset of Alzheimer's. Comforters may give this kind of advice unconsciously, not for the welfare of mourners, but to bring comfort to themselves. For mourners, however, it is often disorienting to be urged to erase their memories. Mourners should be reassured that no researcher has yet documented that people forget those they lose. Rather, what researchers sometimes find is that a loss may be so painful that the mourner will temporarily repress the memory of loved ones. Yet what is repressed remains in the mourner's memory and, in time, will likely reappear in a time and place of its own choosing.

MOURNERS ARE ABLE TO CONTROL THEIR EMOTIONS

Many of us tend to think that people can control their faculties and senses at all times. We may believe that, if we set our minds to it—"if we buck up, so we won't take it so hard"—we can control our feelings at will, and that grief will not take so severe a toll on us. But no matter how hard we try to control our feelings and thoughts, a loss may simply be very hard on us. It is also not true that those who are more intellectual are psychologically stronger or spiritually superior. This is nonsense. We are at bottom, all of us, the children, and only the children, of the loving God.

Rabbi Samson Raphael Hirsch expressed it this way: "The pain suffered when an immediate relative dies cannot be dismissed any more than can physical suffering when a limb is amputated." Accordingly, comforters should not praise mourners solely for their bravado in the face of suffering or, contrarily, condemn them for being "cool" or light-hearted. Typically, mourners are trapped between two reactions: On the one hand, if they appear stoic, people wonder, "Why are they taking it so lightly?" On the other, if they show their emotions, people conclude, "This is not a very strong person." For both mourners and for comforters, it is simply better not to judge.

A Parting Consolation

It is the universal custom of synagogues not to conclude a public reading of the Bible from any of the prophets on a note of sorrow, chastisement, or ominous prediction. If a passage does indeed end on a negative note, a previous sentence is repeated, in order to end always with optimism. And so in that spirit, my readers, I conclude this section, not with the problematic consolations you have just read, but with one that is to my mind the most succinct and most potent of all consolations, and one that accompanies us on the spiritual journey beyond grief.

This consolation was composed by the old Psalmist in his "Song of Ascents" (126:5), and continues to echo through history's dark caverns for millennia. I am reminded again and again as I recite these words that, against all odds, even deeply troubled human beings can climb up life's down staircase:

"They that sow in tears shall reap with songs of joy."

Notes

Chapter 1

4   *"The catastrophe is not*   de Saint-Exupéry, Antoine. *The Little Prince*. Harcourt, 2000.

4   *In Albert Camus's graphic words*   Camus, Albert. *The Fall*. Vintage Books, 1991.

4   *They come and go fitfully*   Singh, Kathleen Dowling. *The Grace in Dying: How We Are Transformed Spiritually As We Die*. HarperSanFransisco, 2000.

4   *"Midnight. No waves*   Dogen Zenji, founder of Soto-Zen. Babylonian Talmud, *Shabbat* 106a; Midrash *Ruth Rabbah* 2,8.

7   *"Light grief*   Hercules Forens, Jerusalem Talmud, *Mo'ed Katan*, Chapter 3, *Halakhah* 7.

7   *Va'yidom—nothing moved*   See *Mikra'ot Gedolot*. Rashi, on the other hand, thinks it is a matter of Aaron's strong will, and an *aggadah* therefore states that he will be rewarded. Apparently, Rashbam does not believe Aaron's will, no matter how strong, could still an emotional convulsion.

8   *Outside the mourners' gate*   *Pirkei d'Rabbi Eliezer* 17, quoted in *Beit Yosef* to *Tur Yoreh De'ah*, 378, 10; see also Babylonian Talmud, *Soferim* 19 (end).

8   *"The holiest attribute*   de Unamuno, Miguel. *The Tragic Sense of Life*. Dover Publications, 1954. Rabbi Mordecai Jaffe, *Levush Ateret Zahav*, to *Tur Yoreh De'ah* 378.

8   *"Le seul bien*   de Musset, Alfred. "Tristesse." *Poésies Nouvelles*. 1850.

8   *"With my tears*   John Welch, "The Puppet" (often attributed to Gabriel García Márquez).

9   *"Everything nailed down*   Hudson, W.H. *Green Mansions.* Reprint edition. Oxford University Press, 1998.

11   *Grudges sometimes begin here*   Curiously, such disagreements suffer from the very irreversibility of death itself. Everything surrounding this tragic moment seems to be set in concrete, partaking of the quality of this moment. And many attempts at reconciliation break down because though the aggrieved may be prepared to forgive, the accused is not prepared to be forgiven.

13   *"The deep pain*   Schopenhauer, Arthur. "Psychological Remarks." *Parerga und Paralipomena.* Edited by E.F.J. Payne. Oxford University Press, 2001.

Chapter 2

18   *While the roots*   Cassel, Erich. *Nature of Suffering and the Goals of Medicine.* Reprint edition. Oxford University Press, 1991.

18   *The great scholar*   Oral Transmission.

19   *Ancient sources*   For the theme of desiring and acting out one's own death through ritual, see Emanuel Feldman, "Death as Estrangement: The Halakhah of Mourning." *Judaism,* 21 (Winter, 1972).

19   *"If one in a group*   Jerusalem Talmud, *Shabbat* 110

19   *"To a stone arch*   Mishnah *Mo'ed Katan* (end).

19   *It is called seudat havra'ah*   Mishnah *Mo'ed Katan* 3:7

20   *For a full year*   *Yoreh De'ah* 94:3.

21   *In T.S. Eliot's*   Eliot, T.S. *Four Quartets,* third quartet, part v.

23   *So profound and universal*   *Mo'ed Katan* 22; Shachter, Hershel. *Nefesh Ha'rav.* Reishis Yerushalayim, 1994.

25   *In fact, Victor Frankl*   Frankl, Victor. *Man's Search for Meaning.* Touchstone Books, 1984.

26   *In mourning, as P.N. Furbank writes*   cited by P.N. Furbank, "Unenlightenment: A Review of *Building a Bridge to the 18th Century: How the Past Can Improve Our Future* by Neil Postman." *The New Republic* (November 29,1999).

26   *And there is the custom*   *Shibbolei ha'Leket, Semachot, #23.*

Chapter 3

33   *Mourning is especially traumatic*   *Beyond the Innocence of Childhood.* Edited by David W. Adams and Eleanor J. Deveau. Baywood Publishing Co., Inc., 1995.

34   *Only in childhood*   Erna Furman, cited by Neil Chethik in *FatherLoss* (Hyperion Books, 2001).

34   *Sociologist Lynn Davidman writes,*   Davidman, Lynn. *Motherloss.* University of California Press, April 2000.

36   *A very important goal*   See James Fogarty, *The Magical Thoughts of Grieving Children.* Baywood Publishing Co., Inc., 2000.

36   *A recent study*   Conducted by Columbia University and New York University, 1999.

36   *The profoundly sad moments*   Jonathan Vos Post cited this anonymous classic poem in *Family Dynamics and the Chicago Institute for Psychoanalysis* (Emerald City Publishing, 1995).

38   *Psychologists often observe*   "Marital conflict had produced anger, and perhaps, desire for escape, but coexisting with these feelings were continued attachment to the other and even, perhaps, affection. Anger interfered with grieving, and only with the passage of time did persisting need for the lost spouse emerge." Institute of Medicine. *Bereavement: Reactions, Consequences, and Care.* Edited by M. Osterweis, F. Solomon, and M. Green. National Academy Press, 1984.

Chapter 4

45 *Shakespeare's "dark backward* Shakespeare, William. *The Tempest.* Reprint edition. Edited by Stephen Orgel. Oxford University Press, 1998.

45 *To appreciate the Jewish tradition* In addition to being a central feature of Buddhist meditation, *Mindfulness* is the title of an important work by Ellen J. Langer (Perseus Books, 1990).

46 *It is, after all* Lamm, Maurice. *The Jewish Way in Death and Mourning.* Jonathan David Publishers, 2000.

47 *The anthropologist Victor Turner* Turner, Victor. *The Ritual Process: Structure and Anti-Structure.* Aldine de Gruyter, 1995.

57 *Male mourners often intentionally* Golden, Bernard. *Healthy Anger: How to Help Children and Teens Manage Their Anger.* Oxford University Press, 2002.

58 *"make yourself a heart* Tosefta, Sotah 7:12.

Chapter 5

62 *There should not* Rambam *Hilchos Avel*, perek 5. I learned much from the insights into this law proffered by Dr. Norman Lamm in an unpublished *shiur kelali* he gave to faculty and students at Yeshiva University, 2000.

62 *They say: "We are going* See Rosh to Babylonian Talmud, *Sukkah* 25b: "The mourner wants to be separated and sit in a dark and uncomfortable place where he can dwell on his suffering." Also see Rabbi J. B. Soloveitchik on Mo'ed Katan 3b: "The laws of mourning are akin to the laws of excommunication and the leper"—in that in all of them a common theme is to distance themselves from the community of men. Until his friends intervene, and plead with him, "Come with us," thereby indicating

that until that intervention by the friends, the mourner wanted to be by himself, and they insist, "No, come with us."

63 *For Ezekiel, silence was a fasting* The phrase is a well-known traditional Taoist concept.

64 *I sometimes hold it* Alfred, Lord Tennyson. *In Memoriam A. H. H.* 1850.

65 *There is no* Chopra, Deepak. *The Seven Spiritual Laws of Success.* Amber-Allen Publishers, 1995.

67 *"The more one* Passover haggadah.

68 *Roger Rosenblatt* Rosenblatt, Roger. "I Am Writing Blindly," *Time* magazine (November 6, 2000).

74 *A leading exponent of humanistic psychology* Maslow, Abraham. *Religions, Values, and Peak Experiences.* Viking Press, 1994.

74 *It is curious, Anthony Storr says* Storr, Anthony. *Solitude: A Return to the Self.* Ballantine Books, 1989.

76 *When from our* Wordsworth, William. *The Prelude: The Four Texts (1798, 1799, 1805, 1850).* Penguin Classics, 1996.

77 *"even if there are no words* *Responsa of Adret,* Part I, 478.

78 *The Oxford theologian* Lewis, C.S., *A Grief Observed.* Bantam Books, 1983.

79 *"no man is an island"* Donne, John. "Meditation XVII." *Devotion Upon Emergent Occasions.* Edited by Anthony Raspa. Oxford University Press, 1987.

Chapter 6

82 *Sigmund Freud affirmed* Freud, Sigmund. *Mourning and Melancholia.* 1917.

82 *Joshua Loth Liebman* "Traditional Judaism, as a matter of fact, had the wisdom to devise almost all of the procedures for healthy-

minded grief which the contemporary psychologist counsels, although Judaism naturally did not possess the tools for scientific experiment and systematic case study, nor did it always understand, as we now can, the underlying reasons for its procedures." Liebman, Joshua Loth. *Peace of Mind*. Simon & Schuster, 1946.

86   *Judaism placed this*   Soloveitchik, Joseph. *Worship of the Heart: Essays on Jewish Prayer*. Edited by Shalom Carmy. KTAV Publishing, 2003.

87   *For example, Midrash recognizes that*   Midrash *Yalkut Shimoni* to Exodus 156.

88   *This is clear*   Soloveitchik, J.B. *She'urei ha'Rav al inyanei avelus ve'Tisha b'Av.*

88   *The duration of*   Soloveitchik, J.B. *She'urei ha'Rav al inyanei avelus ve'Tisha b'Av.*

89   *The dead person*   See Naftali Eskries and Maurice Lamm, "Viewing the Remains" in *The Journal of Religion and Health*. See also Mitford, Jessica. *The American Way of Death*. Fawcett Books, 1987.

90   *Moreover, it is psychologically futile*   Lamm, Maurice. *The Jewish Way in Death and Mourning*. Jonathan David Publishers, 2000.

92   *Early twentieth-century Austrian writer*   Borkenau, Franz. *The Spanish Cockpit: An Eyewitness Account of the Political and Social Conflicts of the Spanish Civil War*. Pluto Press, 1986.

92   *The effects of inappropriate grieving*   Gray, Francine Du Plessix. "The Work of Mourning," in *The Best American Essays*. Edited by Kathleen Norris. Houghton Mifflin Co., 2001

92   *In Antigone's words*   Sophocles, *Antigone*. Reprint edition. Dover Publications, 1993.

98   *The prophet Samuel*   Ha'ne-ehavim ve'haneimin be'chayehem, u'vemosam lo nifradu (2 Sam. 1:23).

99   *Ashley Davis Prend wrote:*   Prend, Ashley Davis. *Transcending Loss: Understanding the Lifelong Impact of Grief and How to Make It Meaningful.* Berkeley Publishing Group, 1997.

99   *After death there*   Brener, Anne. *Mourning and Mitzvah: A Guided Journal for Walking the Mourner's Path Through Grief to Healing.* Jewish Lights Publishing, 1993. I read this fine book and found that Brener wrote of the *Kaddish* in the very same vein as I did in this book and in my *The Jewish Way in Death and Mourning.* Her other observations are equally commendable.

Chapter 7

104   *Rabbi Eliyahu Dessler*   Dessler, Eliyahu. *Strive for Truth: Michtav Me'Eliyahu.* Phillip Feldheim, 1985. *Tanchumei Avelim.*

104   *Midrash calls this kiflayim*   Midrash *Eikhah Rabbati,* end Ch 1.

104   *Isaiah speaks of two levels*   See *Shem M' Shmuel,* Nitzavim, 5677.

106   *All three are provided*   1.Ch. 40—*Nachamu, Nachamu*; 2.Ch.49—*Azavani Ha'shem*; 3.Ch. 54:11–17 and Ch.55:1–5—*Lo Nuchamah!*; 4.Ch. 51:12–23 and Ch. 52:1–12—*Anochi, Anochi, Hu*; 5.Ch. 54:1–10—*Rani Akarah*; 6.Ch. 60:1–22—*Kumi Ori, Ki Va Orech*; 7.Ch. 61:10–11, Ch. 62:1–12, and Ch. 63:1–9—*Sose Assis.*

106   *This corresponds to shiva*   It also reflects the "seven," which Judaism holds is civilization's characteristic number, symbolizing a turning of the wheel of time—a full week—when we end with the Sabbath and we begin to count the days over again until the next Sabbath.

106   *An ancient midrash explains*   Rashi to Genesis 6:6. See *Tosafos.*

109   *The Zohar declares*   Perhaps Rachel is speaking about her husband who is not next to her to console her as he had always done.

109   *The medieval commentator*   Ramban to Genesis 48:7.

109   *"Rachel cries incessantly*   Zohar—vol. 2, Va'era, 29b.

111   *Consoling mourners, Maimonides said*   Rambam, Mishnah Torah, *Shoftim*, Chapter 14, *Halakhah* 7.

113   *Phillips Brooks once said*   Brooks, Phillips. *Joy of Preaching*. Kregel Publications, 1989.

114   *Upon leaving, we traditionally recite*   Note that the Hebrew text varies to accommodate the second person, masculine or feminine, and singular or plural.

Chapter 8

118   *The Nobel prize-winning physicist*   Quoted by W. Heisenberg in his article "Theory, Criticism, and a Philosophy," in *From a Life of Physics* (World Scientific Publishing Co., 1989).

120   *It means being ready*   See Gray, Francine Du Plessix. "The Work of Mourning," in *The Best American Essays*. Edited by Kathleen Norris. Houghton Mifflin Co., 2001.

121   *Robert Frost said*   Frost, Robert. "A Servant to Servants." *North of Boston*. Henry Holt, 1915.

122   *The great Harvard philosopher*   James, William. *Varieties of Religious Experience*. Touchstone Books, 1997.

122   *The Pain: Wasting Afflictions*   This section follows in the style of the great preacher Harry Emerson Fosdick.

123   *Someday, at the*   Rilke, Rainer Maria, *Duino Elegies* "Tenth Elegy."

124   *Sir Thomas Browne*   Browne, Sir Thomas. *Religio Medici*. 1646.

126   *Joshua Weinstein has*   Weinstein, Joshua. "The Uses and Advantages of Pain," *Azure* 1 (Summer, 1996). I have not found a clearer description of the usefulness of pain than this.

127   *The psychiatrist Rollo May*   May, Rollo. *The Meaning of Anxiety.* Revised Edition. W.W. Norton and Co., 1996.

128   *The existentialist philosopher*   Sartre, Jean Paul. *The Flies (Les Mouches); In Camera (Huis Clos).* Translated by Stuart Gilbert. Penguin Books Ltd., 1946.

129   *As George Eliot*   Quoted by C. E. M. Joad in *Shaw* (Folcroft Literary Editions, 1972).

131   *Throughout our lives*   Penfield, Wilder and Phanor Perot. "The Brain's Record of Auditory and Visual Experience." *Brain*, 86, 1963.

133   *"Healing" and "curing"*   See Erich Cassel, *Commentary* (1983).

135   *This is designed to teach*   The Jerusalem Bible (since 1985, the "New" Jerusalem Bible) was published originally in French and then, in 1966, in English.

Chapter 9

140   *The philosopher Friedrich*   Quoted by Victor Frankl in *Man's Search for Meaning* (Touchstone Books, 1984).

140   *Carl Jung noted*   Jung, Carl. *Psyche and Symbol: A Selection of the Writings of C.G. Jung.* Edited by Violet de Laszlo. Translated by R.F.C. Hull. Princeton University Press, 1991.

142   *Blaise Pascal, the*   Pascal, Blaise. *Pensées.* Translated by A.J. Krailsheimer. Penguin Classics USA, 1995.

142   *Ralph Waldo Emerson*   Quoted in *The Laws on Nature: Excerpts from the Writings of Ralph Waldo Emerson.* Edited by Walt M. Laughlin. Wood Thrush Books, 2001.

146   *Israel Baal Shem Tov*   The story, of course, is a traditional parable. In actuality, some deaf people do dance; they can feel the beat and can dance quite well.

148   *In the ninth century*   Saadia Gaon, *Selichot Prayer Book*.

Chapter 10

153   *A report on spiritual wellness*   C. J. Chandler, J. M. Holden, and C. A. Kolander, "Counseling for Spiritual Wellness: Theory and Practice," *Journal of Counseling and Development* 72 (1992).

155   *Sigmund Freud had a picture*   From Ernest Becker, *The Denial of Death* (Free Press, 1997).

Chapter 11

162   *In the summer*   See, for example, *The Jewish Standard of New Jersey* (August 18, 2000).

162   *There is as much truth*   This section on heaven originally appeared *The Jewish Way in Death and Mourning* (Jonathan David Publishers, 2000).

163   *In a handful of sparse Hebrew sentences*   My original version of this parable has been reprinted verbatim in at least sixteen books, and that pleases me. I hope that it continues to be used. But I ask that Rabbi Tuckachinsky, who originated the idea behind the parable but who did not speak English, not be cited as the author of these words. He died many years ago, and I do not know whether he would have consented to my elaboration and English rendition.

166   *Potentially we will be able*   Becker, Ernest. *The Denial of Death.* Free Press, 1997.

166   *Will Simple People Achieve Immortality*   This section is adapted from *The Jewish Way in Death and Mourning* (Jonathan David Publishers, 2000).

167   *Indeed, the Mishnah expressly excludes*   Sanhedrin 10:1.

167   *Although Jewish philosophers changed the formulation*   For example, Hasdai Crescas, fifteenth-century Spanish philosopher.

170 *"I Believe"* Words and music by Ervin Drake, Jimmy Shirl, Al Stillman, and Irvin Graham TRO–© Copyright 1952 (Renewed) 1953 (Renewed). Hampshire House Publishing Corp., New York, NY. Used by permission.

172 *Nowhere in the archives* Epstein, Isadore. *Judaism.* Penguin Books, 1959.

173 *Any attempt to describe life after death* For much of this section, I have relied on the work of Simcha Paull Raphael. See his *Jewish Views of the Afterlife* (Jason Aronson Publishers, 1995).

174 *At the hour of a man's departure* Zohar 2, 218a.

174 *Rabbi Yochanan ben Zakkai* Berachot 22b.

174 *Jewish tradition speaks* Rabbinic literature (*Pesikta Rabbati* 2:3), medieval Midrash (*Massekhet Hibbut Ha-kever* 1, 3), and Kabbalah (Zohar 1, 79a) all have references to three angels who appear after death and greet the departed being.

175 *It is a cosmic drama* See Thomas Cahill's fine description in *The Gifts of the Jews* (Anchor Books, 1999).

176 *In a "spherical"* Georg Reimann, *Geometry.* Reimann geometry is also called elliptic geometry and is the mathematical concept underlying Einstein's theory of relativity. Fundamentally, it uses the axiom that says it is impossible for any two lines to be parallel—*all* lines intersect one another.

176 *Two worlds kiss* Jerusalem Talmud, Y'vamot 15:21.

178 *Virginia Woolf* Woolf, Virginia. *To the Lighthouse.* Harvest Books, 1989.

178 *From a variety* Bava Batra 58a, Bava Metzi'a 85b, Ta'anit 16a.

179 *In the literature* Raphael, Simcha Paull. *Jewish Views of the Afterlife.* Jason Aronson, 1995.

179 *"They that love* Penn, William. "Union of Friends." *Harvard Classics: Some Fruits of Solitude.* P.F. Collier and Son Co., 1909–1914.

180   *The Babylonian Sage Rav*   Shabbat 152b.

180   *As he was dying*   Berachot 22b.

180   *Simcha Paul Raphael*   Raphael, Simcha Paull. *Jewish Views of the Afterlife*. Jason Aronson Publishers, 1995.

181   *In the Talmud*   Babylonian Talmud, *Sotah* 49A.

182   *What Is Death?*   This section is adapted from *The Jewish Way of Death and Mourning* (Jonathan David Publishers, 2000).

Chapter 12

190   *"The road uphill*   Kahn, C.H., *The Art and Thought of Heraclitus*. Cambridge University Press, 1981.

192   *Rather, the role of spiritual healers*   Karasu, T. Byram. "Spiritual Psychotherapy." in *American Journal of Psychotherapy* 53, no. 2 (1999).

197   *In fact, he took immediate action*   See S. R. Hirsch on *ohaloh*, Genesis 35:21. See also his comments on *"ohaloh"* in Genesis 9:21 and 13:3.

200   *"The Rabbis learned*   Judah David Eisenstein, Midrash.

201   *They instituted memory-sparking events*   See Rambam, Mishnah Torah, *Hilchot Evel*, 13:11–12.

201   *Mourners ideally should learn*   Dessler, Eliyahu. *Strive for Truth: Michtav Me'Eliyahu*. Phillip Feldheim, 1985.

203   *Essentially, "souls" here*   See, for example, Baruch Halevi Epstein, *Torah T'mimah*. Many commentators ascribe this to the spiritual protection every person needs.

208   *A story is told*   Martha Whitmore Hickman, *Healing After Loss: Daily Meditations for Working Through Grief*. HarperCollins, 1994.

210   *One ancient source*   *Yalkut Shimoni*, cited by Yeshayah Liebowitz, *Parshat ha'shavua*. See Norman Lamm, *The Religious Thought of Hasidism*. Yeshiva University Press, 1999.

Chapter 13

213 *Ashley Davis Prend* Prend, Ashley Davis. *Transcending Loss.* Berkeley Publishing Group, 1997.

215 *The Torah says, "lasu'ach ba'sadeh"* See *Torah T'mimah*, Genesis; 4:67. Ch. 36.

219 *Psychologist Victor Frankl* Frankl, Victor, *Man's Search for Meaning.* Touchstone Books, 1984.

222 *Maimonides said as much in the strongest terms* Maimonides, Moses. *The Guide of the Perplexed.* Translated by Shlomo Pines. The University of Chicago Press, 1963.

222 *In essence, what we are saying in this prayer* Berachot 60b.

223 *The Rabbis of the Talmud highlighted* Berachot 54a.

225 *My brother, Dr. Norman Lamm* Lamm, Norman. *The Religious Thought of Hasidism.* Yeshiva University Press, 1999.

225 *This explains the custom* The custom is recorded in *Bet Lehem Yehudah* to *Yoreh De-ah* 338:1 and is attributed to *Sefer Terumot.* The explanation that death is treated as a *mitzvah* because it is the will of God was provided orally by Rabbi Yehoshua Baumol.

225 *Rabbi Abraham Isaac Kook* Moshe Zevi Neriyah, *Mo'adei ha-Reiyah.*

226 *The landmark psychological study* G.H. Pollock in "On Migration—Voluntary and Coerced," in *The Annual of Psychoanalysis* (1989). See also "Process and Affect: Mourning and Grief," in the *International Journal of Psychoanalysis* 59 (1978).

226 *What he discovered* Yes, it is true that creative geniuses reacting to childhood bereavement have also grown to be ingeniously destructive of the whole human enterprise. It is bone chilling to read the names, but they include Vladimir Lenin, Joseph Stalin, Ho Chi Minh, and Adolph Hitler, and the twisted effect of unresolved grieving may have been the cause for the deaths of tens of millions of people in Nazi Germany and the Soviet Union.

227   *The psychologist Hannah Siegel*   Siegel, Hannah. "A Psychoanalytic Approach to Aesthetics," in *International Journal of Psychoanalysis* (1952).

227   *Ralph Keyes*   Keyes, Ralph. *The Courage to Write*. Henry Holt, 1995.

229   *C.S. Lewis, the theologian*   Lewis, C.S. *A Grief Observed*. Bantam Books, 1983.

230   *Actor Matthew McConaughey*   Quoted by Neil Chethik in *FatherLoss*. (Hyperion Books, 2001).

231   *In fact, a 1978 study*   Pollock, G.H. "Process and Affect: Mourning and Grief." *International Journal of Psychoanalysis* 59 (1978).

Chapter 14

235   *"You Have Transformed*   Psalms 30:12.

236   *When the eminent scholar*   Berachot 42b, quoted in Joseph B. Soloveitchik, *Man of Faith in the Modern World*. Edited by Abraham Breslin. KTAV Publishing, 1989.

236   *Both sinners and mourners*   Sefer ha-Chinuch 264, which explicitly equates mourning with repentance. See Solveitchik, Joseph. *Man of Faith in the Modern World*. Edited by Abraham Besdin. KTAV Publishing, 1989.

237   *In a poignant book*   Neuberger, Roy. *From Central Park to Sinai*. Jonathan David Publishers, 2000.

255   *Dr. Norman Lamm*   Lamm, Norman. *The Royal Reach: Discourses on the Jewish Tradition and the World Today*. Feldheim, 1970.

Words for a Loss, When at a Loss for Words

258   *The French writer Charles Baudelaire*   Baudelaire, Charles. *Fusées.* French and European Publications, 1986.

259   *Nathaniel Hawthorne*   Hawthorne, Charles. *American Notebooks 1841–1852.* Edited by Bill Ellis and Claude Simpson. Ohio State University Press, 1973.

265   *To pray directly to the deceased*   Rabbi Judah Aryeh Leib Alter of Gur, *S'Fat Emet,* to Lekh Lekha, Jerusalem Ed.

266   *Eric Lindemann, in his classic paper*   Lindemann, Eric. "The Symptomatology and Management of Acute Grief." *The American Journal of Psychiatry,* 1944.

274   *The king employed day-workers*   Jerusalem Talmud, *Berachot,* Ch. 2, *Halakhah* 8.

277   *Once you realize you are children*   Comments on Deuteronomy 14:1.

278   *Elie Wiesel, the writer*   Wiesel, Elie. documentary by PBS, *Elie Wiesel: First Person Singular.* Public Broadcasting Station, October 24, 2002.

281   *Carl Sandburg*   Sandburg, Carl. *Abraham Lincoln: The Prairie Years.* Harcourt Brace, 1926.

282   *A saint grows*   An interpretation given me by Chief Rabbi Immanuel Jakobvitz.

283   *The noted naturalist Loren Eiseley*   Eiseley, Loren. "The Judgment of the Birds." *The Immense Journey.* Random House Trade Paperbacks, 1959.

285   *Man comes from dust*   Machzor, following the *U-netanneh Tokef* prayer. Babylonian Talmud *Mo'ed Katan* 28a.

286   *We are not like the shadow*   Bereshit Rabbah 86:2.

288   *A fox searches for a way*   Mendel, Nissan. *The Complete Story of Tishrei.* Kehot Publications, 1998.

288 *The Midrash teaches that Moses' head*   Shemot Rabbah 47:6.

290 *The English scholar*   Pater, Walter. *The Rennaissance: Studies in Art and Poetry.* Oxford University Press, 1998.

292 *The Rabbis, despite their love of life*   Horeb, vol. 2.

292 *Rabbi Samson Raphael Hirsch noted*   Comments on Leviticus 1, 25.

293 *The Talmud refers to this*   Babylonian Talmud, Sanhedrin 104A.

298 *My Place Is with You*   This translation was written by Leon Wieseltier and originally appeared in *The New Republic.* Leon Wieseltier is the author of *Kaddish.*

300 *Indeed it may be*   Some may consider this "romantic semantics," but occasionally we need to think intuitively, even homiletically, to find similarities—though this may take us outside scientific exactitude.

301 *Why must I die now?*   Midrash.

305 *Rabbi Israel Salanter*   Katz, Dov. *The Mussar Movement.* Orly Press, 1958.

307 *An insightful Hasidic anecdote*   Berger, Israel. *Zechut Yisrael ha-nikra eser tsachtsachot.* 1910.

312 *As Arthur Quiller-Couch*   Armistice Day anniversary sermon, given by Arthur Quiller-Couch in Cambridge, England, in November, 1923.

313 *Seamus Dean, Irish poet and novelist*   Dean, Seamus. *Reading in the Dark.* Vintage Books, 1998.

314 *As James J. Lynch*   Lynch, James J. *The Broken Heart: The Medical Consequences of Loneliness.* Basic Books, 1985.

316 *Rabbi Samson Raphael Hirsch*   Horeb, vol. 1.

Index